NOV 2 2 2006

D0147479

Everyday Law
for Individuals
with Disabilities

3 1170 00721 6868

The Everyday Law Series
Edited by Richard Delgado and Jean Stefancic
University of Pittsburgh Law School

Everyday Law for Individuals with Disabilities
Ruth Colker and Adam Milani (2005)

Everyday Law for Children
David Herring (2006)

Forthcoming
Everyday Law for the Elderly
Lawrence Frolik

Everyday Law for Latino/as
Steve Bender, Joaquin Avila, and Raquel Aldana-Pindell

Everyday Law for African Americans
Harold McDougall III

Everyday Law for Gays and Lesbians
Anthony Infanti

Everyday Law for Consumers
Michael Rustad

Everyday Law for Individuals with Disabilities

Ruth Colker
Heck-Faust Memorial Chair in Constitutional Law
The Ohio State University Moritz College of Law

Adam A. Milani
Former Associate Professor of Law
Mercer University Law School

Glenview Public Library
1930 Glenview Road
Glenview, Illinois

Paradigm Publishers
Boulder • London

All rights reserved. No part of the publication may be transmitted or reproduced in any media or form, including electronic, mechanical, photocopy, recording, or informational storage and retrieval systems, without the express written consent of the publisher.

Copyright © 2006 Paradigm Publishers

Published in the United States by Paradigm Publishers, 3360 Mitchell Lane Suite E, Boulder, CO 80305 USA.

Paradigm Publishers is the trade name of Birkenkamp & Company, LLC, Dean Birkenkamp, President and Publisher.

Library of Congress Cataloging-in-Publication Data
Colker, Ruth.
    Everyday law for individuals with disabilities / Ruth Colker, Adam A. Milani.
        p.   cm.—(The everyday law series)
    Includes bibliographical references and index.
    ISBN 1-59451-144-6 (hc)—ISBN 1-59451-145-4 (pbk)   1. People with disabilities—Legal status, laws, etc.—United States.   2. Discrimination against people with disabilities—Law and legislation—United States.   I. Milani, Adam. II. Title. III. Series.
    KF480.C649 2005
    343.7308'7—dc22

                                                                            2005021803

Printed and bound in the United States of America on acid free paper that meets the standards of the American National Standard for Permanence of Paper for Printed Library Materials.

Designed and Typeset by Mulberry Tree Enterprises

10   09   08   07   06   1   2   3   4   5

In Memoriam

This book is dedicated to the memory of Adam Milani, who passed away shortly before this book went to press. Adam was a tireless advocate and role model for individuals with disabilities. This book should help continue his spirit of advocacy.

Contents

Preface

In the last three decades, we have seen the law of disability discrimination have a transformative effect on society: Buildings have ramps, there are services that allow people with hearing impairments to use telephones, and children with disabilities go to school with their peers. However, people with disabilities still face problems in employment, education, transportation, and access and accommodation, and we have also seen that individuals facing these issues are often better served by engaging in self-advocacy than by going through the traditional legal system.

Ruth's vantage point has been that of the mother of a boy who was diagnosed as "developmentally disabled" at age 3. This diagnosis was frightening to Ruth, in part, because she knew that her great-uncle, who is mildly retarded, received no education whatsoever after he was diagnosed as retarded. Like many disabled children of his generation, he lived with his parents in a very protective, family-oriented atmosphere, and thus it was exciting for him to learn how to venture out on his own, as when he took a bus to dust furniture at his uncle's furniture shop. Yet despite the love and support of his extended family, his opportunities in life were limited. Further, it must have been frightening to his parents to send their son out into the world to earn a living at a time when most families hid children with mental retardation.

Thanks, in part, to a federal law enacted in 1975 called the Individuals with Disabilities Education Act (IDEA), the life of Ruth's son has been entirely different. At age 3, he was entitled to free, special education services from the county and received several years of small-class instruction for nearly three hours a day. Ruth had to learn to navigate the medical and education system to help get him the right array of resources, but she could engage in this advocacy against the backdrop of a federal statute that entitled her preschooler to a free and adequate education. The mantra of the special education movement is that early intervention is the key to success for many children. Ruth's son could be the poster child for that mantra because, with the support of special services under IDEA, he has flourished in grade school. Ruth's knowledge of his rights and her willingness to advocate for her son in a supportive public school atmosphere has made it possible for her son to have opportunities that would not have been imaginable for her uncle, who is now nearly 90 years old.

Adam, too, has been able to see not only the effectiveness of advocacy outside the legal system for individuals with disabilities but also the transformative effect of disability laws. He was paralyzed from the chest down playing ice hockey as a senior in high school in December 1983. When he started college at Notre Dame in August 1984, he was very new to living with a disability and had no idea what obstacles he would face as a student who used a wheelchair. Neither did the people at the school. The woman assigned to assist students with disabilities tried her best, but she had no training in disability issues. Also, her office was on the second floor of a building without an elevator—kind of hard for a wheelchair user to go see her. Fortunately, Adam's parents were tireless advocates who talked to and worked with people on all levels of the university administration to make sure he would have physical access to campus buildings and a support system of caregivers. It was still a struggle at times, but with the help of his parents' advocacy, Adam was able to graduate in four years and then go on to law school.

In 1993, less than ten years after he enrolled at Notre Dame, Adam and his parents were contacted by a senior administrator at the school. The Americans with Disabilities Act (ADA), which was passed in 1990, had just gone into full effect, and the school wanted assistance on disability issues. Adam prepared a proposal with several recommendations, which included hiring a full-time director of an Office for Students with Disabilities. That person was hired in 1995, and the difference between then (when Adam enrolled) and now—in terms of the accessibility of the Notre Dame campus and the services offered for students with disabilities—was like that between night and day. The parents of students with disabilities, and the students themselves, still have to be effective advocates, just as Ruth is doing with her son; but as a result of ADA's enactment and schools' responses to it, there are often services already in place and people knowledgeable about how, when, and where they must be provided.

Because of our successful experiences with self-advocacy for individuals with disabilities, we were receptive when Richard Delgado and Jean Stefancic suggested that we consider writing a practical book that would not only describe, in lay terms, the law of disability discrimination but also give readers examples of how to find solutions to such problems without having to find a lawyer and file a lawsuit. Ruth had worked with Richard in the past and knew of his excellent reputation for putting together innovative books and other material. We surveyed the existing literature and realized that there was a need for such a book. And then, after much discussion, we decided we would find the time in our busy schedules to write it.

We believe a practical book that not only describes the legal rights of individuals with disabilities but also suggests nonlegal solutions to disability discrimination issues is important because of how the legal system interacts with such problems. Legal representation is often difficult to obtain and legal recourse is often ineffective. On the other hand, public and private entities sometimes are willing to modify their behavior to correct a problem of discrimination if that problem is brought to their attention. Hence, individuals with disabilities and their advocates can benefit from having both legal and practical knowledge in thinking about problems of disability discrimination.

Why is legal representation often difficult to obtain and traditional legal recourse often so ineffective? One factor is that lawyers often take a personal, financial risk in filing disability cases. In the employment discrimination area, the average monetary award for a successful plaintiff is less than $100,000, partly because individuals with disabilities often have low-paying jobs. Lawyers are rarely able to afford to take such cases on a contingency basis (whereby they collect 30 percent or so of the plaintiff's monetary award as a fee for their service), because the time-consuming nature of these cases means that the contingency fee award often will not even cover the lawyers' expenses. Lawyers can also take cases and, if they prevail in court, seek to obtain their fees from the opposing party. Although juries are often favorably disposed toward such cases, most of these cases are dismissed by judges before trial. So, again, few lawyers can afford to take an employment discrimination case based on the hope that they *might* get paid by the opposing party after several years.

Other kinds of disability discrimination cases present similar problems with finding formal legal representation. In cases involving a denial of access to facilities or services open to the public, the complaining party is only rarely entitled to receive money damages as a form of relief. Hence, contingency award agreements are usually out of the question. Indeed, since few people with disabilities can afford to pay a lawyer for such cases, the only viable form of payment for a lawyer representing the person alleging discrimination is an award of fees to be paid by the opposing party—and that occurs only when the attorney for the complaining party helps his or her client prevail in the lawsuit. Because many blatant inaccessibility problems still exist, however, some lawyers do earn a living engaging in that kind of litigation. For instance, we have good friends who make a living as lawyers in the disability discrimination field, primarily doing accessibility work.

Although lawyers are often denounced for being too greedy in their litigation strategies, it is hard to criticize lawyers who are reluctant to take cases involving disability discrimination, especially employment discrimination cases. If they are in private practice and must pay the bills themselves, they cannot afford to take too many employment discrimination cases because of the risk that they will not get paid for their work.

"Self-help," therefore, may often be the most viable strategy for many individuals with disabilities who face discrimination problems. But they cannot proceed with a self-help strategy without knowing what the law requires (even if the law is underenforced). Voluntary resolution of legal claims usually happens in the "shadow" of the law. Thus, we try in this book to give readers a broad overview of the applicable legal requirements while also suggesting self-help strategies. We hope this combination assists people with disabilities (or their families and friends) to be more effective advocates.

Although the scope of the book is ambitious—we discuss employment, education, transportation, housing, voting, health insurance, and access to and accommodations by government and private entities—it doesn't cover every area of law that might be relevant to individuals with disabilities. In particular, we have not tackled the Social Security system, the health care system (outside of the insurance area), or worker's compensation, even though each of those areas of law, among others, might be relevant to individuals with disabilities. Rather, the focus of our book is the law of disability *discrimination.* Those other areas of the law do not necessarily involve issues of discrimination. Other books in the *Everyday Law* series on health care or the elderly might be more helpful in apprising individuals of their rights in those areas.

Too little knowledge, however, can be a dangerous thing. We don't want people to believe that simply reading this book makes them "experts" on the law of disability discrimination. But the information in this book *can* be an important beginning as individuals try to understand problems and think of creative solutions. In both the individual chapters and the extensive Appendix, we mention federal and state-by-state resources that readers can use to further supplement their knowledge. Patience and diligence are necessary ingredients to successful self-advocacy. We wish our readers good luck in becoming successful advocates in the area of disability discrimination, and we hope to hear of new success stories as people try to implement our suggestions.

Ruth Colker and Adam A. Milani

Acknowledgments

We would like to thank Richard Delgado and Jean Stefancic for urging us to write this book. Paradigm editor Michael Peirce and Paradigm publisher Dean Birkenkamp have been tremendously helpful at every stage of this production. We thank them, too, for their personal interest in this venture.

We have been fortunate to write this book within a supportive atmosphere at our educational institutions. Ruth was able to devote some time to this project during her sabbatical from the Moritz College of Law. She also benefited from the research assistance of Cricket Nardacci, who compiled most of the information found in the Appendix. Cricket's research was funded through a generous Distinguished Scholar Award made available to Ruth at Ohio State University. Scott Lissner, who is Ohio State's ADA coordinator, also offered useful suggestions throughout the project. The K–12 education chapter benefited from resources made available by Vanessa Coterel, a former student of Ruth's who now works in the disability rights field as a lawyer. Mark Weber helped Ruth understand the recent amendments to federal education law. Ruth's secretary, Carol Peirano, also helped in innumerable ways with this project.

Adam's work on this project was assisted by a summer research grant from the Mercer University School of Law. His colleagues at Mercer have supported his decision to focus on disability issues throughout the years.

The book has also benefited from our many conversations with individuals with disabilities, and their lawyers, over many years. Those people are too numerous to recount, but we thank them all for being our teachers in this struggle. We are especially indebted to those who responded to our request for stories to be included in this book.

Acronyms

ABA	Architectural Barriers Act
ACAA	Air Carrier Access Act
ACPD	Aviation Consumer Protection Division
ADA	Americans with Disabilities Act
ADAAG	ADA Accessibility Guidelines for Buildings and Facilities
ADAPT	American Disabled for Accessible Public Transit
ADD	attention deficit disorder
ADHD	attention deficit hyperactivity disorder
ALJ	Administrative Law Judge
AMPHL	Association of Medical Professionals with Hearing Losses
CDC	Centers for Disease Control and Prevention
CRO	Complaints Resolution Official
DOE	Department of Education
DOJ	Department of Justice
DOL	Department of Labor
DOT	Department of Transportation
DSM-IV	Diagnostic and Statistic Manual of Mental Disorders, 4th ed.
EEOC	Equal Employment Opportunity Commission
EIT	electronic and information technology
ETS	Educational Testing Service
FAA	Federal Aviation Administration
FAPE	free and appropriate public education
FHA	Fair Housing Act
FHAA	Fair Housing Amendments Act
FTA	Federal Transit Administration

GAO	Government Accounting Office
GRE	Graduate Record Exam
HAVA	Help America Vote Act
HUD	Department of Housing and Urban Development
IDEA	Individuals with Disabilities Education Act
IEP	individualized education program
IFSP	Individualized Family Service Plan
ITP	Individualized Transition Plan
LD	learning disabilities
LSAT	Law School Admissions Test
MCAT	Medical College Admission Test
MFE	multifactored evaluation
OCR	Office for Civil Rights
OTRBs	over-the-road buses
SAT	Scholastic Aptitude Test
SSDI	Social Security Disability Insurance
TDD	telecommunication device for the deaf
TSA	Transportation Security Administration
TTY	text telephone
UFAS	Uniform Federal Accessibility Standards
VAEHA	Voting Accessibility for the Elderly and Handicapped Act

1

Introduction

Many laws exist to protect the rights of individuals with disabilities, but few of them are very effective when implemented through the traditional judicial system. Those people who are well informed about their legal rights, however, are often better able to resolve matters voluntarily and informally. In this book, we strive to provide information that will make such informal resolutions possible. We discuss the variety of federal statutes that purport to protect the rights of individuals with disabilities and provide readers with basic details about how to file a formal legal complaint under these statutes. We also suggest, however, other less formal mechanisms that may be more effective in these areas. Legal enforcement includes more than just formal judicial proceedings. It also entails many strategies that are successful when carried out in the "shadow" of the law.

We do not expect that many readers of this book will hire a lawyer to protect their legal rights (although that is certainly an option they should sometimes consider). Instead, we assume that our readers want to know more about the rights of individuals with disabilities so that they can help protect those rights. Such readers might be parents or friends of individuals with disabilities or individuals with disabilities themselves.

We also do not assume that the readers of this book have had any legal training, so we try to describe—in lay terms—the rights that exist under federal disability discrimination law. Nonetheless, it is virtually impossible to discuss legal concepts without some legal jargon. When possible, we define legal terms for readers who may not understand them. For some people, a good legal dictionary might be a helpful companion while reading this book in case we do not define terms that require further explanation.

Focus on Federal Disability Discrimination Laws

This book focuses on the federal law that exists in the area of disability discrimination. Each of the fifty states and the District of Columbia also have some law in this area that applies only to the individual states. Readers might want to supplement the information from this book with research into state law in their particular state. (We do offer a list of federal and state resources in the Appendix.) In general, however, federal law is more protective of the rights of individuals with disabilities than state law. So, the information in this book should provide a good beginning for readers who want to become more informed about these rights.

When talking about individuals with disabilities, we find that the legal landscape is quite broad. There are laws relating to health insurance benefits and Social Security payments, as well as to the law of discrimination. In this book, we are addressing only the law of *dis - ability discrimination*. What legal recourse is available if an individual with a disability has faced what might be considered discrimination? Discrimination can take many forms—including outright exclusion from services, failure to make reasonable accommodations, and problems relating to inaccessibility. We discuss these three forms of discrimination as well as others ranging from employment and education to voting accessibility. Readers who want to learn more about health law topics as they relate to individuals with disabilities might benefit from the *Everyday Law for the Elderly* book in this series.

History and Overview of Federal Disability Discrimination Laws

What are the laws that prohibit disability discrimination? The first federal statute enacted on the issue was the Architectural Barriers Act of 1968 (ABA), 42 U.S.C. § 4151–4157. It requires that federally owned, leased, or financed buildings be accessible to people with disabilities. The coverage of the ABA, however, is limited to buildings directly used or funded by the federal government.

The earliest and most prominent broad-based statute barring disability discrimination was the Rehabilitation Act of 1973. Sections 501, 503, and 504 of the Rehabilitation Act, 29 U.S.C. § 791, 793, 794, prohibit federal agencies, federal contractors, and recipients of federal financial assistance from discriminating against qualified individuals with disabilities on the basis of disability. The original text banning discrimination in the Rehabilitation Act, however, was a little-noticed sentence in a comprehensive statute that provided rehabilitation services. For nearly a decade, there was virtually no judicial enforcement of this statutory requirement. In fact, some members of the disability community had to go to court to get the U.S. Department of Justice to begin enforcing this statute in the 1980s.

Today, the Rehabilitation Act is an important form of legal protection for individuals with disabilities, given the large variety of services funded, in part, by the federal government. If individuals with disabilities are attending a university or using hospital services, they are most likely utilizing the services of an entity that receives federal funds in the form of student financial aid or Medicare/Medicaid payments. The individual with a disability does not have to be using those aspects of the entity's services that receive federal financial assistance in order to have a claim of discrimination under the Rehabilitation Act.

In 1975, Congress enacted the next important federal statute in the disability discrimination area. Originally called the Education of All Handicapped Children Act, it has subsequently been renamed the Individuals with Disabilities Education Act (IDEA), 20 U.S.C. § 1400 *et seq.* IDEA is a process-oriented civil rights statute that guarantees that each child with a disability shall have an individualized education program (IEP) so that he or she can receive a free and appropriate public education (FAPE). This statute applies only to children from ages 3 to 21 while they are in preschool, primary school, or secondary school. It does not apply to university students. Discrimination claims by college students are typically heard under the Rehabilitation Act or the Americans with Disabilities Act; nearly all institutions of higher education receive federal financial assistance in the form of student financial aid that makes them subject to the Rehabilitation Act.

IDEA is not a pure antidiscrimination statute because the rights that apply to students with disabilities have no parallel for students without disabilities. Under federal law, only students with disabilities are entitled to individualized education plans as well as a free and appropriate public education. In some sense, IDEA provides *more rights* to students with disabilities than to other students. This can be frustrating for parents if their child is on the borderline between "disability" and "nondisability." If the student is deemed disabled under the definition found in IDEA, then a whole set of rights attaches to that student. If the student is struggling in school but does not meet the definition of disability, then the parents have fewer tools for advocating that additional resources be devoted to the student. Therefore, parents who want to secure extra educational resources to help their child need to have a clear understanding of how to have the child qualified as disabled for the purposes of IDEA.

IDEA was a landmark statute in that it forced school districts to accept nearly all students into their classrooms, thus preventing them from refusing to serve students with disabilities. Most of the positive results achieved under this statute, however, have not arisen as a result of litigation. Litigation is a slow and burdensome process that is unlikely to solve educational issues quickly for children in primary and secondary school. Hence, it is crucial for parents to have effective advocacy skills when asserting the rights guaranteed by IDEA in order to avoid having to resort to litigation. Chapter 3 discusses IDEA extensively, offering pointers for effective, informal advocacy.

In the 1980s several other important federal statutes were enacted, including the Voting Accessibility for the Elderly and Handicapped Act of 1984, 42 U.S.C. § 1973ee; the Air Carriers Access Act of 1986, 49 U.S.C. § 41705; the Fair Housing Act Amendments of 1988, 42 U.S.C. § 3601 *et seq.*; and the Child Abuse Amendments of 1984, 42 U.S.C. § 5101 *et seq.*

The Voting Accessibility statute requires states to promote the fundamental right to vote by improving access for handicapped and elderly individuals to registration facilities and polling places for federal elections. The Air Carriers Access Act prohibits air carriers from discriminating on the basis of disability. The Fair Housing Act Amendments expanded the coverage of the Fair Housing Act to prohibit discrimination on the basis of disability in private and public real estate transactions. The Child Abuse Amendments were intended to prevent the withholding of medical treatment to infants with disabilities.

Despite the sheer number of statutes enacted in the 1980s to protect the rights of individuals with disabilities, all of these statutes, other than the Fair Housing Act Amendments, are toothless. The Voting Accessibility statute, for example, provides individuals with a right to sue only *after* they have given the chief election officer of the state forty-five days to comply with its statutory obligations. Moreover, if the individual with a disability satisfies this notice requirement and achieves a successful outcome in court, the only relief that can be awarded is declaratory or injunctive relief (i.e., an order to require the state to make its voting places accessible in the future). Accordingly, a lawyer with such a case cannot hope to have his or her fees come out of a contingency fee award (whereby the lawyer would typically get 30–40 percent of a financial award), because no financial awards are possible under this statute. In contrast to situations involving the Rehabilitation Act and IDEA, which require a losing defendant to pay the plaintiff's attorney's fees, a state defendant who loses a case under the Voting Accessibility statute is *not* liable for attorney fees.

Thus, in the 1980s individuals with disabilities had little hope of finding a lawyer to bring a case under the Voting Accessibility statute. The lawyer would have had to take the case on a pro bono basis with no possibility of collecting attorney fees from the opposing party, even if the suit were successful. The Voting Accessibility statute also gave states no incentive to make their polling places accessible. The *worst* remedy that states had to fear was an order requiring them to make their voting places accessible in the future when, of course, federal law already imposed that requirement on them.

The Voting Accessibility statute is one of the "sounds good" statutes enacted by Congress in the disability rights area in the 1980s that had few practical implications. The only exception to this pattern, as noted above, is the Fair Housing Act Amendments of 1988, inasmuch as that statute provides for effective compensatory and punitive damages for individuals with disabilities and the possibility of attorney fees for their lawyers. Enactment of the Fair Housing Act Amendments of 1988 suggested that Congress was ready to move from "sounds good" legislation to strong legislation with effective and meaningful remedies.

Enactment of the Americans with Disabilities Act of 1990 (ADA), 42 U.S.C. § 12101–12213, reflected a genuine commitment by

Congress to enhance the substantive rights of individuals with disabilities. As of early 1990, no federal statute prohibited the majority of employers, program administrators, owners and managers of places of public accommodation, and others from discriminating against people with disabilities. In that year, more than 8 million Americans with disabilities who wanted to work were unable to obtain jobs. Individuals with disabilities also faced enormous transportation problems. Public transportation was rarely accessible to individuals with disabilities despite their disproportionately heavy reliance on such transportation. In fact, very few rail cars and only one-third of the public buses in the United States were accessible to riders with disabilities.

ADA was enacted in 1990 to assist in remedying the problems relating to access by persons with disabilities to public facilities, employment, and transportation services. Although it was enacted by an overwhelming majority in a bipartisan Congress, it has received a cool reception from judges. Moreover, it contains some fundamental flaws that has made implementation through the courts difficult.

In the employment area, which is discussed in Chapter 2, individuals with disabilities are protected by Title I of ADA. The average monetary award under this title of the statute, however, is less than $100,000, partly because individuals with disabilities often have low-paying jobs. These awards are too small for lawyers to take the cases on a contingency fee basis; because of the time-consuming nature of these cases, the contingency fee award often will not even cover the lawyer's expenses. If plaintiffs do prevail, their lawyers can seek attorney fees from the losing party, but a hostile judiciary has made it difficult for plaintiffs to succeed in many ADA cases that are taken to court. It is usually a poor bet for a lawyer to take an ADA Title I case in the hope of winning an attorney fee award from the opposing party. It is therefore crucial for individuals with disabilities to contemplate remedies other than judicial recourse to protect their rights under ADA Title I.

In the accessibility area, which is discussed in Chapter 5, we find that individuals with disabilities have very limited legal alternatives when they have been denied access to places of public accommodation due to inaccessible design features. In theory, ADA Title III bans discrimination in access to public accommodations such as restaurants, hotels, and supermarkets. But ADA Title III, like the Voting Accessibility statute, permits only suits for declaratory and injunctive relief; plaintiffs cannot bring claims for monetary damages. In other words, the best an individual can hope for, when suing to gain accessibility to a facility or to receive an accommodation, is that the court will order the change to be made; the individual will not receive any compensation for the problem that led to the suit. In contrast, however, in situations involving the Voting Accessibility statute, an individual's lawyers can be awarded attorney fees if they are successful on behalf of their client. Hence, there are lawyers who specialize in accessibility lawsuits and seek their fees from the defendant when they prevail. Unfortunately, some of these lawyers have been criticized by the media for receiving substantial attorney fee awards. Nonetheless, architects are increasingly sensitive to accessibility issues, so most new buildings comply with ADA accessibility. Further, some business owners consider it to be good business for their facility to be accessible to individuals with disabilities. But ADA provides few incentives for owners of public accommodations to make their facilities accessible when they need only fear suits for declaratory and injunctive relief.

Despite the limited remedies available under ADA Title III, however, we have seen a major transformation in many private facilities in the United States. Restaurants, hotels, and supermarkets (along with many other private facilities) are much more likely to be accessible today than they were a decade ago. Arguably, the law contains an important education component that has helped spur private entities to make their facilities more accessible to the public. Remedies, other than judicial remedies, appear to have been successful under ADA Title III. Chapter 5 discusses some successful nonjudicial strategies that have been employed under ADA Title III.

Goals and Outline of This Book

Hence, this book is both descriptive and prescriptive. We describe the existing law on disability discrimination and then suggest methods that one might employ to enforce these rights. Judicial remedies are included along with nonjudicial remedies.

Chapter 2 discusses examples from the employment area. It suggests low-cost accommodations that employees might request to resolve various fact patterns. It also discusses the intersection of Social Security Disability law and ADA Title I, so that readers will understand how to seek Social Security Disability Insurance (SSDI) benefits without jeopardizing their ADA complaints.

Chapter 3 focuses on the K–12 educational area. It walks the reader through the process of attaining an individualized educational program for his or her child. It discusses the conflicts of interest that inherently exist as part of the IEP process and explains how parents can best navigate those conflicts. (Parents have to negotiate with the people who will be providing services during the IEP process and can ill afford to alienate the person who may be educating their child.) This chapter also discusses how one might use the free legal services available in each state to children who are developmentally disabled.

Chapter 4 examines the laws affecting postsecondary educations (colleges and universities). It discusses the dramatic shift in the requirements for obtaining accommodations that occurs when a student moves from high school into postsecondary education. Specifically, it focuses on issues regarding admissions, standardized tests, and accommodations for students with disabilities.

Chapter 5 provides examples from the access and accommodation area, including the story of a young man who needs a personal assistant and is being asked to purchase two tickets for any entertainment event that he attends. The chapter discusses the alternatives that he seeks to resolve this problem—the local media and a public rally, as well as local legal assistance—and, while exploring each of these alternatives, considers why they might or might not succeed in this situation. For example, solo lawyers are often unwilling to take cases against major corporations because they know they will get drowned in paperwork, but, on the other hand, they might take a case against a locally owned proprietor.

This chapter also discusses the federal laws requiring that facilities, programs, services, and transportation be accessible to people with disabilities. It explains how these requirements apply both to private entities that operate public accommodations and to state and local governments.

Chapter 6 addresses problems facing disabled travelers such as the difficulties involved in finding van-accessible buses for long-distance travel or in dealing with airlines when they lose or damage wheelchairs. The Air Carrier Access Act is, unfortunately, a poor vehicle for solving air transportation problems because some federal courts have held that private individuals do not have the right to bring an action to enforce it. Nonetheless, complaints to airlines can sometimes result in vouchers for free air travel.

Chapter 7 explains the laws requiring access and accommodation in housing. The Fair Housing Act Amendments of 1988 provide for effective compensatory and punitive damages for individuals with disabilities and the possibility of attorney fees for their lawyers, but self-advocacy is often the quickest and best route to achieve access.

Voting rights are the focus of Chapter 8. Since voting rights remedies are fairly ineffectual, this chapter focuses on how self-advocacy through the media can be a valuable tool for increasing voting accessibility among individuals with disabilities. This chapter also emphasizes the importance of being aware of voting problems *in advance of* an election so that corrective action can be taken in a timely way. Indeed, individuals with disabilities *should* vote. At present, they are disproportionately unlikely to do so. It is estimated that individuals with disabilities could have created a different outcome in the 2000 election if they had voted in numbers proportionate to the rest of the voting-age population.

Chapter 9 concludes the book by retrospectively examining the lessons learned from previous chapters. Following that is an Appendix that provides a list of state and federal resources to assist individuals with disabilities. In theory, the United States has powerful laws banning disability discrimination. In practice, these laws are difficult to enforce. Nonetheless, voluntary efforts to make facilities, programs, services, and transportation accessible to people with disabilities have changed markedly in the past two decades as a result of publicity about the problem of disability discrimination. We sincerely hope that the readers of this book will emerge with a stronger sense of their own capability for addressing some of these problems in their personal lives.

It is easy to lose sight of the progress we have made in the disability area, due to frustrations with the recalcitrance of the judiciary's response to ADA. Joseph Shapiro, in his compelling book on the history of ADA, tells the story of a man who was being honored as the National Multiple Sclerosis Society Man of the Year in Manhattan, New York, in 1988.[1] At the time, curb cuts did not exist, many taxi drivers were unwilling to transport people in wheelchairs, and buses lacked wheelchair lifts. Although the man was staying in a hotel across the street from the award ceremony, the conference organizers had to hire a van with a special hydraulic lift to get him across the street! Today, by contrast—as a result of ADA's passage, extensive litigation against cities that have resisted installing curb cuts, and voluntary compliance—that ride across the street is likely to be less cumbersome. We have made the transition from no curb cuts at all to crumpled curb cuts that need repairing. Cities now understand that they have the responsibility to install and even maintain curb cuts, while individuals with disabilities have learned to assert their rights to independent living.

Our aim is to provide the readers of this book with comprehensive information about the rights of individuals with disabilities so that they can seek to have these rights enforced more rigorously. It is hard work, but knowledge of one's rights can be an important starting point on that voyage.

Notes

1. Joseph Shapiro, *No Pity: People with Civil Rights Forging a New Civil Rights Movement* (1993), p. 8.

2
The Law of Employment Discrimination

The Americans with Disabilities Act generally provides that an employer may not discriminate against an individual with a disability "in regard to job application procedures, the hiring, advancement, or discharge of employees, employee compensation, job training, and other terms, conditions, and privileges of employment."

Discrimination can be *intentional* or *unintentional.* Unlawful *intentional* discrimination, for example, would be a refusal to consider an individual for a job as a truck driver because he or she is deaf. Unlawful *unintentional* discrimination could include requiring all applicants for a teaching position to have a valid driver's license. Although the rule requiring a driver's license may not have been created to exclude individuals with disabilities, it will have that unintended consequence for some individuals with disabilities because they cannot drive for a disability-related reason. Another common form of unintentional discrimination is lack of physical accessibility. A business may not have installed steps to its entrance to exclude individuals who use wheelchairs from working there, but the steps have that unintended consequence.

In order to bring a successful claim of discrimination against an employer, one typically must

- be an *individual with a disability*;
- be *qualified* for the position one seeks or holds *with or without reasonable accommodations;*
- have been *discriminated* against *because of* one's disability; and

- *not* pose a direct threat to self or others because of one's disability.

If an individual is *not* disabled, then an employer is entitled to treat that person arbitrarily, so long as such treatment does not violate any other federal or state law. For example, an employer could decide that he does not want to hire a receptionist who wears eyeglasses because he thinks that people who wear glasses are unattractive. The mere fact that someone needs to wear eyeglasses does not constitute a disability under federal law. Thus, a typical eyeglass wearer could not challenge that (silly) rule under federal disability law because she is not an individual with a disability. On the other hand, if the eyeglass wearer is legally blind and could perform the essential functions of the job (i.e., greeting people) if she were allowed to wear eyeglasses, then she could bring a claim under federal disability law. Her argument would be that she

- is an individual with a disability due to her blindness;
- is qualified for the position in question with the reasonable accommodation of being permitted to wear eyeglasses;
- is being discriminated against because of her disability and her consequent need to wear eyeglasses; and
- poses no threat to self or others because of her need to wear eyeglasses.

Relevant Statutes

The principal federal statute that protects individuals who have faced employment discrimination on the basis of disability is Title I of the Americans with Disabilities Act (ADA). Title I forbids employers with fifteen or more employees from discriminating against qualified individuals with disabilities in the full range of employment-related activities. ADA is divided into three main titles: Title I covers employment discrimination, Title II covers discrimination by public entities such as state and local government, and Title III covers discrimination by what are called public accommodations such as restaurants, hotels, and grocery stores.

In theory, an individual who is a victim of employment discrimination by a public entity could sue under ADA Title I or Title II, because ADA Title I covers both public and private employment discrimination and ADA Title II covers all discrimination by public entities. In practice, however, employment discrimination lawsuits are typically brought under ADA Title I, irrespective of whether the defendant is public or private.

Although ADA Title I is the principal statute that prohibits employment discrimination, the Rehabilitation Act of 1973 is also sometimes relevant. Section 504 of the Rehabilitation Act prohibits discrimination in programs or activities that receive federal financial assistance. It also prohibits discrimination by federal agencies. ADA does *not* prohibit discrimination by federal agencies. A victim of discrimination by the federal government would bring suit under Sections 501 and 505 of the Rehabilitation Act. Section 505(a) of the Rehabilitation Act provides that an individual has a private right of action under Section 501 against a federal employer [29 U.S.C. § 7941(a)(1)].

In addition, each state has a state law that bans employment discrimination on the basis of disability. This fact is particularly important in cases where the defendant is the *state* itself. The leading case on this issue is *Board of Trustees of the University of Alabama v. Garrett*, 531 U.S. 356 (2001). In that event, the plaintiffs who were alleged victims of employment discrimination, sued the state in federal district court for monetary damages under ADA Title I. (ADA Title I expressly provides that individuals may sue states for employment discrimination.) The Supreme Court ruled that Congress did not have the constitutional authority to allow plaintiffs to bring such a lawsuit. ADA Title I is unconstitutional, the Court held, to the extent that it permits private plaintiffs to sue a state for monetary damages in federal court for employment discrimination. This ruling, however, applies only to suits against the *state* as defendant when the plaintiff is seeking *monetary damages.* The *Garrett* decision still left in place many remedies for individuals who are victims of employment discrimination by the states. They may

- sue under ADA Title I for *injunctive and declaratory relief;*[1]
- file a complaint with the U.S. Department of Justice, asking it to investigate the alleged acts of employment discrimination;[2]
- sue under Section 504 of the Rehabilitation Act, if the entity receives federal financial assistance; or
- sue under state disability discrimination law.

In sum, the principal statute banning employment discrimination is ADA Title I, but if the individual is suing a public entity such as state or federal government, then it may be necessary to proceed under the Rehabilitation Act or other relevant statutes. In this chapter, we will assume the individual is suing under ADA Title I because the substantive requirements under each of these statutes is virtually the same.

Who Is Covered

Definition of Disability
In order to file a lawsuit under ADA or the Rehabilitation Act, one must be an "individual with a disability." These federal laws define an individual with a disability as one who

1. has a physical or mental impairment that substantially limits one or more of the individual's major life activities;
2. has a record of such impairment; or
3. is regarded as having such an impairment.

Most of the successful cases brought under federal law involve individuals who meet the first definition: They actually *are* disabled.

The second definition applies to someone who used to have a disability and is now cured, but is being discriminated against on the basis of that prior disability. For example, Gene Arline, a schoolteacher, lost her teaching job because she had tuberculosis when she was younger. The Supreme Court ruled that she could bring a claim of discrimination under the Rehabilitation Act under a *record of theory*, because she had a record of a disability that was the basis of an adverse employment decision [*School Bd. of Nassau Cty. v. Arline*, 480 U.S. 273 (1987)].

The third definition applies to someone who is healthy but is *falsely regarded* as disabled. For example, employers have sometimes falsely regarded gay men as disabled by presuming they are HIV-positive. Because HIV is a disability itself, these men have been able to bring ADA claims under the theory that they were falsely regarded as having a disabling condition. The "regarded-as" theory, however, is extremely difficult to use successfully, because it requires the plaintiff to get into the mental mindset of the defendant. The defendant can simply deny that he or she regarded the plaintiff to be disabled and, instead, suggest another rationale for the adverse job action. As of April 2005, no ADA plaintiff has successfully used a regarded-as theory of disability in a successful case brought to the U.S. Supreme Court, although a few successful cases have been heard in the federal courts of appeals.

Mitigating Measures Rule

Most successful lawsuits are brought under the first definition of disability, but even this definition is a hard one to pursue because the Supreme Court has ruled that a court has to determine whether someone is disabled *after* considering the effects of any assistive devices or medication he or she might use. Oddly enough, that rule applies even when the employer decides not to hire someone based on his or her condition *before* the person uses an assistive device. For example, twin sisters Karen Sutton and Kimberly Hinton were not hired by United Airlines because they failed the vision screening, which they underwent *without being able to wear their corrective lenses*. Uncorrected, their vision was 20/200 and 20/400 respectively. Their vision was 20/20, however, with the use of corrective lenses. The sisters brought suit against United Airlines, alleging that they were discriminated against on the basis of their disability (poor vision). They lost because the courts found them not to meet the statutory definition of disability. In *Sutton v. United Air Lines, Inc.*, 527 U.S. 471 (1999), the Supreme Court held that "[a] person whose physical or mental impairment is corrected by medication or other measures does not have an impairment that 'substantially limits' a major life activity." Under that interpretation of the word *disability,* they were not disabled because their condition was corrected with eyeglasses.

Lower courts have applied this holding to other corrective devices such as hearing aids and to various medications that one might take for psychological impairments on the grounds that these corrective devices permit a person not to be "substantially limited" in a major life activity. Thus, for instance, the courts have ruled that individuals who have auditory impairments or seizure disorders or psychological impairments are not disabled. It does not matter whether the employer treated them adversely because of their symptoms in an uncorrected state. Some lower courts, however, have taken this interpretation of *disability* too far, resulting in successful appeals. For example, an appellate court recently overturned a lower court that had concluded that an individual with cerebral palsy was not disabled. The court of appeals ruled that the fact that the individual had worked hard to participate actively in society, including working at the same company for twenty-five years and serving as a volunteer firefighter and mediator, did *not* mean that he was not disabled due to his substantial physical impairments.

A narrow interpretation of the word *disability* has made it difficult for plaintiffs to demonstrate that they are both "disabled" and "qualified" for employment. If the individual's disability is so severe that mitigating measures do not alleviate the symptoms, then the individual is often not qualified for the particular position in question. But if the disability is relatively mild after the use of mitigating measures, then the person is not sufficiently limited to be disabled. This is the "Catch-22" of the law of disability discrimination. Courts are currently wrestling with the issue of whether to broaden the interpretation of the word *disability* to avoid this Catch-22.

The narrow interpretation of this word means that employees need to think twice before pursuing litigation against an employer. It is quite possible that a court will conclude that they are either not disabled or not qualified for the position in question. Given the tendency of trial courts to rule against plaintiffs on the question of whether they are disabled and qualified, few lawyers will take disability discrimination cases on a pro bono basis. These facts put pressure on disabled employees to find mechanisms *other* than litigation to pursue their complaints about discriminatory treatment.

Importance of Medical Evidence

We have found that medical evidence is extremely important in ADA cases, irrespective of whether a plaintiff ever files a formal complaint in court. It is usually advisable for a disabled employee to receive a *written report* from a *licensed medical professional* documenting that he or she is a qualified individual with a disability. This letter, if possible, should state the medical diagnosis, the limitations imposed by the disability, and the conclusion that the individual is qualified to perform the essential functions of the position in question with or without accommodations. Such a letter should be placed in the *personnel file* of the individual with a disability so that the employer cannot later claim to have been unaware of the employee's disability status.

When requesting a letter from a medical professional, the disabled employee needs to make sure that the medical professional is aware of the essential requirements of the job. The letter should state that the treating professional has been given the written job description for the position in question (if one is available), and that the employee is disabled as well as physically or mentally qualified for the position in question. If appropriate, the letter can also identify reasonable accommodations that should be offered to the employee. It is crucial that the letter state that the individual is *both* disabled and qualified. Otherwise, the employer can try to use the letter to suggest that the individual is not qualified for the position in question.

Medical documentation needs to be included in the personnel file for two important reasons:

• The employer cannot later deny having knowledge that the individual is disabled.
• An employee cannot request reasonable accommodations without first establishing that he or she is disabled. Medical documentation is often necessary to ascertain disability status.

Susan Abdo's experience in her lawsuit against the University of Vermont exemplifies the key role that medical documentation can play in an ADA complaint [*see Abdo v. University of Vermont*, 263 F. Supp.2d 772 (D. Vt. 2003)]. Although her case involved educational discrimination rather than employment discrimination, the same factors apply with regard to the importance of good medical documentation. In 1999, Ms. Abdo enrolled in graduate classes at the University of Vermont. As a result of an earlier car accident, she had serious neck and jaw injuries that made it difficult for her to sit for long periods of time. Ms. Abdo obtained a letter from her treating physician that described the nature of her disability and specifically requested accommodations that would allow her to maintain her status as a qualified individual with a disability. However, her physician's first letter did not entirely satisfy the university because it was not thorough enough for the university to determine whether she was substantially limited in a major life activity. Further, the initial letter did not specify the "degree and range of functioning." When Ms. Abdo learned of the university's problems with her medical documentation, she obtained a letter from a second treating physician that was much more specific. It stated how long she was able to sit, how long she was able to engage in upright activities, and how much time she could take without rest.

Despite the specificity of the second letter, the university continued to refuse to agree that Ms. Abdo was disabled as defined by

ADA. It claimed that both letters were insufficient because the treating physicians did not identify a precise medical diagnosis of the disability. In hindsight, it probably would have been better for the physicians' letters to have specified a medical diagnosis, but that failure was not fatal to her legal claim. The trial court found that the letters were adequate to support her claim of being disabled because they "set forth the functional limitations imposed by her disability."

Ms. Abdo did not prevail on her ADA case until four years after the university refused to accommodate her. Litigation was her only alternative because the university refused to cooperate to attain a voluntary resolution of her complaint. At many universities, including the one she was attending, Ms. Abdo would have been able to obtain the requested accommodations if she had supplied the medical information earlier and been more forthcoming about her diagnosis and degree of limitations. Doctors are often not aware of the ADA requirement to demonstrate a substantial limitation of one or more major life activities. Individuals with disabilities need to work closely with their physicians in order to ensure that medical documentation is sufficiently complete to resolve cases without recourse to litigation. But they also need to be careful not to overstate the extent of their impairment, because if they do so the employer or other entity may suggest that they are not qualified. *Specificity rather than over - statement* is the key to successful documentation of disability.

Unfortunately, the documentation of disability can be expensive. In the case under discussion, Ms. Abdo had to pay to see a second physician in order to acquire adequate documentation. Health insurance plans do not always cover these services. In the Appendix, we have included a list of state-by-state resources. Some of these resources might help individuals locate qualified physicians who can diagnose disabilities; others may help reduce the costs of health care. For the most part, however, individuals with disabilities themselves must bear the expense of providing medical documentation.

Qualified Individual with a Disability

In order to bring a claim of discrimination, a plaintiff must be a *qual - ified* individual with a disability. A qualified individual with a disability is an "individual with a disability who, with or without reasonable accommodation, can perform the essential functions of the employment position that such individual holds or desires" [42 U.S.C. § 12111(8)].

Notice that this "qualified" assessment occurs *after* the effectiveness of reasonable accommodations has been considered. (Reasonable accommodations are discussed under "Request for Reasonable Accommodation" later in this chapter.) Let us assume, for example, that Susan Fish, a woman with a hearing impairment, is seeking a position as a secretary, and one of her job duties would be answering the telephone and taking messages. She is a proficient typist but cannot talk on the telephone without an amplification device. She would be a qualified individual with a disability because she can perform the essential functions of the employment position *with reasonable accommodation* (the amplification device).

An important aspect of the "qualified" assessment is whether the individual can perform the essential functions of the employment position. The courts have consistently held that an employer's *written job description* that is prepared *before advertising or interviewing applicants* should be given strong weight in determining the essential functions of the employment position [42 U.S.C. § 12111(8)].

Returning to the previous hypothetical scenario, let us assume, for example, that Susan's hearing impairment is so severe that she cannot communicate on the telephone even with the use of an amplification device. She can communicate with a TTY (a telecommunication device for the deaf), but that process is too slow and cumbersome to be effective at the workplace because it would involve an operator interceding in her calls. Can Susan still be considered a qualified individual with a disability if she is a competent typist? The answer may depend on the content of the employer's written job description prepared in advance of advertising for the position. If the written job description specifies that the secretary must be a competent typist but does not specify that the person must answer the telephone, then Susan might successfully argue that telephone answering is not an *essential* function of the job— in other words, that it is a secondary task that could be assigned to someone else, with Susan, in return, receiving extra typing work. On the other hand, if telephone answering *is* listed in the written job description as a primary task in the job, then Susan needs to be able to demonstrate a way that she can perform that task with reasonable accommodation. If she cannot perform that essential task with reasonable accommodation, then she is not a qualified individual with a disability.

General Types of Discriminatory Practices

ADA Title I forbids a wide variety of discriminatory practices. Typically, ADA Title I covers only those *employees* or *applicants for employment* who meet the definition of disability. It generally forbids discrimination in regard to job application procedures; the hiring, advancement, or discharge of employees; employee compensation; job training; and other terms, conditions, and privileges of employment. More specifically, 42 U.S.C. §12112(b) lists seven types of actions that constitute discrimination on the basis of disability:

1. limiting, segregating, or classifying a job applicant or employee in a way that adversely affects the opportunities or status of such applicant or employee (e.g., an employer adopts a separate track for employees with disabilities based on the presumption that employees with disabilities are uninterested in, or incapable of, performing particular jobs)
2. participating in a contractual or other arrangement or relationship that has the effect of subjecting a covered entity's qualified applicant or employee with a disability to prohibited discrimination (e.g., an employer hires a training company to do training for its employees and the training company picks an inaccessible site for that training)
3. utilizing standards, criteria, or methods of administration (a) that have the effect of discrimination on the basis of disability or (b) that perpetuate the discrimination of others who are subject to common administrative control (e.g., an employer requires a job applicant to show a valid driver's license to be considered for employment even though the job does not require driving)
4. excluding or otherwise denying jobs or benefits to a qualified individual because of the known disability of someone with whom the qualified individual is known to have a relationship or association (e.g., an employer refuses to hire a woman because he knows that her son is HIV-positive)
5. (a) not making reasonable accommodations to the known physical or mental limitations of an otherwise qualified individual with a disability who is an applicant or employee, unless such covered entity can demonstrate that the accommodation would impose an undue hardship on the operation of the business of

such covered entity; or (b) denying employment opportunities to a job applicant or employee who is an otherwise qualified individual with a disability, if such denial is based on the need of such covered entity to make reasonable accommodation to the physical or mental impairments of the employee or applicant (e.g., an applicant for a job with a law firm requires a machine that magnifies print in order to perform the job but the firm refuses to consider purchasing such equipment)

6. using qualification standards, employment tests, or other selection criteria that screen out or tend to screen out an individual with a disability unless the selection device is shown to be job-related and consistent with business necessity (e.g., an employer requires applicants for a secretarial position to use a particular computer keyboard for testing when the applicant could demonstrate his computer skills effectively if allowed to use a modified keyboard)

7. failing to select and administer tests concerning employment in the most effective manner to ensure that the test results accurately reflect the skills and abilities of the individual with a disability rather than reflecting the impaired sensory, manual, or speaking skills of such employee or applicant, except where such skills are the factors that the test purports to measure (e.g., an employer requires applicants to take a written math test for a position as a cashier even though, if allowed to take the test orally, the applicant could have demonstrated her qualifications for the position)

It is *not* necessary to prove that employers *intentionally* engaged in discrimination in order for their activities to be covered by ADA Title I. Indeed, rules that have an *adverse effect* on the opportunities or status of a job applicant or employee are also covered by the statute. For example, an employer might require job applicants to take a pencil/paper test before making an employment decision. That type of exam was probably not chosen for the purpose of discriminating against someone on the basis of a disability. But if the design of the testing instrument precludes an individual with a disability from showing that he or she is qualified for the position in question, then the disabled individual could allege discrimination on the basis of disability.

Associational Discrimination

Although individuals typically have to be disabled in order to bring a complaint under ADA Title I, there are two situations in which that status is not necessary. The first of these situations is when discrimination occurs because of someone's *relationship or association* with an individual with a disability [42 U.S.C. §12112(b)(4)]. For example, if a parent is fired because an employer is concerned that she will miss too much work to care for her child with a disability, then the parent has a claim of *associational* discrimination.

Claims of associational discrimination are hard to prove. For example, Joan Ennis adopted a boy who was HIV-positive. Shortly before she adopted her son, the employer sent around a memo reminding employees that they were self-insured and stating that it would be in everyone's interest to keep down health insurance costs. Ms. Ennis was fired within six months of adopting her son, supposedly for inferior job performance. When she claimed that her discharge was due to her employer's concern that her adopted son might incur large doctor's bills, the employer denied having that concern. When she challenged the employer's position through litigation, she lost [*Ennis v. National Association of Business and Educational Radio, Inc.,* 53 F.3d 55 (4th Cir. 1995)].

The facts of the situation need to be unambiguous if one is to be successful under an associational theory of discrimination. In the late 1980s, Professor Colker was able to help resolve a case successfully involving an extreme fact pattern. When Brian Lowe's fellow hotel/restaurant employees learned that Brian's best friend was dying of AIDS, they started wearing white gloves at work and said they were scared they would catch the "plague" from Brian. Brian was soon discharged from his job as a waiter out of the stated concern that he could not "get along well with others." Yet before the AIDS scare had occurred, Brian had received no negative performance evaluations. When Brian contacted me to assist him on this matter, Professor Colker immediately called the employer to discuss the situation. The personnel manager was not even aware that the other employees were shunning Brian because of the AIDS scare. She agreed to provide some compensation to Brian and to educate the other employees about HIV transmission once she heard the whole story. It was very helpful that one of Brian's supervisors was able to corroborate his version of the story. Because the employees' behavior had been so extreme—wearing white gloves and overtly discussing getting the "plague"—it was easy to demonstrate that Brian was being treated adversely because of his relationship with another person. In resolving this case, it was also helpful that Brian did not desire reinstatement. He simply wanted some money to tide him over until he could obtain further employment. The hotel was happy to pay Brian some money to avoid adverse publicity, and the public interest was served through some AIDS education. Had Brian insisted on reinstatement, Professor Colker may have had more difficulty resolving the case voluntarily.

Medical Examinations and Inquiries

The other situation in which a plaintiff in an ADA case does not actually have to be disabled to file a complaint is the medical examination and inquiry situation [*see* 42 U.S.C. § 12112(d)]. There are two main rules with respect to medical examinations and inquiries.

Under the first rule, an employer may not conduct a medical examination or make inquiries of a job applicant as to whether such individual has a disability *before* making an offer of employment. However, once an employer has made an offer of employment, the employer may *condition* the offer of employment on the successful completion of a medical examination. That medical examination

- must be given to *all* entering employees regardless of their disability status; and
- must be treated as a confidential medical record and maintained separately from the personnel file.

All applicants for employment are covered by this rule, not simply applicants who are disabled.

This rule is particularly advantageous to individuals with *invisible* disabilities. Let us assume, for example, that an individual, Rhonda, with a seizure disorder applies to be a schoolteacher. The school district makes an offer of employment conditioned upon the successful completion of a medical exam. Rhonda submits to the medical examination, at which time the school district physician learns that she has a seizure disorder that she successfully controls with medication. If the school district then rescinds its offer of employment, Rhonda would know that the rescission has occurred because of her disability and would be in a good position to file a complaint about her adverse treatment. Alternatively, if the school district had been able to require her to take a medical examination *before* making its offer of employment, it could have invented another reason for denying her employment, hiding its true disability-based reason.

Under the second medical-exam rule, an employer may make inquiries of incumbent employees as to the nature or severity of their disabilities. These inquiries do *not* have to be made to all employees. Nonetheless, the employer may use the results of the examination only in ways that are *job-related and consistent with business neces - sity*. Let us assume, for example, that Rhonda was hired as a schoolteacher and the school district was aware that she had a seizure disorder. The school district could request that Rhonda undergo a periodic medical exam to make sure that her seizure disorder was under control. The school district might argue, for example, that it is important that Rhonda be able to help safely evacuate children in the event of a fire and that she not suffer from a seizure disorder in those circumstances. But the school district must use the results of the medical exam in a way that is job-related and consistent with business necessity. If the results of the exam indicate that Rhonda's seizure disorder will not interfere with the essential functions of her job, then the school district cannot use those results to terminate her employment.

Request for Reasonable Accommodation

It is unlawful for an employer to fail to make reasonable accommodations to the *known* physical or mental limitations of a qualified individual with a disability, unless the employer can demonstrate that the accommodation would impose an undue hardship on the operation of the business [*see* 42 U.S.C. § 12112(b)(5)]. ADA Title I defines an "undue hardship" as an "action requiring significant difficulty or expense" when considered in light of four factors specified by the statute: (1) the nature and cost of the accommodation, (2) the overall financial resources of the facilities, (3) the overall financial resources of the covered entity, and (4) the type of operation or operations of the covered entity.

The undue hardship exception gets complicated when an individual works for a franchise. In that event, a court has to investigate the financial relationship between the franchisor and the franchisee. If a franchisee simply pays an annual franchise fee to the franchisor and receives no financial support from the franchisor, then, according to the Equal Employment Opportunity Commission (EEOC), a court should consider only the financial resources of the franchisee in determining whether or not providing an accommodation would be an undue hardship [*see* ADA Title I, EEOC Interpretive Guidance, 29 C.F.R. Part 1630, Appendix § 1630.2(p)].

In determining whether a financial expenditure would constitute an undue hardship, however, the employer needs to evaluate all potential sources of funding. If funding is available from a state vocational rehabilitation agency or if tax credits are available to offset the cost of the accommodation, such monies are considered part of the financial resources of the covered entity. An employee may also offer to pay part of the cost of an accommodation in order to secure employment. In that event, only the remaining cost of the accommodation should be considered in making the undue hardship inquiry.

When an employee makes a request for a reasonable accommodation, the employer is supposed to engage in an interactive dialogue with the employee to determine what accommodation would be reasonable and effective. Suggested reasonable accommodations under the federal laws include (but are not limited to): (1) making existing facilities readily accessible to and usable by people with disabilities (including both work areas and nonwork areas such as lunchrooms, restrooms, and training rooms); (2) job restructuring (by reallocating or redistributing nonessential job functions); (3) development of part-time or modified work schedules; (4) reassignment to a vacant position (when accommodation within an employee's current job cannot satisfactorily be made); (5) acquisition or modification of equipment or devices; (6) modification or adjustment of examinations, training materials, or policies; and (7) provision of auxiliary aids such as qualified readers or interpreters for blind or deaf employees. This list of suggested accommodations is not exhaustive, nor would all of the suggested accommodations be reasonable in every situation. What constitutes an appropriate accommodation in a given case must be determined by utilizing a fact-based case-by-case approach, considering all relevant factors. The reasonable accommodation mandate does not require an employer to provide personal items for an employee's use, such as eyeglasses, wheelchairs, or prosthetic limbs, unless such items are specifically designed or required to meet job-related rather than personal needs.

There are numerous resources that can help people locate reasonable accommodations. These resources include the following:

- the Job Accommodation Network at http://www.jan.wvu.edu
- links on the Department of Labor's Office of Disability Employment Policy website at http://www.dol.gov/odep
- links on the National Center on Workforce and Disability/Adult website at http://www.onestops.info
- links on the DisabilityInfo.gov site at http://www.disability info.gov/digov-public/public/DisplayPage.do?parent FolderId=5064 and http://www.disabilityinfo.gov/digov-public/public/DisplayPage.do?parentFolderId=13

The reasonable accommodation rule is not triggered until

- the employee identifies him- or herself as an individual with a disability; and
- the employee requests a reasonable accommodation.

The employer should *not* be the person to initiate the discussion about reasonable accommodation. That is the responsibility of the employee. If an employee is not able to perform the essential functions of the job and requests no accommodation to facilitate performing those functions, then the employer is entitled to terminate the employee's employment.

To understand the importance of requesting an accommodation, let us reconsider the previous example involving a secretarial position with telephone answering duties. This time, let us assume that Tom Fish has developed a hearing impairment after being hired for a secretarial position that includes telephone answering duties. Because Tom cannot hear telephone conversations well, let us assume that he is not adequately performing his telephone answering duties. Tom, however, has not told his employer about his hearing loss. The employer may legitimately fire Tom for failing to perform the essential functions of the job.

Now let us assume that Tom brings to his employer's attention the fact that he has a hearing impairment. Further, he requests a reasonable accommodation to permit him to perform his telephone answering duties. These accommodations might include an amplified phone. Once Tom makes a request that is reasonable (i.e., not unduly costly) and effective (i.e., would permit him to perform the essential functions of the job), then the employer has the responsibility to reply. The employer could suggest another solution or argue that the proposed solution is not effective. For example, Tom's hearing impairment might be so severe that even an amplified phone would not permit him to perform the essential functions of the job. That would be a fact question that the employer and employee would try to resolve. If the employer believes that Tom's requested accommodation would not be effective, then the employer could suggest an alternative accommodation.

It is usually best if the employee himself can suggest at least one accommodation that is both reasonable and effective, because the employer may be unable to suggest any accommodations at all. The employer is unlikely to conduct extensive outside research to discover accommodations that might be effective, so the employee is well advised to do his homework before making reasonable accommodation recommendations. For example, a group of firefighters sued under ADA, claiming that they had a skin disorder that precluded them from being able to comply with the employer's "no-beard" policy. The purpose of the no-beard policy was to ensure that the firefighters' face masks had a tight fit to their faces. The firefighters asked to be excused from the no-beard policy, but the employer responded that such a rule would jeopardize their safety. From a trade publication the firefighters learned of a mask that had been developed that could provide a tight seal even over a bearded face. But by the time they made this discovery, they had already lost their case. If they had extensively reviewed the trade magazines *before* filing their complaint, they may have been able to propose a reasonable and effective accommodation.

In thinking about what accommodations would be reasonable and effective, we need to remember that an employee must be able to perform *all* the *essential* functions of the job with reasonable accommodations. Hence, in our example concerning Tom Fish, we assumed that answering the telephone was an essential function of his job as secretary. As a reasonable accommodation, Tom could *not* request that his telephone duties be eliminated from his job description. Instead, he needed to figure out what kinds of accommodations would permit him to perform the essential functions of the job.

The key points about reasonable accommodations are as follows:

- They must be reasonable.
- They must be effective.

- They are required only for individuals who have identified themselves as disabled.
- They permit the individual to perform all the essential functions of the job.

Ultimately, after following this problem-solving approach, the employer has the discretion to choose the accommodation that will be provided and may choose the least expensive accommodation or the accommodation that is easiest to provide, so long as the accommodation provided is effective. Because ADA Title I does not specify a time frame within which an employer must provide an accommodation, and courts have considered the following factors in determining whether a delay in providing one violates ADA: (1) the length of the delay, (2) the reasons for the delay, (3) whether the employer has offered any alternative accommodations while evaluating a particular request, and (4) whether the employer has acted in good faith [*see, e.g., Selenke v. Medical Imaging of Colorado*, 248 F.3d 1249 (10th Cir. 2001)]. Further, since Title I contemplates an interactive process between employer and employee, *both* have responsibilities in this regard. Thus it has been held that employees who fail to fulfill their responsibilities in this process cannot prevail in an action under Title I.

Defenses

ADA Title I contains two major defenses that are available in all employment discrimination cases:

1. A test or selection criteria that screens out individuals with disabilities has been shown to be *job-related and consistent with business necessity.*
2. An individual may pose a direct threat to the health or safety of others at the workplace by performing the essential functions of the job.

Of these two defenses, the second one—the direct threat defense—has proven particularly difficult for plaintiffs.

The direct threat defense does *not* state that an individual may not pose a direct threat to *himself or herself* at the workplace. It only references threats to *others* at the workplace [42 U.S.C. § 12113(b)]. Nonetheless, the Supreme Court has concluded that employers may refuse to hire someone out of fear that the workplace may exacerbate that person's disability.

For example, Mario Echazabal applied for a position with Chevron at one of its oil refineries. He was offered a job that was conditioned upon his being able to pass the company's physical examination. (See "Medical Examinations and Inquiries" earlier in this chapter for a discussion of job offers conditioned upon passing a physical examination.) However, when the test results revealed a liver abnormality or damage caused by Hepatitis C, he was denied employment. Chevron claimed that his condition would be aggravated by exposure to toxins at its refinery. Echazabal countered that Chevron's decision reflected the kind of workplace paternalism that ADA was meant to outlaw. Because his employment would not harm others, Echazabal argued, he, rather than the employer, should be able to evaluate the level of risk that he chose to accept as a condition of employment. The Supreme Court disagreed [*Chevron U.S.A. Inc. v. Echazabal*, 536 U.S. 73, 81 (2002)]. In doing so, it approved an EEOC regulation stating that an employer may preclude employment of an individual due to the potential harm to the employee's own health presented at the workplace, so long as the employer is acting on the basis of "a reasonable medical judgment that relies on the most current medical knowledge and/or the best available objective evidence" and upon an expressly "individualized assessment of the individual's present ability to safely perform the essential functions of the job" [29 C.F.R. § 1630.2(r)]. The *Echazabal* decision provides the employer, rather than the employee, with the final say in how much risk to self an individual should accept at the workplace as a condition of employment.

When faced with a problem involving the direct threat defense, an employee needs to ensure that the inquiry is particularized to that fact situation. The case law under ADA emphasizes that application of the direct threat defense is supposed to be based on an *individual - ized* inquiry. Professor Colker was able to use that fact to informally resolve an ADA case involving a paramedic. When the city learned that one of its paramedics was HIV-positive, it wanted to either reassign him to telephone dispatch duties or discharge him. The employee had worked as a paramedic for twenty years, felt healthy, and wanted to maintain his current employment. The city argued that the employee could pose a threat to others because he might perform procedures that involved possible transmission of his bodily fluids to others if he was cut during the emergency procedure.

In theory, of course, it is possible that a health care worker might perform a procedure that could result in the transmission of bodily fluids from the health care worker to the patient. The Centers for Disease Control and Prevention (CDC), which has guidelines on that situation, cautions that extra care must be exercised when working in dark spaces with sharp instruments. But the city's response needed to be based on a particularized inquiry. Was there any genuine risk that this employee might have found himself in a situation where performance of his duties could create a risk to the health of others? Professor Colker therefore asked the city to identify all of the medical procedures performed by a paramedic that could possibly lead to fluid transmission from health care provider to patient. She then interviewed her client and was able to determine that he had not performed any of those procedures in his twenty years of work as a paramedic. Armed with that information, she was able to persuade the city that it did not have a sound legal basis for using the direct threat defense.

The Supreme Court has said that the "direct threat defense must be based on a reasonable medical judgment that relies on the most current medical knowledge and/or the best available objective evidence, and upon an expressly individualized assessment of the individual's present ability to safely perform the essential functions of the job, reached after considering, among other things, the imminence of the risk and the severity of the harm portended" [*Chevron U.S.A., Inc. v. Echazabal,* 536 U.S. 73. 86 (2002)]. A hypothetical risk that is contrary to twenty years of the employee's actual work experience does not meet that test.

One reason that Professor Colker had some leverage to resolve this direct threat case voluntarily was that the city had violated ADA's confidentiality rules. The employee had not informed the city that he was HIV-positive; yet when the city learned that fact through its health insurance provider, it made no attempt to keep the information confidential. Professor Colker agreed to not seek damages for the city's failure to keep medical records confidential if it allowed the employee to continue working as a paramedic. Further, although she had learned that the employee had never been put in a situation where he was at risk of transmitting bodily fluids to a patient, she agreed that the employee would refrain from putting himself in such a situation in the future. She learned that paramedics always work in teams of two and, therefore, that it would be possible for her client to refrain from engaging in an "exposure-prone" procedure if one were to arise on the job. Her client had no interest in exposing the public to any possible harm, so he was happy to reach that accommodation. By keeping the lines of communication open, then, Professor Colker was able to offer a concession to the city while protecting her client's interests. Her client was able to return to work very quickly and to maintain employment while his health was still good. Had she pursued litigation, her client may have achieved a successful outcome, but the stress of litigation may have had an adverse effect on his health. Further, he may have won back his right to work at a time when his health no longer permitted him to work. A quick, voluntary resolution of this case was invaluable to her client.

Interaction Between ADA Title I and Social Security Disability Insurance

Many individuals who file claims of discrimination under ADA Title I have also filed claims for compensation under Social Security Disability Insurance (SSDI). The Social Security Act provides monetary benefits to every insured individual who "is under a disability." The act defines disability as an "inability to engage in any substantial gainful activity by reason of any . . . physical or mental impairment which can be expected to result in death or which has lasted or can be expected to last for a continuous period of not less than 12 months" [42 U.S.C. § 423(d)(1)(A)].

In some situations, individuals who allege that they have been unlawfully terminated from employment because of a disability also file for benefits under SSDI. On the one hand, for the purposes of ADA, they are arguing that they should not have been terminated because they are qualified individuals with a disability; on the other hand, they are arguing that they are "unable to engage in employment by reason of a long-term disability." Seizing upon inconsistent statements like these, employers have argued that such individuals cannot be qualified for employment and, hence, that their discharge was lawful under ADA Title I.

This argument puts discharged employees in a quandary: They may need the financial security of SSDI but may also want to pursue a lawsuit under ADA Title I for an unlawful discharge. Can a former employee apply for SSDI benefits while continuing to pursue an ADA Title I lawsuit?

Depending on the facts of the individual situation, it may be possible to pursue both claims. As the Supreme Court noted in *Cleveland v. Policy Management Systems Corporation* [526 U.S. 795 (1999)], there are important differences between the ADA Title I inquiry and the SSDI inquiry. Most important, ADA defines a qualified individual to be an individual who can perform the essential functions of the job *with reasonable accommodation.* SSDI does not reference reasonable accommodations in defining who is disabled. In addition, the ADA Title I inquiry is a highly individualized inquiry, based on the facts relating to the specific employee and employer. By contrast, the Social Security Administration receives more than 2.5 million claims for disability benefits each year; it cannot make judgments based on highly specific factual disputes about the workplace.

It is in an individual's best interest to be careful about what he or she says in an SSDI application if the individual also desires to pursue an ADA claim. Let us assume, for example, that Douglas Parker sustains a back injury on the job that precludes him from standing for long periods of time. In his current position as a technical service employee, he does often stand while performing his work. Parker undergoes back surgery to improve his condition and misses six months of work while recuperating. He seeks to return to work under modified work conditions, but the employer discharges him. Parker files an ADA Title I charge of discrimination and at the same time seeks SSDI benefits. In his SSDI application, it is accurate to say that he is currently unable to work due to disability because he has been discharged due to his disabling condition. Nonetheless, that statement is not inconsistent with his allegation in an ADA Title I lawsuit that he is capable of working *with reasonable accommoda- tion.* To protect himself further, Parker could state in his SSDI application that he is unable to work due, in part, to his employer's unwillingness to accommodate his disabling condition. The courts, however, have not required employees to make such explicit statements in order to sustain their ADA lawsuits [*see Parker v. Columbia Pictures Industries,* 204 F.3d 326 (2d Cir. 2000)].

Remedies

Injunctive and Declaratory Relief
Injunctive and declaratory relief is available in all ADA cases, irrespective of whether the defendant is a public or private employer. Injunctive and declaratory relief is *prospective* relief whereby the indi-

vidual asks the employer to refrain from certain future conduct or asks the court to make a declaration about the unlawfulness of certain conduct. For example, one might request that a business entrance be made accessible in the future or that the employer refuse to engage in certain conduct in the future.

As discussed in "Relevant Statutes" earlier, injunctive and declaratory relief *are* available in suits brought by private individuals against the *state*, even though monetary damages are not available in such employment discrimination suits. The full set of remedies—including compensatory and punitive damages—are available in suits against local government as well as private employers. Those principles are discussed below.

Compensatory and Punitive Damages

As specified in the Civil Rights Act of 1991, Congress provides for compensatory and punitive damages under ADA and the Rehabilitation Act against an employer who engages in unlawful intentional discrimination. A plaintiff may recover compensatory damages for future pecuniary losses, emotional pain, suffering, inconvenience, mental anguish, loss of enjoyment of life, and other nonpecuniary losses, as well as punitive damages. Those damages are capped based on the size of the employer. The cap is $50,000 when the defendant employer has between 15 and 100 employees, $100,000 when the defendant employer has between 101 and 200 employees, $200,000 when the defendant employer has between 201 and 500 employees, and $300,000 when the defendant employer has more than 500 employees. Compensatory and punitive damages are *in addition* to relief such as back pay and lost benefits that restore the individual to the economic position he or she would have enjoyed if there had been no discrimination.

The Civil Rights Act of 1991 also provides that compensatory damages are *not* available in a situation where an employee has requested reasonable accommodations and the employer has made a good-faith attempt to identify a reasonable accommodation. The reasonable accommodation rule gives employers a strong incentive to engage in a good-faith, interactive dialogue about reasonable accommodations. Even if no agreement is reached, the employer will not be liable for compensatory or punitive damages if a good-faith discussion has occurred.

Procedural Requirements

Before an individual can bring suit in federal court under ADA, he or she must file a charge of discrimination. There are two ways to file a charge:

- A charge of discrimination may be filed with the U.S. Equal Employment Opportunity Commission within 180 days of the date of discrimination. Field offices of the EEOC are located in fifty cities throughout the United States and are listed under the U.S. government header in most telephone directories. For the appropriate EEOC field office in your geographic area, contact 800-669-4000, 800-669-6820 (TTY), or http://www.eeoc.gov/facts/howtofil.html.

- A charge of discrimination may be filed with a designated state or local fair employment practice agency within 300 days of the date of discrimination. That office should be listed under the state government header in the phone book. Nearly every state has a fair employment practice agency, and filing with the state agency rather than with the federal government allows one to take advantage of the additional time allotted for filing charges of discrimination. There are some notable exceptions, however. For example, Georgia and Alabama do not have state fair employment practice agencies, so residents of those states *must* file a charge with the EEOC *within 180 days* of the employer's alleged discriminatory acts. Accordingly, we recommend that individuals who are contemplating filing an employment discrimination investigate whether their state has a fair employment practice agency as soon as possible.

It is *not* necessary to hire a lawyer before filing a charge of discrimination. Note, however, that any information contained in the charge of discrimination will be admissible evidence if a formal complaint in a federal court is ever filed. In addition, the employer will receive a copy of the charge of discrimination, so it is very important for all information to be complete and accurate. You do not have to fill out the form at the EEOC or Fair Employment Practices office. It can be taken home and completed later.

The federal or state agency then must investigate the alleged discrimination to determine whether there is reasonable cause to believe that discrimination occurred. If the agency determines that there is reasonable cause, then it seeks either to resolve the matter voluntarily or to resolve it through litigation. It is rare for the EEOC to pursue a case through litigation, but the EEOC often does try to encourage a voluntary resolution during the investigatory stage. It always makes sense for the individual who has filed the charge of discrimination to stay in contact with the EEOC investigator and to provide as much information as possible. For an overview of the EEOC's charge processing procedures, contact http://www.eeoc.gov/charge/overview_charge_processing.html.

If the EEOC is unable to resolve the matter voluntarily and decides not to pursue the case in court, it issues a "right-to-sue" letter *within 180 days of the date it received the charge of discrimination.* An individual has 90 days to file a complaint in federal court after receiving the right-to-sue letter.

If an individual is confident that she wants to file a claim of discrimination in court and does not want to take advantage of the EEOC's informal voluntary resolution process, she can request a right-to-sue letter when she files her original charge of discrimination. In that situation, the EEOC will typically forego its investigation and issue the right-to-sue letter promptly. This option is not always a good one, in that it precludes the claimant's opportunity to take advantage of "free" discovery or fact-finding by the EEOC. But EEOC offices vary, so claimants should make a decision based on the competence of their local EEOC office. If the local office has a reputation for performing poor and slow investigations, then the claimant might want to seek a right-to-sue letter immediately. On the other hand, if the local EEOC office has a good reputation, then it makes sense to take advantage of its free discovery process. In our experience, there is such a variety of practices at local EEOC offices that it is hard to generalize about the best possible strategy. A local lawyer who does employment discrimination cases should have a good sense of what strategy makes the most sense in a particular local community.

Once an individual receives a right-to-sue letter from the EEOC, she only has *90 days* to file a claim of discrimination in court. It is therefore *very important* not to seek a right-to-sue letter before securing an attorney.

Conclusion

Litigation is often not a desirable path in claims involving employment discrimination. The available evidence suggests that plaintiffs fare poorly when they pursue litigation in ADA cases. Trial courts too readily conclude that plaintiffs are not disabled and do not qualify to bring a discrimination claim under ADA.

The litigation statistics, however, do not reflect the large number of ADA cases that are resolved voluntarily when individuals with disabilities work cooperatively with their employers. Accurate and particularized medical evidence is often essential to the voluntary resolution of ADA cases. Individuals with disabilities should make sure that their treating physician is aware of ADA's definition of disability, and of the essential functions of the job in question, before writing a letter on an employee's behalf. Doctors, as well as lawyers, need to have some ADA expertise in order for cases to be resolved voluntarily without recourse to litigation.

Notes

1. In a suit for injunctive or declaratory relief, a person is asking a judge to *enjoin* or *stop* a defendant from engaging in a certain activity, or is asking a judge to *declare* that a certain conduct is illegal. For example, if the entrance to a workplace is inaccessible to an individual who uses a wheelchair, the individual could seek a declaration that the defendant must install a ramp. Alternatively, if a defendant refuses to hire someone for a position because she is HIV-positive, the individual could seek an *injunction* to prevent the defendant from applying that rule. In both examples, the plaintiff is seeking not *monetary* relief but, rather, an order or statement from the court.

2. Complaints of discrimination against state and local entities may be filed with the Department of Justice within 180 days of the date of discrimination. For more information, contact the U.S. Department of Justice Civil Rights Division, Disability Rights Section, 950 Pennsylvania Avenue, N.W., Washington, D.C. 20530.

3

The Law of Special Education: Preschool–12

Three major federal statutes typically regulate the law of special education for children in preschool through twelfth grade: Section 504 of the Rehabilitation Act, Titles II and III of the Americans with Disabilities Act (ADA), and the Individuals with Disabilities Education Act (IDEA). For most children with disabilities, IDEA is the primary source of legal protection; hence, that statute will be the focus of this chapter.

IDEA provides a cause of action for a *parent* or *guardian* to bring a legal claim on behalf of his or her *child with a disability*. Unlike the other statutes discussed in this book, IDEA is *not* an antidiscrimination statute. The quality of education offered to typically developing children is usually not relevant in a claim under this statute. Instead, IDEA is a statute that gives children with disabilities certain procedural protections (through their parents or guardians) as well as certain substantive guarantees.

IDEA's provisions are as follows:

- Children who meet the statute's definition of having a *disability* are entitled to *special education and related services.*
- The content of those special education services is determined by a *team* that writes what is called an *Individualized Education Program* (IEP) or, for preschoolers, an *Individualized Family Service Plan.* The parent is part of that team.
- Each school district must provide a *free and appropriate public education* (FAPE) to each child in the *least restrictive environ-*

ment. A least restrictive environment is one in which children with disabilities and other children are educated together as much as is appropriate.

- A school district must exercise special caution when disciplining children with disabilities in order to determine if their misbehavior is a manifestation of their disability. "Stay-put" rules preclude a school district from suspending or otherwise changing a child's educational program for more than ten days without significant procedural safeguards.

Relevant Statutes

The Individuals with Disabilities Education Act, 20 U.S.C. § 1400 *et seq.*, is the major federal statute that guarantees that each child under the age of 21 receives an "appropriate education." (A child must be at least 3 years of age but not yet 22 years old to qualify for services.) This statute applies only to preschool and primary and secondary (high school) education. It does not apply to postsecondary (college) education. IDEA was first enacted into law in 1975 under the Education for All Handicapped Children Act. The name was changed in 1990 to the Individuals with Disabilities Education Act. This statute was enacted to end an era when many children with disabilities were either completely denied an education or received a segregated, warehoused education that was entirely inadequate. In its findings, Congress noted that more than half of the approximately 8 million children with disabilities were not receiving appropriate educational services and 1 million were excluded entirely from the public schools. The purpose of IDEA is "to ensure that all children with disabilities have available to them a free appropriate public education that emphasizes special education and related services designed to meet their unique needs and prepare them for employment and independent living" [20 U.S.C. § 1400(d)(1)].

Although IDEA contains significant substantive protections for children with disabilities, the heart of this statute is a complex set of procedural requirements. IDEA is made up of four parts. Part A contains the general provisions of the act, including definitions. Part B sets forth the formula grant program that requires each state receiving federal financial assistance under IDEA to develop a plan to ensure a free and appropriate public education to all children with disabilities. Part C authorizes states to receive grants from the federal government to develop and implement statewide systems to provide early intervention services for infants and toddlers (ages 0 to 3) with disabilities. And Part D provides for state program improvement grants for children with disabilities.

Parts A and B are the heart of IDEA and will be the focus of this chapter.

Other statutes that are sometimes relevant in the educational context are Section 504 of the Rehabilitation Act and ADA Title II or Title III. Section 504 of the Rehabilitation Act prohibits discrimination in programs or activities that receive federal financial assistance; virtually all public schools are covered by Section 504 because they receive some form of federal financial assistance. ADA Title II covers discrimination by public entities such as state and local governments, including public schools. Title III covers discrimination by what are called "public accommodations"; this category includes private schools, with the exception of educational institutions that are controlled by religious entities. If a child does not meet the definition of disability under IDEA (i.e., because his or her disability does not require special education services), the child may still qualify for accommodations under Section 504 or ADA Title II (or, at a private school, under ADA Title III).

> EXAMPLE: Suzie is a child with attention deficit hyperactivity disorder (ADHD) who is in fourth grade at the local public school. She takes medication for her condition and is achieving in the average range for her age and grade. Nonetheless, even with medication, she has trouble concentrating for sustained periods of time and is easily distracted by background noises like room fans or hallway sounds. Her parents want the school district to make some accommodations for Suzie in the classroom by placing her desk in a comparatively quiet area; they also want Suzie to take exams in a quiet setting. Because Suzie does not need special education services, her parents must make those requests under Section 504 or ADA Title II rather than under IDEA.

Below we provide a sample letter that a parent might use to trigger an evaluation for disability services. Note that we have worded the letter in such a way as to include references to Section 504, ADA, and IDEA, so that all possibilities are considered.

Strategically, it is important for parents to realize that children might go back and forth between receiving protection under IDEA and receiving it under Section 504 or ADA Title II. In this example, Suzie may have had sufficient emotional and psychological problems stemming from her ADHD in the early grades, before she began to take medication, to qualify as disabled under IDEA. During this time, she received special psychological services to help her deal with frustration and improve her social skills. As she became more mature and better able to deal with the demands of the regular classroom, she no longer qualified for services under IDEA. Nonetheless, she may still require accommodations and should therefore still be covered under Section 504 or ADA Title II for those purposes.

For the purposes of Section 504 or ADA, the definition of disability is the definition covered in Chapter 2 of this book. In fact, ADA uses the same definition of disability for all three of its major titles, and Section 504 and ADA have identical definitions of disability. (This chapter will not repeat that discussion of the definition of disability.) In order to be effective advocates for their children, it is important that parents understand not only the definition of disability under Section 504 and ADA discussed in Chapter 2 but also the definition of disability under IDEA discussed below. This understanding is particularly important for parents whose child needs *accommo-dations* but does not need *special educational services*. That child is covered by Section 504 and ADA, but not by IDEA.

Definition of Disability

Like ADA, IDEA contains its own definition of disability. Only children who are *educationally* disabled fall within the scope of IDEA. A child does *not* need to prove that he or she is educable to qualify for services under IDEA. And, to make matters even more complicated, the statute provides a different definition for preschoolers than for school-age children.

In general, a child in K–12 is disabled for the purposes of IDEA if he or she has

- mental retardation;
- hearing impairments;
- speech or language impairments;
- visual impairments;
- serious emotional disturbance;
- orthopedic impairments;

- autism;
- traumatic brain injury; or
- other health impairments, or specific learning disabilities;
- *and*, "by reason thereof, needs special education and related services."

EXAMPLE: Jimmy was born without a left arm and wears an artificial prosthesis. He performs at an average academic level in second grade and does not need special educational services. His school offers physical education twice a week. Jimmy can participate in most activities but is in need of special assistance. He also would benefit from physical therapy to improve his balance and the use of his prosthetic arm. Because gym is part of the regular curriculum, Jimmy may qualify under IDEA as a child who needs special education or related services because of his disability.

EXAMPLE: Marta is blind in one eye. She performs at an average academic level in seventh grade and does not need special education services. If her visual impairment causes her to tire easily and need additional breaks, she could qualify for accommodations under Section 504 or ADA Title II. But she is not disabled for the purposes of IDEA.

Regarding children aged 3 through 9, a state may, at its discretion, include children who are not specifically labeled as disabled under one of the categories listed above but who are experiencing developmental delays in one or more of the following areas:

- physical development
- cognitive development
- communication development
- social or emotional development or
- adaptive development

and who, for that reason, need special education and related services. This more lenient standard allows states to provide services to young children who may not have a disability diagnosis but who are significantly delayed in their development. Most states take advantage of this latitude to provide services to preschool children, although, in theory, states could take advantage of this latitude up to age 9.

EXAMPLE: Jeremiah is 3 years old. He has very limited language skills and poor motor skills and does not seek to socialize with other children his age. His pediatrician indicates that Jeremiah is "developmentally delayed" but cannot provide a diagnosis to explain his developmental delays. Jeremiah is likely to qualify for preschool services under IDEA even though he has no diagnosis. If he is to continue receiving services in grade school, however, his doctors will have to provide a diagnosis fitting into one of the categories listed for K–12 education.

If the parents of a preschooler who is developmentally delayed are wondering whether their child is covered by IDEA, a good first step is to go to their state's website for the department of education's Office for Exceptional Children (or whatever it is called in their state). There they should be able to determine if the state has taken advantage of the latitude to cover children who are developmentally delayed but do not yet have a specific disability diagnosis. For example, Ohio's department of education has a website at http://www.ode.state.oh.us, which, in turn, provides a link to the Operating Standards for Ohio's Schools Serving Children with Disabilities website. These operating standards contain many definitions, including the definition of preschool child with a disability. That definition applies to a child between the ages of 3 and 6 who has a "disability demonstrated by a documented deficit in one or more areas of development, which has an adverse effect upon normal development and functioning." Similarly, a search of the New York department of education's website leads to the following useful link: http://www.vesid.nysed.gov/specialed/publications/lawsandregs/part200.htm#200.1. This link contains the definitions for disability in New York. Preschoolers without a specific diagnosis of disability are covered under New York law as disabled if they

(i) exhibit a significant delay or disorder in one or more functional areas related to cognitive, language and communicative, adaptive, socioemotional or motor development which adversely affects the student's ability to learn. Such delay or disorder shall be documented by the results of the individual evaluation which includes but is not limited to information in all functional areas obtained from a structured observation of a student's performance and behavior, a parental interview and other individually administered assessment procedures, and, when reviewed in combination and compared to accepted milestones for child development, indicate:

(a) a 12-month delay in one or more functional area(s); or

(b) a 33 percent delay in one functional area, or a 25 percent delay in each of two functional areas; or

(c) if appropriate standardized instruments are individually administered in the evaluation process, a score of 2.0 standard deviations below the mean in one functional area, or a score of 1.5 standard deviations below the mean in each of two functional areas.

New York has one of the more sophisticated definitions of disability for preschoolers. New York's third definition—a score of 2.0 standard deviations below the mean (i.e., a delay) in one area or of 1.5 standard deviations in two areas—is a formula typically used by states to identify preschoolers who are disabled. In practice, that means a child must be in the first or second percentile in one area, or in the fifteenth percentile or lower in two areas to qualify for special education services as a preschooler. Because of the difficulties involved in accurately testing preschoolers, these are only rough estimates. As discussed below, the school district has the responsibility for testing a child who has been identified as potentially disabled. But it is important for parents to understand the definition of disability so that they can seek to interpret the test results, especially if the testing is done by the school district itself.

Testing

There are many situations that trigger a school district's responsibility to test a child with a disability at public expense. These include the following:

- an initial evaluation to determine whether a child qualifies for special education services
- a reevaluation of a child who has been previously identified as disabled
- an independent educational evaluation
- further testing in a particular area
- a functional behavior assessment

Initial Evaluation

If a parent believes that his or her child may be eligible for special education services, the *state* has the obligation to test the child at taxpayers' expense. This initial evaluation is called a multifactored evaluation (MFE). Note, however, that a parent is always entitled to have the child privately tested by an appropriate professional, even if the state provides free testing. If the parent can afford private testing, that is often preferable to having the state do the testing itself because the state has a financial incentive for concluding that a child is not disabled.

Parents should put their request *in writing* to the school district if they desire to have their child tested for special education services. The evaluation must be completed within ninety days of receipt of a parent's permission to test. It is always important for parents to keep copies of all correspondence with the school district because IDEA is a very procedurally driven statute. If the school district ignores a request for testing or delays testing for an inappropriate period of time, that would give rise to a procedural violation of IDEA.

The following is a sample letter that a parent could use to request testing:

Dear [*Principal*]:

I am the parent of [*child*] who is in the __ grade at [*name of school*]. My child is not performing successfully in the regular education classroom. [*Specifically state problem such as failing grades, unable to do homework, emotional problems at school, etc.*]

I am requesting a timely and complete multifactored evaluation as defined by IDEA to determine whether my child qualifies for special education and related services. [*Having consulted with my child's treating physician*], I suspect that my child has a disability and qualifies for Special Education services or a Section 504/ADA Title II Accommodation Plan.

Please consider my signature on this letter as my permission to test my child. I understand that a school district is required to complete an evaluation within ninety days of receiving a parent's permission to test. Because I am also requesting an evaluation under Section 504 of the Rehabilitation Act and ADA Title II, I understand that my procedural rights under each of these statutes have been triggered. Please send the relevant written material to me at the address below.

Thank you for your attention to my request. I may be reached at [*best phone number to reach you during regular business hours*]. I will expect to hear from you within five school days of receipt of this letter.

Sincerely,

[*Full name and address*]

Reevaluation

Once a child has been identified as disabled, he or she is eligible for an IEP for *three years*. At the end of the three-year period, a multi-factored reevaluation must be discussed by the IEP team. A school district or parent may request that a reevaluation occur more often than every three years if conditions warrant. Sometimes, the initial evaluation does not discover problems that emerge later, such as social-emotional problems that are interfering with the learning process. In such instances, the parents should modify the sample letter above to include language such as "Due to changes or concerns [be specific], I am requesting that a multifactored reevaluation be given to my child."

Independent Educational Evaluation

Sometimes a parent is not satisfied with the testing conducted by the school district on behalf of his or her child. In such circumstances, the parent is entitled to request an "independent educational evaluation" at the school district's expense. When the school district consents to an independent evaluation, the school provides the parent with a list of eligible providers, and the parent schedules the appointment. In the letter requesting an independent educational evaluation, the parent should state the basis for believing that an independent evaluation is appropriate. Further, the parent should use language like this: "It is my understanding that IDEA requires that the school district provide me with a list of locations where the Independent Evaluation may take place and the qualifications necessary for the evaluator." It is important that a parent take a child to a *qualified* professional. Otherwise, the school district may disregard the results of the evaluation.

Further Testing in a Particular Area

Sometimes, parents may believe that more specific testing is needed in certain areas that were not examined during the initial multifactored evaluation. If the parents believe the school district is competent to conduct that testing, then they should request further testing in the particular area or areas in question rather than an independent educational evaluation. The letter they write to the school should be very specific regarding both the basis for their belief that further testing is appropriate and the areas in which further testing is needed.

For example, the preliminary testing may have suggested a learning disability but further testing is warranted to determine the precise nature of the learning disability.

Functional Behavior Assessment

A parent should request a "functional behavior assessment" when a child who has already been identified as disabled is exhibiting behaviors that are interfering with his or her learning. Typically in such situations, the child was not previously identified as having a social-emotional problem that might lead to disruptive behavior. Instead, the child may have been identified as having other disabilities. The functional behavior assessment is a mechanism for modifying the existing IEP to include a positive intervention plan to deal with disruptive or other antisocial or inappropriate behavior. IDEA requires that a school district conduct an assessment after the first time it suspends a disabled student for ten days in a school year or when anyone on the IEP team requests that such an assessment be done. The goal of a functional behavior assessment is to identify a positive intervention plan that will allow the student to stay in school.

A letter requesting a functional behavior assessment should state specifically the nature of the problem that the child is experiencing. Further, it should state: "It is my understanding that this assessment will provide the IEP team with the information necessary to establish a Positive Intervention Plan that will be incorporated into the IEP."

Free and Appropriate Public Education

IDEA requires all states to provide children with disabilities between ages 3 and 21 with a free and appropriate public education that is designed to meet the children's unique needs and prepare them for employment and independent living. A FAPE comprises free, special education and related services provided in conformity with an IEP. Because the education is free, a school district cannot charge parents for costs that are not charged to students without disabilities.

A cornerstone of these rules is the requirement that the education be appropriate. The Supreme Court has ruled that *appropriate* is not synonymous with *best*. Its conclusion, instead, is that IDEA establishes a "basic floor of opportunity" consisting of "access to specialized instruction and related services which are individually designed to provide educational benefit to the handicapped child" [*Board of Education v. Rowley*, 458 U.S. 176 (1982)]. Accordingly, an individualized program should be developed for each child that assists the child in making reasonable academic progress.

The mere fact that a child might *benefit* from a related service does not obligate the school district to provide it. IDEA does not require school districts to *maximize* the potential of disabled students. Thus, the Supreme Court found that the school district was not required to provide a sign language interpreter for Amy Rowley, a deaf student, because Amy was able to perform better than the average child in her class and was advancing easily from grade to grade without an interpreter. The *Rowley* case is a bit unusual in that most deaf students qualify for sign language interpreters. It is necessary, however, to show that a child will not make appropriate progress in school without a sign language interpreter in order to qualify for one. The school district does not have to provide the best possible education for a child.

In cases involving children with severe disabilities, it can be particularly difficult to assess whether the children are making adequate progress, but the courts have emphasized the importance of making such an evaluation in all such cases. Hence, the Third Circuit reversed a ruling in favor of a school district in a case involving the right of a severely disabled child to receive hands-on physical therapy each week from the school district [*Polk v. Central Susquehanna Intermediate Unit 16*, 853 F.2d 171 (3d Cir. 1988)]. In that case, the Third Circuit was troubled by the fact that the school district appeared to have a policy precluding hands-on direct physical therapy for any child. Such a blanket rule was inconsistent with the nature of an IEP and, on the basis of that particular fact pattern, made it unlikely that the child was receiving adequate educational services.

Related Services

IDEA defines a free and appropriate education in terms of special education and the "related services" necessary to meet the child's needs [20 U.S.C. § 1400(d)(1)(A)]. Related services are those services a student requires in order to benefit from special education. They include

- transportation services;
- corrective and other supportive services designed to assist the disabled child in benefiting from special education;

- speech pathology;
- audiology;
- physical therapy;
- occupational therapy;
- recreation (including therapeutic recreation and social work services);
- counseling (including rehabilitation counseling);
- psychological services;
- medical services provided solely for diagnostic and evaluative purposes;
- assistive technology devices and services; and
- orientation and mobility services.

As this listing of related services is not intended to be exhaustive, other services may be included or required under this category. For example, transition services may be considered a related service.

Courts have struggled to determine whether services related to health care are covered under this mandate. For example, consider Garrett F., who is ventilator dependent and cannot attend school unless he receives health care services throughout the school day. For his first five years of schooling, the family used settlement proceeds from an automobile accident to pay for a licensed practical nurse to assist him during the day. Eventually, however, the parents requested that the school district pay for this care. When the school district refused, his parents sued.

This was a hard legal issue because IDEA exempts school districts from paying for "medical services." One might argue that the continuous nursing care that Garrett required to attend school was a medical service. However, the Supreme Court ruled that the "medical services" exclusion refers specifically to services that must be performed by a *physician* [*Cedar Rapids Community School District v. Garret F.*, 526 U.S. 66 (1999)]. In general, children are entitled to what the regulations call "school health services," which are defined as "services provided by a qualified school nurse or other qualified person" [*see* 34 C.F.R. § 300.13(a), 300.13(b)(10)]. If the services can only be performed by a physician, however, then the school district does not need to provide them under IDEA.

The Court in *Garrett F.* also ruled that the fact that the services he requires might be costly was no defense because the services *were necessary to Garrett's attendance at school.* The Court noted that IDEA does not include cost in its definition of related services, and it refused to read an "undue burden" exception into IDEA.

The Individualized Family Service Plan and Individualized Education Program

Part C of IDEA provides grant money from the federal government to develop and implement statewide systems to provide early intervention services for infants and toddlers (ages 0 to 3) with disabilities. Such early intervention services must be provided in a "natural environment," which the regulations define as "settings that are natural or normal for the child's age peers who have no disabilities." Natural environments are typical places, contexts, activities, and experiences that may include the child's home or child care and preschool settings. These settings could also extend to visiting the grocery store, going to a park, eating in a restaurant, reading a book at the library, and attending a church or synagogue service.

Children in this age group get an Individualized Family Service Plan (IFSP) rather than an IEP, but the IFSP can act as an IEP when the child is entering preschool if it meets the requirements of an IEP. An IFSP is to be developed following "a multidisciplinary assessment of the unique strengths and needs of the infant or toddler" and "a family-directed assessment of the resources, priorities and concerns of the family." This plan must include:

- a statement of the infant's or toddler's present levels of development;
- a statement of the family's resources, priorities, and concerns;
- a statement of the major outcomes expected to be achieved for the child and family;
- a statement of the specific early intervention services needed to meet the unique needs of the child and family;
- a statement of the natural environments in which early intervention services are to be provided;
- projected dates for initiation, and anticipated duration, of services;
- the name of the service coordinator; and
- the steps to be taken to support transition services available to children 3 years of age and above.

A similar process is initiated to create an IEP for each *school-aged* child with a disability who qualifies for services under IDEA. IDEA requires that the IEP document must contain, at a minimum, the following information:

- the child's present educational performance levels
- the annual goals for the child, including short-term instructional objectives
- a statement of the special education, related services, and supplementary aids and services to be provided to or for the child
- an explanation of the extent, if any, to which the child will not participate with nondisabled children in the regular classroom
- a statement of any special modifications in student assessment procedures that the child may require
- the dates on which it is anticipated that the services listed will be initiated, and the expected frequency, location, and duration of those services
- beginning at age 14, and every year thereafter, a statement of the child's needed transition services related to the child's course of study (to ensure that the child's educational program is planned to help the child reach his or her goals for life after secondary school)
- if appropriate, beginning at age 16, a statement of needed transition services for the child, including a statement pertaining to the responsibilities of various agencies to provide such services
- a statement of how the child's progress toward annual goals will be measured, and how the child's parents will be regularly informed of the child's progress [20 U.S.C.A. § 1414(d)(1)(A)]

In addition, beginning at least one year before the child reaches the age of majority under state law (i.e., 18 or 21, as the state law provides), the IEP must include a statement that the child has been informed of his or her rights under Part B of IDEA.

IDEA authorizes parents to participate in developing the IFSP and IEP. School districts must attempt to arrange meetings at a time that is acceptable to parents and the school district. If parents are having difficulty finding a convenient meeting time, they should keep records of their requests so that, if necessary, they can establish a procedural violation on the part of the school district.

Until recently, school districts were required to have *yearly* meetings with parents to develop either the IFSP (for preschoolers) or the IEP (for K–12). On December 3, 2004, President Bush signed into law the Individuals with Disabilities Improvement Act of 2004, which went into effect on July 1, 2005. Under this revised version of IDEA, parents and school districts may waive the entitlement to a reevaluation of each child with a disability at least once every three years if both parties agree that a reevaluation is unnecessary. However, we recommend that parents *not* consent to such a waiver because children with disabilities constantly undergo changes; it is hard to imagine why a child would not benefit from a yearly reevaluation.

IDEA places considerable weight upon the process used to develop the IFSP and IEP. The sequence of events typically commences when a child is suspected of being disabled. School districts have an affirmative obligation to seek an evaluation of any child suspected of having a disability. The school district must provide a detailed notice to the child's parents and seek to obtain consent from the parents to conduct an evaluation of the child. After this evaluation is complete, a meeting is held to determine whether the child should be classified as disabled and, if so, what placement and services should be provided in order to furnish the child with a FAPE. This information, and more, is included in the child's IFSP and IEP.

With respect to information included in the IEP, the multidisciplinary team must consider

- the child's strengths, the parents' concerns for enhancing the education of their child, and the results of the child's initial or most recent evaluation;
- in the case of a child whose behavior impedes his or her learning or that of others, the strategies (including positive behavioral intervention) and supports needed to address that behavior;
- in the case of a child with limited English proficiency, the language needs of the child as they relate to the IEP;
- in the case of a child who is blind or visually impaired, provision of instruction in Braille and the use of Braille unless the IEP team determines that instruction in Braille or the use of Braille is not appropriate for the child;
- the communication needs of the child and, in the case of a child who is deaf or hard-of-hearing, the child's language and communication needs, opportunities for direct communications

with peers and professional personnel in the child's language and communication mode, academic level, and full range of needs, including opportunities for direct instruction in the child's language and communication mode; and
- the child's need or lack thereof for assistive technology devices and services.

Before a school district (or educational agency) may propose to initiate or change the identification, evaluation, or educational placement of a child, the school district (or agency) must first provide notice, in writing, to the child's parents. Similar notice is required before a school district may refuse to initiate or change the identification, evaluation, or educational placement of a child. This notice must fully explain all procedural safeguards and must contain, among other things, descriptive information concerning the proposed action or refusal to act by the school district.

The IFSP and IEP process is the cornerstone of IDEA. If parents can arrive at a good educational plan with the assistance of the school district, then they are most likely to be pleased with their child's educational experience. Many parents, however, find it difficult to have a productive exchange at the IFSP and IEP meeting; indeed, it is very helpful to come into that meeting with an understanding of what to expect.

At a typical IFSP or IEP meeting, the school district may have between six and ten people present to represent its point of view. The special education teacher, intervention specialist, principal, and experts in speech and communication, physical therapy, occupational theory, or psychology may be present at the meeting. The parent may come by him- or herself or accompanied by a spouse or friend. Parents routinely report that it is an intimidating and overwhelming process.

Parents need to come to the IFSP or IEP meeting fully prepared to participate actively. They need to request to see all documentation regarding their child *before* the meeting so that they are well informed. The documentation that is prepared in advance of the meeting is often written in jargon that parents find difficult to understand, and there may be test results with indications of percentiles, norming data, and standard deviations. We thus encourage parents to seek parent advocates or other people in their community who might help them understand the content of these reports in advance of the meeting.

In addition, parents may want to come to the meeting with a draft of the kinds of services they think their child might need. This wish list should be reasonable and consistent with the kinds of services that the parent is aware have been made available to other children.

> EXAMPLE: Johnny has a speech impediment and qualifies for speech therapy. Does the parent want to insist on two sessions of one-on-one speech therapy for a half-hour each week? Or would a group session (two to four children) be acceptable? Is twice a week necessary, or would once a week be sufficient? Does the speech therapy need to be delivered by a licensed professional? Or can the speech therapist act as a consultant to the regular classroom teacher, who might incorporate speech therapy into the regular curriculum? Parents should consider these questions in *advance* of the meeting so that they can propose a reasonable educational program.

We have found that school districts frequently want to offer services on a consultative basis because that method of service delivery permits their specialists to service more students. Parents worry that no consultation is in fact taking place, and that the child is not receiving any services at all. If parents consent to consultative services, then they should (1) insist that the IFSP or IEP specify the frequency of consultation and (2) have some mechanism to evaluate whether the delivery of services in this manner is effective. For example, the IEP could say that the child is expected to learn how to pronounce the "th" sound by January through consultative services. If the child cannot correctly say the "th" sound in four out of five prompts, then direct services will be immediately initiated. The important point here is that parents are more likely to achieve concrete IEPs that serve their child's needs if they think about what should be in the content of the IEP *before* the meeting.

At the IFSP or IEP meeting itself, parents need to take good notes and *not* agree to an educational plan that is not satisfactory. Parents need to have a cooperative but firm attitude. They should not come alone, as it is very helpful to confer with someone else about decisions that are made during the meeting. One of the most important things for parents to remember during the IFSP or IEP meeting is that they are the experts on their child. They live with their child every day and usually have the best sense of anyone in the room as to what motivates or works with their child. For example, Joyce Majewski tells a story about a school psychologist who wanted to draw a ridiculous conclusion from her son's drawing of a hockey goalie with a mask.[1] The school psychologist insisted that this drawing reflected the boy's effort to hide his feelings behind a mask, like the goalie. Joyce knew, however, that her son was an avid hockey fan and was drawing a goalie realistically. She was able to point out that the psychologist's conclusion was inconsistent with other reports and personal observations about her son. She realized that the psychologist did not know her son at all. She was the expert on her son and could offer a more realistic interpretation of the drawing than could the psychologist.

There are several websites that give tips on preparing for an IFSP or IEP meeting. Some examples for an IFSP are http://nncf.unl.edu/nncf.go.ifsp.html, http://www.answers4families.org/IFSPWeb, and http://ericec.org/digests/e605.html. Others can be found by doing an Internet search on "preparing for IFSP." Some examples for an IEP are http://www.parentsunitedtogether.com/page22.html, http://www.geocities.com/Athens/Oracle/1580/preparing_for_iep.html, and http://add.about.com/cs/education/a/iepmeetings.htm. Others can be found by doing an Internet search on "preparing for IEP." Books on IFSP or IEP preparation can be found using the same searches; they are also available at your local library.

It is normal to feel emotional during an IFSP or IEP meeting, but it is best to try to remain calm. Emotional outbursts can make team members feel uncomfortable and undermine the effectiveness of the meeting. If a parent feels upset, he or she can ask for a short break to gain some composure.

Although we recommend against getting too emotional, we have found that "I" statements can actually enhance the process. For example, Chris was a parent at an IEP meeting involving his third-grade daughter, Sarah, who had various cognitive and physical disabilities. When negotiations appeared to be breaking down, Chris decided to switch to "I" statements and said: "I feel very worried that if we miss this opportunity to push Sarah, we won't get it back again. I need to know that we tried everything we could to help her succeed." The tone in the room changed instantly, and by the end of the session, the participants had worked out a provisional mainstreaming plan that satisfied everybody's needs. The father's "I" statements were effective because they were personal yet not overly emotional. Parents who can maintain that tone often encounter success at IEP meetings.

Sometimes, a school district will cite budgetary limits as an excuse not to give a child a needed educational service. But a lack of money or financial hardship is never a reason why a school can deny a child a *necessary* educational service. Recall that medical services that must be performed by a licensed physician are excluded from the coverage specified by the statute. And bear in mind that a child is entitled to an appropriate education, which may not be the best possible education. Higher expenditures sometimes correspond with a better education, but not one that the school district must provide. The expense issue, therefore, often arises in distinguishing between appropriate and best, rather than as a direct defense.

Another issue that some parents may wish to consider is whether their child is being inappropriately characterized as disabled. Various studies suggest that African American boys are disproportionately labeled as "severely emotionally disturbed" and are segregated in special education. By contrast, Latino and Asian American children are disproportionately *not* labeled as disabled, including those who actually are in need of special education services. The labeling of children as "disabled" or "nondisabled" is subjective, and parents need to be wary of overgeneralizations that may be affecting their children. For that reason, parents should seek to obtain third-party confirmation of their child's disability status rather than relying on the school district's assessment. Unfortunately, a lack of access to affordable health care can make it difficult for parents to obtain such verification.

Finally, there are cases where parents complain about an abuse of the disability labeling system in an attempt to get extra time on tests — that is, to enhance their children's performance rather than to accommodate their disability. This problem can frustrate parents of children who are not labeled as disabled as well as teachers who feel that their exam process has been compromised through inappropriate labeling. Indeed, ADA and IDEA do not permit "reverse discrimination" lawsuits, so nondisabled children cannot sue a school district over this mislabeling issue.

One solution to this "extra time" problem is for teachers to stop giving examinations that are time pressured so that everyone has an opportunity to complete them. For example, as a law professor, Professor Colker gives only take-home exams with a strict word limit so as to discourage students from spending unlimited amounts of time answering the test questions. She has found that such a system benefits all students because everyone gets to write a complete answer that reflects his or her understanding of the subject. (There are rumors that the SAT may move to a less time-pressured format in response to numerous requests for extra time as an accommodation.) When parents think that their child is being disadvantaged by not having enough time to take a test, they might ask the teacher to reconsider the time limit itself, for the benefit of everyone in the class, rather than using the disability model for just some of the students.

Least Restrictive Environment

IDEA requires that a child with a disability is to be removed from the regular educational environment only when the "nature or severity of the disability of the child is such that education in regular classes with the use of supplementary aids and services cannot be achieved satisfactorily." In addition, every child with a disability must be placed in the least restrictive environment "to the maximum extent *appropri - ate*." Appropriateness is therefore a very important factor in determining the extent to which an integrated environment is required. Not all children with disabilities are required to be educated in a regular education setting.

The terms *least restrictive environment* and *mainstreaming* are sometimes thought to be synonymous, but such an interpretation is incorrect. The term *mainstreaming*, which does not actually appear as a formal term in IDEA, has become common jargon in the educational community. It is typically accepted as meaning the placement of a disabled child in a regular educational setting. Mainstreaming can be achieved in all aspects of a child's educational program or in just some portions of that program, such as in a particular academic class, in a special area of instruction (e.g., art, music, or physical education), or simply in the cafeteria at lunchtime.

Mainstreaming, therefore, is only part of the larger concept of least restrictive environment. The distinction between mainstreaming and least restrictive environment is particularly highlighted whenever parents or educators grapple with incorporating the concept of "integrated education" or "inclusion" into an IEP. This concept involves placement of a disabled child primarily in the regular classroom. In contrast to a child who is being mainstreamed, however, the disabled child in an integrated educational setting is not expected to keep pace with the nondisabled children in the class; nor is the disabled child expected to fulfill all the regular educational requirements in order to be placed into the next grade level. Rather, the disabled child is to be provided an adapted curriculum and will move on to the next grade level if he or she achieves enough success as measured against his or her own IEP.

In determining whether a child is being educated in the least restrictive environment, courts consider the child's social as well as educational needs. For example, Neill Roncker was severely mentally retarded. He had the educational abilities of a 2- or 3-year-old and needed special education services for his academic work. Nonetheless, his parents wanted him to be with typical children for lunch, gym, and recess. The school district insisted that Neill be educated in a county school where he would have no contact with typical children. His parents challenged the school district's decision and ultimately prevailed. They were also successful in having their child placed in a local school where he had contact with typical children while the lawsuit was being litigated [*Roncker v. Walter*, 700 F.2d 1058 (6th Cir. 1983)].

In the *Roncker* case, the parents were not seeking to have their son educated with typical children for the academic subjects. Requests for mainstreaming can be more difficult when parents desire to have a severely handicapped child educated with typical children for the academic subjects. One court has stated that "regular educational instructors [are not required] to devote all or most of their time to one handicapped child or to modify the regular educational curriculum beyond recognition." Accordingly, it found that the school district did not have to place Daniel R. R. in a regular prekindergarten classroom because Daniel could not participate without constant, individual attention from the teacher or her aide and failed to master any of the skills that the teacher was trying to teach her students. Modifying the prekindergarten curriculum and her teaching methods sufficiently to reach Daniel would have required the teacher to modify the curriculum almost beyond recognition [*Daniel R. R. v. Bd. of Education*, 874 F.2d 1036 (5th Cir. 1989)]. Both the *Roncker* and the *Daniel R. R.* cases involved children with severe mental retardation. Courts are more sympathetic to academic mainstreaming with higher-functioning children.

Discipline Issues

Children with disabilities may be disciplined like other children if their discipline problem is not a manifestation of their disability. Further, they may be disciplined like other children by having a change in placement for less than ten days. However, if a change in placement is contemplated for *more than* ten days, rigorous procedural safeguards must be followed.

In short, if disciplinary action is contemplated that will result in a change of placement of more than ten days for a child with a disability, then the school must arrange for a "manifestation review." The procedures involved include the following:

- A parent must be notified of the decision.
- A parent must be notified of the procedural safeguards that exist *before* the change in placement is to occur.
- Upon request by the parent, a review must be held of whether the inappropriate behavior was a manifestation of the disability.
- The manifestation review must be conducted immediately and, if possible, no later than ten school days after the decision to take action was made.
- The manifestation review must be conducted by the IEP team and other qualified personnel.
- If the parent disagrees with the results of the manifestation review hearing, then the parent can appeal through the state's due process procedure. This hearing should occur on an expedited basis.

In carrying out a manifestation review, the IEP team and other qualified personnel may determine that the behavior was not a manifestation of the child's disability only if the team first evaluates all the diagnostic and other information available concerning the child and then ascertains that (1) the assistance the child was receiving was consistent with the child's IEP and placement, (2) the child's disability did not impair his or her ability to understand the impact and consequences of the behavior subject to disciplinary action, and (3) the child's disability did not impair his or her ability to control the behavior subject to the disciplinary action. If the team determines that the child's behavior is not a manifestation of the child's disability, the child can be suspended or expelled to the same extent that nondisabled students would be disciplined for the same behavior.

If the IEP team determines that the behavior was a manifestation of a disability, then the team has to conduct a functional behavioral assessment and implement a behavioral intervention plan, if no previous assessment exists. If an assessment does already exist, then the existing plan needs to be reviewed and modified. Unless the danger-ousness exception (discussed next) is met, the school must return the child to his or her previous placement, unless the parent and school agree to a change.

> EXAMPLE: Philip is a seventh grader who has been diagnosed with a severe emotional disorder. He has a behavioral intervention plan to help with his sometimes disruptive behavior in the classroom. After school one day, Philip goes to his garage and retrieves a can of brown paint that his mother had used to paint their mailbox. He pours it all over his math teacher's car, which is in the school parking lot. The school suspends him for ten days pending a manifestation review. The manifestation review team concludes that his behavior was not a man-ifestation of his disability, and Philip is suspended for the remainder of the semester by being placed in an alternative educational setting. His parents appeal that determination. While the appeal is pending, Philip would stay in the alternative educational setting.

> EXAMPLE: The details are the same except that, this time, the mani-festation review committee determines that Philip's behavior *was* a manifestation of his disability. He would then be returned to his regu-lar classroom unless the parent and school agree to a change of place-ment as part of the modification of his behavioral intervention plan.

School districts have more latitude with respect to discipline when there are incidents involving weapons, drugs, or dangerous behavior. In 1997, Congress amended IDEA to provide that schools may uni-laterally remove children with disabilities to an interim placement if the child carries or possesses a weapon, uses illegal drugs, or sells or solicits the sale of a controlled substance while at school, on school premises, or at a school function, regardless of whether the alleged be-havior is a manifestation of a disability. IDEA's 2004 amendments ex-panded this category to include children with disabilities who had "inflicted serious bodily injury upon another person while at school, on school premises, or at a school function." In such situations, the school district may move the student to an interim alternative educa-tional setting that allows the student to progress toward meeting the goals set out in his or her IEP. This alternative placement can last for no more than forty-five*school* days. (The 2004 amendments increased the duration from forty-five days to forty-five *school* days.) The child is also supposed to receive a functional behavioral assessment and behavioral intervention services and modifications that are designed to address the behavior violation so that it does not recur.

> EXAMPLE: The previous details are modified to state that Philip accosts the math teacher as he is leaving the building and breaks his arm. Because the behavior involves the infliction of serious bodily harm, the school may remove Philip to an alternative education placement for forty-five school days regardless of whether the behavior is determined to be a manifestation of his disability.

In general, the 2004 version of IDEA gives more latitude to school districts when children with disabilities engage in disruptive behavior. Previously, broader protections for the child existed so that he would have to "stay put" in his regular placement pending an appeal if the school determined that the adverse behavior was not a manifestation of the child's disability. Now, the child stays in the alternative educational placement pending the appeal of the manifestation determination. The statute does require that the school arrange for an expedited hearing within twenty school days after the hearing is requested and that a determination be reached within ten school days after the hearing itself. Given the ten-day initial alternative placement, then, a child can now be in alternative placement for up to forty school days: ten days (initial alternative placement pending manifestation determination) plus twenty days (period after the request for a hearing appealing manifestation determination) plus ten days (period after the hearing and before determination) equals forty days.

It is therefore crucial for parents to be actively engaged at the manifestation review stage, so that they can seek a determination that the misbehavior was a result of the disability.

Private Schooling

Children may find themselves in private schools for two different sets of reasons: (1) The parents and school district have agreed that the private school is the only appropriate educational option for the child or (2) the parents have voluntarily chosen a private schooling option even though the school district has made available an appropriate public school option.

In the first instance, the school district bears the cost of education because all children are entitled to a *free* and appropriate education. In the second instance, the placement is considered *voluntary* and the parent, rather than the school district, is responsible for the tuition. Nonetheless, even in the second instance, the state education agency and the local education agency (in the area where the child resides) have some responsibility to ensure that the child with disabilities receives appropriate special education and related services. The school district is required to allot a proportional amount of *federal* funds for special education and related services for children with disabilities in private schools, based on the number and location of disabled students residing in their jurisdiction. But the school district is not required to allocate any state or local money to these children, who are being "voluntarily" educated in private schools. Services that are offered with these federal funds may be offered on the premises of the private (or parochial) school, or they may be offered at an alternative site. If the school district chooses an alternative site, then it must provide the child with transportation from the private school to the service center. School districts are *not* required to provide transportation from the child's home to the private school.

In practice, these rules concerning private schools typically mean that children with disabilities can receive a full array of services only if they attend their local public school. The only exception is when the child is so severely disabled that the public schools cannot provide an appropriate education. In that rare situation, the school district may pay for the child to attend a school for children with severe disabilities. Such residential placements can be very expensive, and the school district will typically do its utmost to find a public school placement for the child.

Parents who are dissatisfied with their child's public school placement sometimes decide to enroll their child in a private school that they believe better suits her needs. Such parents are entitled to reimbursement for expenses incurred for the unilateral placement of their child if it is ultimately determined that attending the private school was necessary to provide a FAPE for their disabled child. For example, in *School Committee of the Town of Burlington v. Department of Education of Massachusetts*, 471 U.S. 359 (1985), the school district recommended placing a child with a disability in a highly structured class within the school district. Relying upon evaluations from outside experts, the parents wanted the child placed in a state-approved special education private school, unilaterally placed their child in the private school, and then sought reimbursement for the cost of the school. In allowing the reimbursement, the Supreme Court stated:

> A final judicial decision on the merits of an IEP will in most instances come a year or more after the school term covered by the IEP has passed. . . . [It] would be an empty victory to have a court tell [parents] several years later that they were right but that these expenditures could not in a proper case be reimbursed by the school officials.

The expenses for which parents are entitled to reimbursement presumably include all those necessary to enable the child with a disability to receive a FAPE. A variety of expenses have been ordered to be reimbursed, including tuition expenses, costs of residential placement, expenses for related services, expenses for other services required to permit a student to receive a FAPE, lost earnings by a parent for time expended relating to protecting the child's rights, and even interest on payments made for a unilateral placement or interest on borrowings in order to make such payments. The balancing of equities can also result in a situation where neither party gains a total victory but the court imposes a Solomon-like decision concerning who shall bear the costs.

In order to obtain reimbursement for private school expenses (which would include reimbursement for tuition), parents must comply with the following requirements: (1) At the last IEP meeting prior to removing their child from public school, the parents must inform the IEP team that they are rejecting the school district's proposed placement and intend to place their child in private school. (2) Alternatively, parents must provide the school with *written* notice of their decision to place the child in private school.

Parents are *required* to follow one of these two options; if they do not, they will be denied reimbursement for private school expenses.

If the school district provides the parents with notice of the district's intent to evaluate the child, the parents must make the child available for such evaluation or they may not recover reimbursement for private school expenses. Such reimbursement for private school expenses will also be denied if a court finds that the parents acted unreasonably in placing their child in private school.

Complaint Process

In theory, parents and the school district should be able to develop an effective IEP through an informal, interactive process at the IEP meeting. When the IEP process is not attaining a satisfactory result, parents have many procedural options.[2]

1. A parent can request a *case conference*. A case conference is an informal procedure designed to provide parents and the school district with an opportunity to discuss and resolve issues related to the provision of appropriate educational services for a child. It is appropriate to request a case conference when a parent disagrees about identification, evaluation, placement, or the provision of a free, appropriate public education.

2. If a case conference is unsuccessful in resolving a problem, the next step is to request an administrative review. The review is requested from the school superintendent. When the superintendent receives a written request for an administrative review, he or she must contact the parent and schedule a meeting without undue delay and at a convenient place and time. After the meeting is scheduled, the superintendent must inform the parties involved of his or her decision within twenty days.

3. An optional next step is for a parent to request mediation by a representative of his or her state department of education. Both the parent and the school district must consent to this process. If a parent desires this process, then the parent should send a letter to both the Office for Exceptional Children (or whatever it is called in his or her state) and the Superintendent of Schools. The letters should be addressed individually to each of these recipients and should include the following information:

- the name of the child, the type of disability, the grade level of the child, and the name of the school attended by the child
- a request for mediation with a clear statement of the issue that the parent wants mediated, such as the content of the IEP
- how the parent can be reached

This letter should be sent by certified mail with return receipt requested to both the Superintendent and the Office for Exceptional Children. A parent might consider also sending a copy of the Superintendent's letter to the President of the School Board. A receipt is not necessary for the School Board letter.

4. The next possible step is to request an *impartial due process* hearing. The state department of education typically employs impartial hearing officers who convene due process hearings. Federal law requires a decision from the hearing officer within forty-five days of the request for a hearing. Note the following considerations regarding impartial due process hearings:

- A special timetable exists in situations where a child has been disciplined by being removed from the regular classroom and there is a dispute about whether the misbehavior was a manifestation of the child's disability.
- The school district has ten days to make a manifestation review of whether the misbehavior was a result of the child's disability. If the parent is unsatisfied with the result of the manifestation review, the parent may seek an expedited hearing, which must occur within twenty school days of the request. The hearing officer must then reach a decision within ten school days after the hearing. (As noted above, the child can therefore be removed from the regular classroom for forty school days when the school district concludes at the manifestation hearing that the behavior was not a manifestation of the child's disability.)

The parties to the hearing have a right to counsel and traditional due process rights to present evidence, to confront and cross-examine witnesses (as well as to compel attendance of witnesses), and to obtain a verbatim record of the hearing. Either party may prohibit the production of any evidence that has not been disclosed to that party at least five days before the hearing. The hearing officer must reach a final decision within forty-five days after receipt of the request for a hearing (unless the rules for expedited reviews apply). The hearing officer's decision must be in writing and must include written findings of fact.

In those states that provide for a hearing at the local level, the losing party may appeal to the state department of education. The decision at the state level may be appealed by commencement of a civil action in either a state or a federal court, at which the court may receive additional evidence.

Parents need to be cautious in requesting a due process hearing because doing so can create ill feelings between the parents and the school district. One of the difficulties with IDEA is that parents and the school district must have an ongoing long-term relationship; repeated disagreements make it difficult to maintain a cooperative atmosphere for the benefit of the child. Nevertheless, a due process hearing is sometimes the only available mechanism to resolve a dispute and should be considered.

If a parent desires a due process hearing, the parent should send separate letters to the Superintendent of Schools and the Office for Exceptional Children stating the *specific factual reasons why the parent is requesting a due process hearing*. The letters should conclude with the statement that: (1) the child is not being provided with a free and appropriate public education or (2) the child is not being educated in the least restrictive environment. Both of these letters should be sent by certified mail with return receipt requested.

5. Instead of requesting a due process hearing, a parent can decide to *file a formal complaint with the state department of education*. This approach should be used only when the school district has engaged in a clear procedural violation of IDEA. For example, if a parent has documentation demonstrating that a request was made for an evaluation and the school district ignored the request, then it would be appropriate to file a complaint.

A complaint may also be filed if the school district is engaging in a practice that is violating IDEA for an entire group of children. For example, if the school district is refusing to provide any accommodations for any students during statewide testing, then a complaint could be filed on behalf of all disabled students who need accommodations. The state's department of education should have a website with information about how to file a complaint.

6. A final option is to file a complaint with the U.S. Department of Education's Office of Civil Rights (OCR), which has jurisdiction over enforcement of Section 504 of the Rehabilitation Act. As discussed earlier, that statute may apply if the child has a complaint with regard to *discrimination*. Examples of civil rights violations would be situations in which students with disabilities are treated differently from other children. For instance, they might not be allowed to go on field trips or attend graduation due to accessibility problems or other concerns. The Office for Civil Rights accepts electronic or

written complaints. For further information, go to http://www.ed. gov/about/offices/list/ocr/complaintintro.html. If a parent desires to submit a written complaint, that complaint should be sent to the regional office of OCR. Addresses for regional offices are found on OCR's website.

A complaint with OCR must be filed within 180 days from the date of the act of discrimination. OCR must complete its investigation and write its decision within 90 days after receipt of the complaint. If a complaint is sent by regular mail, the parent should request a return receipt to know the date the complaint was received. If an electronic form is used, then the parent should print a copy of the electronic form for his or her records.

The U.S. Department of Education's Office of Special Education Programs has an independent obligation to monitor and enforce IDEA. It conducts monitoring visits to fulfill that obligation and, after each visit, issues a report on the level of compliance for the entire state. These reports are available through its website at http://www.ed.gov/about/offices/list/osers/osep/index.html?src=mr.

Conclusion

IDEA is a landmark statute that has made it possible for nearly all children with disabilities to receive a free public education. The structure of the statute requires a lot of parental initiative. Parents need to be actively involved to help the school district create an effective IEP for their child. Because parents will be working with the same school administrators for many years, it is important that they have an effective and cordial relationship with these people in order for their child to receive a good education. Although parents can hire a lawyer to assist them in developing the IEP, many parents find that they can be even more effective without formal legal assistance. Active participation in the IEP process, coupled with good diagnostic testing and professional support, can produce excellent results. Parents who do not believe they have adequate skills to participate effectively in the IEP process should consider contacting parent support groups in their area. IDEA can be a procedural landmine but, once mastered, can help produce excellent education plans for children with disabilities.

One of the best pieces of advice that Professor Colker received in dealing with special education issues for her son is that the parent is usually the best expert on his or her child. Teachers typically see a child for only one year, and medical professionals have to base their conclusions on short office visits in an unnatural setting. Parents, however, see their children on a daily basis and usually have a good sense of their children's strengths and weaknesses. Although parents do not want to continually second-guess the judgment of educational and medical professionals, they do need to be willing, on occasion, to question authority based on their own knowledge of their child. IEP meetings frequently feel rushed, and school personnel often want to impose a plan they have prepared in advance of the meeting. Thus, parents need to be willing to slow down the process and to make sure that the people in the room have a holistic understanding of their child—the kind of understanding that comes from living with a child. If parents approach the IEP process with a critical yet respectful perspective, they can successfully work with school personnel and medical professionals to develop effective IEPs for their children.

Notes

1. See David M. Engel, "Origin Myths: Narratives of Authority, Resistance, Disability, and Law," *Law and Society Review*, vol. 27, no. 785 (1993).

2. At the time that we wrote this chapter, Congress had recently reauthorized IDEA and made some modifications in the complaint process, and the U.S. Department of Education had not yet written rules implementing the changes. Although the general structure described in this section will probably be retained under the latest version of IDEA, parents should check with their state's department of education before proceeding with the complaint process to make sure they are following the proper procedures. State resources are listed in the Appendix to this book.

4

Postsecondary Education

Transition from High School to Postsecondary Education

The transition from high school to college brings challenges for most students. In college they have more independence regarding (and responsibility for) their own education. For students with disabilities, however, this transition may be especially challenging, because they are no longer covered by the Individuals with Disabilities Education Act (IDEA) (discussed in Chapter 3). The differences between IDEA and the laws that apply to colleges are reflected in a dramatic shift in the respective responsibilities of the school and the student in terms of identifying disabilities and making accommodations for them.

As noted in Chapter 3, IDEA is *not* an antidiscrimination statute. Instead, it gives children with disabilities certain procedural protections (through their parents or guardians) as well as certain substantive guarantees. Among the requirements of IDEA is that the *state* has the obligation to test the children at taxpayers' expense if their parents believe the children may be eligible for special education services. Once a child has been identified as disabled, the *school* must determine the content of special education services by convening a team that develops an Individualized Education Program (IEP).

Recall that a school's responsibility for identifying a disability and determining the appropriate accommodation for it shifts dramatically once a student leaves high school and enters postsecondary education. Both Section 504 of the Rehabilitation Act of 1973 and the Americans with Disabilities Act (ADA) prohibit colleges and universities from *discriminating* on the basis of disability, but they differ from IDEA—and change students' experiences—in many ways. For example, under Section 504 and ADA,

- students are responsible for identifying their disability, providing documentation, and requesting assistance;
- disability service personnel make decisions based on the "reasonable accommodations" requirements of ADA and Section 504, rather than on the individualized focus of IDEA; and
- students with disabilities often have to repeat the process of requesting accommodations each new semester, with new classes and new professors.

Accordingly, it is critical that students with disabilities and their parents begin to plan for the transition from high school to college as early as possible. One way to do so is by contacting the disability services offices at the schools the student is interested in attending to learn what their specific requirements are. There are also a number of websites that provide information on this process. The National Center on Secondary Education and Transition's website at http://www.ncset.org has sections that discuss *Preparing for Postsecondary Education*, http://www.ncset.org/topics/preparing/default.asp?topic=6, and *Post-secondary Education Supports and Accommodations*, http://www.ncset.org/topics/psesupports/default.asp?topic=5. Other helpful websites include The Transition Research Institute, http://www.ed.uiuc.edu/SPED/tri/institute.html; The Transition Coalition, http://www.transitioncoalition.org; the Rehabilitation Research and Training Center at the University of Hawaii, http://www.rrtc.hawaii.edu; LD Online, http://www.ldonline.org/ld_indepth/postsecondary; and U.S. Department of Educatoin, http://www.ed.gov/about/offices/list/ocr/transition.html#reproduction.

Laws Governing Disability Discrimination in Postsecondary Education

Section 504 governs all postsecondary institutions that receive federal financial assistance. Title II of ADA applies to all state-funded or supported institutions, and Title III of ADA covers all private institutions, excluding educational institutions that are controlled by religious entities. With a few exceptions, the same principles will apply under all three provisions.

Generally, a postsecondary institution governed by Section 504 or ADA Titles II or III may not exclude an otherwise qualified student from any part of its program or services or otherwise discriminate against an applicant or student with a disability. The Department of Education (DOE) issued Section 504 regulations in 1977 that prescribe minimum standards for colleges and universities in six areas: (1) admissions and recruitment; (2) treatment of students; (3) academic adjustments, including the provision of auxiliary aids; (4) housing; (5) financial aid and employment assistance; and (6) nonacademic services. Entities covered by Section 504 or ADA Titles II or III must ensure that students with disabilities are informed about how to access appropriate services. Neither Section 504 regulations nor ADA regulations require postsecondary educational institutions to have *written* policies and procedures describing how they will provide services for students with disabilities; however, most institutions have some written material on the subject.

The DOE regulations are available online at http://www.ed.gov/policy/rights/reg/ocr/edlite-34cfr104.html. The DOE also has several publications regarding the rights of disabled students in higher education that can be accessed at http://www.ed.gov/about/offices/list/ocr/publications.html, and it provides an A-to-Z topic index that can be used to find publications or regulations on specific issues at http://www.ed.gov/about/offices/list/ocr/topics.html?src=rt. The DOE's Office for Civil Rights (OCR) headquarters office answers questions on national policy and Freedom of Information requests for information that is national in scope. This office can also be contacted to request publications or other assistance that is not available online: U.S. Department of Education Office for Civil Rights, Customer Service Team, 550 12th Street, S.W., Washington, D.C. 20202-1100; phone: 1-800-421-3481; fax: 202-245-6840; telecommunication device for the deaf (TDD): 877-521-2172; e-mail: OCR@ed.gov. For more information, see http://www.ed.gov/about/offices/list/ocr/index.html.

Admissions

Colleges and universities are not required to engage in affirmative action in admitting students with disabilities. The only requirement is that institutions do not discriminate against *qualified* individuals with disabilities in the admissions process. A qualified individual with a disability is one who is capable of fulfilling the essential functions or requirements of the educational program, with or without the provision of reasonable accommodations, and meets the academic and technical requirements of the program.

> EXAMPLE: Janet applied for admission to her local university. She submitted standardized test scores, grades in classes, and teacher recommendations along with a personal statement. She indicated in her personal statement that she is visually impaired but had performed very well in high school. Although her grades and scores were in the top 10 percent for the applicant pool at the university, she was denied admission. Janet later heard from a friend at the university that she was denied admission because the university was concerned about the cost of accommodating her. She could bring a claim of discrimination in admissions.

> EXAMPLE: Same details as above but, this time, Janet's grades and test scores are in the bottom 10 percent of the applicant pool. Again, she is denied admission. This time, she would have difficulty challenging the admission decision because she has the burden of demonstrating that she is qualified for admission. The university is not required to engage in affirmative action to admit her. (She would have the option of arguing that the grades and tests are not an accurate reflection of her ability, but that is a hard argument to make.)

Pre-Admission Inquiries

A college or university may not make preadmission inquiries as to whether an applicant for admission is disabled. Exceptions to this rule are made where a school is "taking remedial action to correct the effects of past discrimination" or "taking voluntary action to overcome the effects of conditions that resulted in limited participation in its federally assisted program or activity." Even in the latter situations, however, the school must clearly state (1) "that the information requested is intended for use solely in connection with its remedial action obligations or its voluntary action efforts" and (2) "that the information is being requested on a voluntary basis, that it will be kept confidential, [and] that refusal to provide it will not subject the applicant to any adverse treatment." The prohibition against disability-related preadmission inquiries also does not apply to college or university programs operated specifically for students with disabilities.

This prohibition also applies to questions concerning applicants' mental health and known behavioral problems. The Department of Education's Office for Civil Rights has held, however, that an applicant to a counseling program could be asked about past mental health treatment where the purpose of the inquiry is to determine whether the applicant had adequately resolved any personal/therapeutic issues before attempting to counsel others with similar issues.

EXAMPLE: During the course of an admissions interview for a counseling program, the school learns that an applicant had received substantial personal counseling, which included three psychiatrists, several counselors, and nontraditional therapies. The school requests that the applicant grant it access to her mental health professionals in order to determine whether she had adequately worked through her personal problems. This request would not violate the prohibition against preadmission inquiries because its purpose is to determine whether the applicant had adequately resolved any personal/therapeutic issues before attempting to counsel others with similar issues.

The prohibition against disability-related preadmission inquiries also does not apply when a school asks whether a student can perform a discrete task.

EXAMPLE: Philip is visually impaired and is seeking admission to medical school. Students are required to be interviewed as part of the admissions process. It is apparent to the interviewer that Philip is visually impaired. The interviewer could say: "One task that students must complete in medical school is to learn to read X-rays. How would you anticipate completing that task?" The interviewer could not say, "I see that you are visually impaired. Please give me the medical documentation explaining the degree of your impairment."

Applicants may decide on their own to identify a learning, physical, or other disability and ask that it be considered a relevant factor in the admissions process. This is known as "self-identification" and is not barred by Section 504 or ADA. There are several reasons why applicants might choose to disclose their disabilities. First, the disabilities may have impacted their approach to learning, and the ways in which they have dealt with these disabilities can be used to explain the kind of person and student they are. Second, requesting that colleges consider additional or alternative information is reasonable, especially if the student's performance is below a minimum standard (or somewhere below average). Applicants who want this kind of consideration should enclose a letter with their applications that states (1) that they have a disability, (2) which admission requirement(s) they feel it affects and how, and (3) what alternative or additional information they would like to have considered. They should also include documentation of the disability by an appropriate professional. More information on the content of such a letter can be found in this chapter, and a sample letter requesting accommodations in a different context is included here as well.

Admissions Tests

College and universities may "not make use of any test or criterion for admission that has a disproportionate, adverse effect" on applicants with disabilities, unless the test or criterion has been validated as a predictor of success in the program and alternative tests or criteria that have a less disproportionate adverse effect are not available. Admissions tests must be selected and administered so as to ensure that, when a test is administered to an applicant who has impaired sensory, manual, or speaking skills, the test does not reflect those impaired skills but actually measures the applicant's aptitude or achievement level.

The rules governing nondiscriminatory testing apply not only to preadmission tests given by a postsecondary educational institution but also to tests given by other entities such as the Scholastic Aptitude Test (SAT), Graduate Record Exam (GRE), Law School Admissions Test (LSAT), and Medical College Admission Test (MCAT). ADA Title III provides that an entity that offers examinations related to applications for postsecondary educational programs "shall offer such examinations or courses in a place and manner accessible to persons with disabilities or offer alternative accessible arrangements for such individuals."

Courts have concluded that neither the SAT nor the LSAT inherently violates federal antidiscrimination law because they are available in special formats for students with disabilities. The most recent dispute about these and other standardized tests has been over the issue of "flagging." When a test is taken under nonstandard conditions, such as extra time, can the testing service "flag" the test by indicating that it was taken under conditions of accommodation? When a test is flagged, the school receiving the test results becomes aware of the likelihood that the applicant has a disability. In February 2001, the Educational Testing Service (ETS) agreed to stop the practice of flagging scores on several tests, including the GRE. And a year and a half later, in July 2002, the College Board announced that it would stop flagging SAT test scores as of September 2003; the ACT's administrators soon followed suit. However, the groups that give the law school and medical school admissions tests still flag the scores of students who receive accommodations. In *Doe v. National Board of Medical Examiners*, 199 F.3d 146 (3d Cir. 1999), the court held that this practice does not violate Title III since there is no statutory bar against flagging test scores.

The Office for Civil Rights specifies that it is permissible for a postsecondary educational institution to consider a flagged test score *only* so long as the test score is not the only criterion used for admission and the applicant is not denied admission because he or she took the test under nonstandard conditions. The school receiving a flagged test may not ask an applicant why his or her test was taken under nonstandard conditions or what accommodations were provided; this is a backhanded way of asking the applicant about a disability, which is not permitted. Nor may the educational institution ignore or devalue the scores of applicants who took such tests under nonstandard conditions (i.e., with accommodations).

EXAMPLE: An applicant's score on the Medical College Admission Test is marked with an asterisk by the administering body because it has been given under nonstandard conditions. Members of the admissions committee admit that they either devalue asterisked MCAT scores or weight them in a different and lesser manner than other applications. This would violate Section 504.

EXAMPLE: A law school denies admission to an applicant whose Law School Admissions Test score was flagged. The law school uses a number of factors in making admissions decisions, however, and does not give reduced weight to LSAT scores achieved under nonstandard conditions. This process complies with Section 504.

Obtaining accommodations for a standardized test can be a lengthy process, and each testing organization requires different kinds of supporting documentation. Accordingly, students who seek accommodations should consult the appropriate testing organization's requirements and begin the process well before they plan to take the test. Information on how to request accommodations for tests administered by ETS can be found at http://www.ets.org/disability; accommodation information for the SAT and other tests administered by the College Board is available at http://www.collegeboard.com/disabled/students/html/indx000.html; and ACT accommodations are discussed at http://www.act.org/aap/disab/policy.html. The process for the LSAT can be found at http://www.lsat.org/LSAC.asp?url=lsac/accommodated-testing.asp, and MCAT accommodations are explained at http://www.aamc.org/students/mcat/about/ada2003.pdf.

Eligibility Criteria

Schools are not required to lower their admissions standards for applicants with disabilities. An applicant with a disability must be qualified for the program at issue. Courts and the Office for Civil Rights have also held that applicants may be denied admission to clinical programs in situations where they lack physical qualifications deemed essential to participation in the programs. For example in *Southeastern Community College v. Davis*, 442 U.S. 397 (1979), the Supreme Court held that an applicant with a serious hearing disability was not qualified for admission to a registered nursing program after the school presented evidence that her hearing limitations could interfere with her ability to safely care for patients. A state court reached a similar decision concerning a blind medical school applicant [*Ohio Civil Rights Comm'n v. Case Western Reserve Univ.*, 666 N.E.2d 1376 (Ohio 1996)].

Despite the *Davis* decision, having a hearing loss does not automatically bar a person from becoming a medical professional. In fact, the Association of Medical Professionals with Hearing Losses (AMPHL), formed in 2000, specifically targets those with degrees in professional health care fields such as physicians, veterinarians, dentists, nurses, physician's assistants, technicians, audiologists, and therapists, as well as students from these respective fields. The organization's website, http://www.amphl.org, has links for a variety of topics, including guidance on how to apply to a medical professional program and a list of programs that have graduated individuals with a hearing loss or that have such students currently enrolled in their program.

Moreover, not all medical schools have applied blanket exclusions to students with physical limitations. For example, the University of Wisconsin School of Medicine admitted Tim Cordes, a blind student, and he finished in the top sixth of his class [http://www.cnn.com/2005/HEALTH/04/02/seeing.no.limits.ap].

While most physicians with disabilities did not acquire them until after medical school, Cordes is not alone; indeed, a recent article discusses the experiences of several doctors who are deaf, blind, or use wheelchairs [http://www.ama-assn.org/amednews/2005/01/17/prsa 0117.htm]. Another article, however, reports on the experience of Kristianna Matthewis, a blind physician who had great difficulty finding a job after completing medical school at the University of Colorado and a residency program in Michigan [http://www.ama-assn.org/amednews/2001/01/15/prsa0115.htm].

Disclosure and Documentation of Disability

As noted above, an applicant to a postsecondary educational institution may always voluntarily disclose a disability and ask that it be considered in the admissions determination. Further, once accepted, a student who wishes to receive accommodations or adjustments for his or her disability *must* identify the disability. In either situation, the educational institution may require documentation of the disability. The applicant or student is responsible for providing such documentation at his or her own expense. Moreover, the documentation must be fairly recent, come from an appropriate expert, and be sufficiently comprehensive.

Documentation should include

- a diagnosis by an appropriate professional identifying the disability, the date of the most current evaluation, and the date of the original diagnosis;
- a description of the diagnostic tests, methods, and/or criteria used;

- a description of the current functional impact of the disability, including specific test results and the examiner's narrative interpretation;
- information on the treatments, medications, or assistive devices/services currently prescribed or in use;
- a description of the expected progression or stability of the impact of the disability over time, particularly the next five years; and
- information on the diagnosing professionals' credentials.

Postsecondary institutions are often particularly skeptical of requests for disability status when the student has no prior record of having been disabled. Documentation at a young age can be very helpful in alleviating such concerns. Thus, when parents have their child tested at a young age for a disability determination, they need to remember that such documentation may continue to be important even when the child enters postsecondary school. Parents should be careful to keep *all* records of early documentation in case it is needed as the child gets older.

Reasonable Accommodations

Schools must make reasonable accommodations or adjustments for qualified individuals with known disabilities. An accommodation is not reasonable if it would constitute an undue burden or hardship to provide it or if it would require a fundamental alteration to the program at issue.

The leading case dealing with the "fundamental alteration" issue is *Southeastern Community College v. Davis*, 442 U.S. 397 (1979). In that case, the Supreme Court held that a nursing school did not discriminate against an applicant with a hearing-impairment when it refused to admit her. The Court held that Davis was not otherwise qualified for the nursing program because "nothing less than close, individual attention by a nursing instructor would be sufficient to ensure patient safety if [Davis] took part in the clinical portion of the nursing program." The Court concluded that because Davis could not function in clinical courses without close supervision, the nursing school could allow her to take only academic courses. The Court held that "[w]hatever benefits [Davis] might realize from such a course of study, she would not receive even a rough equivalent of the training a nursing program normally gives. Such a fundamental alteration in the nature of a program is far more than the 'modification' [Section 504] requires."

The question of whether accommodations will cause a fundamental alteration is answered in this chapter on a case-by-case basis—specifically, as demonstrated by how the two medical schools discussed in the prior section approached decisions to admit students who were blind. In *Ohio Civil Rights Comm'n v. Case Western Reserve Univ.*, 666 N.E.2d 1376 (Ohio 1996), the court held that the accommodations were not reasonable where the student requested raised-line drawing boards, tutors and faculty assistance, occasional assistance from sighted students, and the waiver of course requirements that she could not perform such as starting an I.V. or drawing blood. The state civil rights commission argued that these requests were reasonable because the skills were not necessary for the student to pursue her chosen field of psychiatry. The medical educators, however, testified that it would be impossible to modify the traditional teaching methods in such a way as to convey the skills and information necessary to allow a blind student to complete the essential course requirements.

By contrast, the University of Wisconsin School of Medicine decided it was able to accommodate blind student Tim Cordes, who planned to pursue an M.D.-Ph.D. and become a medical researcher. The school used technology that converted all the school-produced course material into an electronic format; Cordes, in turn, used a program to convert that material into sound. Line drawings were converted into raised-line drawings, and microscopic images were converted into raised images [http://www.aamc.org/newsroom/reporter/july2000/blind.htm].

While technologically simple, this procedure involved a great deal of faculty time, and not all schools will be willing—or required—to make such an accommodation. Indeed, Wisconsin was the only medical school that accepted Cordes, who had graduated from college with a 3.99 GPA in biology. As discussed next, students who require an accommodation are responsible for requesting it and for supporting it with the necessary documentation. In situations where the accommodation will entail a significant alteration in course requirements or testing, they must also be prepared to show why the alteration does not change a fundamental part of the school's educational program.

Suggested Accommodations

The DOE's regulations suggest three types of accommodations that may be made to assist a student with a disability in obtaining a post-secondary education: academic adjustments, modification or alteration of course examinations, and the provision of auxiliary aids.

With respect to academic adjustments, the regulations provide that modifications may include

- changes in the length of time permitted for the completion of a course or of degree requirements;
- substitution of specific courses required for the completion of degree requirements; and
- adaptation of the manner in which specific courses are conducted or course materials are distributed.

The regulations also cover the modification or alteration of course examinations, requiring a school to "provide such methods for evaluating the achievement of students who have a handicap that impairs sensory, manual, or speaking skills as will best ensure that the results of the evaluation represent the student's achievement in the course, rather than reflecting the student's impaired sensory, manual, or speaking skills." No modification needs to be made, however, where those skills are the factors that the test purports to measure.

Colleges and universities are also required to utilize auxiliary aids to ensure that students with impaired sensory, manual, or speaking skills are not subject to discrimination in postsecondary educational programs. Auxiliary aids may include

- taped texts;
- interpreters or other effective methods of making orally delivered materials available to students with hearing impairments;
- readers in libraries for students with visual impairments;
- Brailled or large-print texts or qualified readers for individuals with visual impairments and learning disabilities; and
- classroom equipment adapted for use by students with manual impairments.

Note, however, that the school does not have to meet this requirement if it can demonstrate that offering a particular auxiliary aid or service would fundamentally alter the course or result in an undue burden. Schools are also not required to provide personal-care attendants, individually prescribed devices, readers for personal use or study, or other devices or services of a personal nature.

Courses must be administered in facilities that are accessible to individuals with disabilities, or the school must make alternative accessible arrangements such as providing the course through videotape, cassettes, or prepared notes. Alternative arrangements must provide conditions comparable to those provided for nondisabled individuals.

Postsecondary institutions are also supposed to offer their programs and activities in the most integrated setting appropriate.

EXAMPLE: A university offers several elementary physics classes. It has moved one class to the first floor of the science building to accommodate students who use wheelchairs and has decided to concentrate students with visual and hearing impairments in that class as well. Concentrating students with no mobility impairments in the same class would be a violation of federal law, although making only one of the physics classrooms accessible is probably permissible.

Scope of Reasonable Accommodations

The extent of accommodations to be provided to students with disabilities is often an issue of dispute. Courts generally have held that postsecondary institutions do not have to accommodate students by lowering required standards. For example, in *McGregor v. Louisiana State University Board of Supervisors*, 3 F.3d 850 (5th Cir. 1993), a student with orthopedic and neurological disabilities who used a wheelchair was provided with numerous accommodations by the law school, including extra time to take exams, a student assistant during exams, a wheelchair-accessible table, and modified class schedules. Despite those accommodations, the student failed to maintain the required grade-point average. The student then requested that he be permitted to continue at the law school without having the requisite first-year grade-point average and that he be allowed to attend law school on a part-time basis and take his examinations at home. The court held that the requested accommodations exceeded the scope of Section 504.

Waiving Required Classes

The DOE's Office for Civil Rights has also held that a college is not required to waive math or language requirements if the school can show that the requirement is necessary to achieve a specific educational purpose. For example, a school did not have to waive a math requirement for a student in an Applied Science Program where it showed that the class's purpose was to provide students with a firm foundation in mathematics for their careers in an increasingly technological society [*City Univ. of New York (NY)*, 3 Nat'l Disab. L. Rep. § 104 (1992)]. Accordingly, students who request that a math or language requirement be waived must be prepared not only to produce evidence of a disability in the area but also to respond to the school's purpose for requiring the course(s).

EXAMPLE: A liberal arts college requires students to take a music appreciation course to graduate. Bonnie is deaf. She requests that the institution substitute an art appreciation or music history course for the music appreciation course. If the university denies her request, she is likely to have a valid claim of an unlawful unwillingness to accommodate her disability so long as she is not seeking to major in music.

EXAMPLE: A liberal arts college has a foreign language requirement for graduation. Billie, who has a learning disability, seeks to be exempted from that requirement. The university may be able to successfully refuse that request, arguing that a foreign language is essential to its undergraduate liberal arts program of instruction.

Changing Test Formats

The extent to which colleges or universities must accommodate students with disabilities by modifying or changing the form of examinations has also been an issue of dispute. In *Wynne v. Tufts Univ. Sch. of Medicine*, 976 F.2d 791 (1st Cir. 1992), the court held that a school's failure to offer the student an alternative format for a multiple-choice biochemistry exam did not constitute a failure to make a reasonable accommodation. The court noted that the school had documented why, in the department chair's words, "the multiple-choice format provides the fairest way to test the students' mastery of the subject matter of biochemistry." The school elaborated upon the unique qual-ities of multiple-choice examinations as they apply to biochemistry, and offered an explanation of the historical record to show the background against which such tests were administered to the student. Similarly, colleges have succeeded in defending a closed-book exam format. Accordingly, students who request an alternative testing format must be prepared not only to produce evidence of a disability that requires such a format but also to respond to the school's purpose for using the current type of testing.

Interpreters

One issue where there has not been much dispute is OCR's requirement that postsecondary educational institutions provide necessary accommodations, including interpreters, for students with hearing impairments. This requirement extends to class-related activities that take place off campus and even to study-abroad programs, and it is the school's obligation to provide such interpreters at no cost to the student if they are not available from outside sources.

> EXAMPLE: A university is having financial problems and does not want to continue offering interpreter services to deaf students. It therefore asks a student to sign a document stating that the provision of an interpreter for 12 credits of coursework is a financial hardship for the school and that "unless we can find other sources of income ... the [school] will not be able to continue this level of service." This requested waiver violates federal antidiscrimination law.

Students who use interpreters also have responsibilities, however. Specifically, they must comply with school policies requiring class attendance when the school has hired an interpreter to sign for them. For example, OCR found that a school was not in violation of Section 504 when it adopted policies that resulted in the suspension of interpreter services for all classes where a hearing-impaired student had two no-shows or late cancellations [*University of California, Davis*, 4 Nat. Disab. L. Rep. ¶108 (1993)]. OCR's investigation showed that the school had to pay for interpreters when a student failed either to show up in class or to provide forty-eight hours' advance notice of a cancellation. According to OCR, suspension of services until the student met with a counselor was a reasonable administrative approach for reducing unnecessary interpreter costs. OCR did, however, find that there must be an exception for "good cause" situations when the student could not reasonably be expected to know in advance that he or she would be missing class so as to provide timely notice of a cancellation.

Interactive Process

ADA and Section 504 contemplate that the student with a disability and the postsecondary educational institution will work together to determine what accommodations can reasonably be provided for that student. A student who fails to cooperate in this interactive process could be denied relief under the federal laws.

Payment for Reasonable Accommodations
A university may not deny the provision of auxiliary aids for students with disabilities based on their ability to pay or their enrollment in specific programs. In *United States v. Board of Trustees for University of Alabama*, 908 F.2d 740 (11th Cir. 1990), the court held that requiring hearing-impaired students to show that they lacked the financial means to pay for their own interpreters (or other auxiliary aids) violated Section 504. It further held that the university is required to be the primary provider of auxiliary aids for students, faculty, or staff with disabilities. Thus, universities cannot require students or employees with disabilities to request assistance from vocational rehabilitation centers. By implication, the university itself must contact those centers for assistance in providing the requisite services. OCR and other courts have followed similar reasoning. A school may, however, charge a special fee in situations where it provides a special program for learning-disabled students that is outside the regular curriculum offered to other students [*Halasz v. University of New England*, 816 F. Supp. 37 (D. Me. 1993)].

There are few disability-specific grants or scholarships available for postsecondary education, and the amounts awarded by those few that are available tend to be relatively small. A resource paper titled "Creating Options: A Resource on Financial Aid for Students with Disabilities," http://www.heath.gwu.edu/PDFs/financialaid.pdf, describes federal aid programs and how they benefit students with disabilities. It also describes assistance available through state agencies for vocational rehabilitation and lists websites where students can conduct online scholarship searches. A comprehensive listing of nationally awarded, disability-specific scholarships is included as well. Another website with links about scholarships for students with disabilities is http://www.familyvillage.wisc.edu/education/scholarships.html.

Safety

Both Section 504 and ADA incorporate a "safety defense." Accordingly, an individual with a disability is not qualified for a postsecondary educational program if his or her participation would pose a direct threat to the health or safety of other individuals. Courts have interpreted the safety defense as applying under Section 504 when an individual with a disability would pose a direct threat to the health or safety *of himself or herself*, as well as to the health or safety *of others*. It is unclear whether threat-to-self reasoning applies to ADA Titles II and III, but the courts have found that it applies to ADA Title I (employment).

In addition to the Supreme Court's decision in *Davis*, discussed earlier in this chapter, several Section 504 cases have addressed the safety issue in the context of postsecondary educational issues. For example, in *Doe v. New York University*, 666 F.2d 761 (2d Cir. 1981), the court held that a medical school did not discriminate against an applicant with a history of mental illness when it refused to readmit the applicant to its program. The court held that the applicable question in determining whether Doe was otherwise qualified to be readmitted to medical school was "the substantiality of the risk that her mental disturbances [would] recur, resulting in behavior harmful to herself and others." The Second Circuit rejected the district court's test that Doe must be found qualified if it appeared "more likely than not" that she could complete her medical training and serve as a doctor without a recurrence of her self-destructive and antisocial behavior. The appellate court reasoned that Congress would not have intended to force colleges to accept students who pose a significant risk of harm to themselves or others even if the chances of harm were less than 50 percent.

A school barring a student for safety reasons, however, must not rely on assumptions about people with disabilities. For example, in *Pushkin v. Regents of the Univ. of Colorado*, 658 F.2d 1372 (10th Cir. 1981), the court held that a university violated Section 504 when it denied a physician with multiple sclerosis admittance to its psychiatric residency program based on incorrect assumptions or inadequate factual grounds. The admissions committee assumed that the plaintiff was angry and so emotionally upset due to his disability that he would be unable to do an effective job as a psychiatrist and that his disability and use of steroids had led to difficulties with mentation, delirium, and disturbed sensorium. Instead, a determination that an individual with a disability poses a direct health or safety threat must be made on a case-by-case basis, through consideration of four basic factors: (1) the duration of the risk, (2) the nature and severity of the potential harm, (3) the likelihood that the potential harm will occur, and (4) the imminence of the potential harm.

Students who are aware that they have a condition that may raise a safety concern should be prepared to show that the risk can be minimized through some type of accommodation. For example, people diagnosed with HIV who are enrolling in a class or program that would involve some kind of hands-on activity should be prepared to show how they will fulfill the class or program's requirements with a minimum of risk to themselves and others.

Academic Deference

The extent to which courts are willing to defer to the expertise of academic personnel in upholding or rejecting a claim for discrimination may be the decisive factor in any postsecondary education case alleging disability discrimination. Courts have generally concluded that an educational institution's academic decisions are entitled to deference because courts are "ill-equipped," as compared with experienced educators, to determine whether a student meets a university's "reasonable standards for academic and professional achievement" [*Wong v. Regents of the University of California*, 192 F.3d 807 (9th Cir. 1999)]. This deference is not absolute; the school has "a duty to make itself aware of the nature of the student's disability; to explore alternatives for accommodating the student; and to exercise professional judgment in deciding whether the modifications under consideration would give the student the opportunity to complete the program without fundamentally or substantially modifying the school's standards." In *Wong*, the court refused to defer to the institution's academic decision because it had not fulfilled this obligation; the school had not shown that it investigated the proposed accommodation to determine whether it could be implemented without substantially altering the school's standards.

Students challenging a school's decision must be prepared for the academic deference argument. To overcome it, they must show that they supported a request for an accommodation with specific documentation and that the school failed to carefully consider the effectiveness of the accommodation.

Nonacademic Programs and Services

The DOE Section 504 regulations also govern access to nonacademic programs and services such as housing, health insurance, counseling, financial aid, physical education, athletics, recreation, transportation, and other extracurricular programs or activities. There are specific regulations governing several areas of nonacademic programs and services. For example, a college or university that provides student housing must provide comparable, convenient, and accessible housing to students with disabilities at the same cost as to others. OCR has found that universities that provide some accessible housing may still violate Section 504 when it is not sufficient to meet the needs of all disabled students who request it.

The regulations also require that "personal, academic, or vocational counseling, guidance, or placement services" be provided to disabled students to the same extent that such services are provided to nondisabled students. Moreover, a school must not counsel qualified students with disabilities toward more restrictive career objectives than it does for students with similar interests and abilities.

Schools that provide financial assistance are barred from dispensing less assistance to students with disabilities than to nondisabled students, from limiting the eligibility of nondisabled students to such assistance or from otherwise discriminating on the basis of disability. A college or university that "provides significant assistance to fraternities, sororities, or similar organizations shall assure itself that the membership practices of such organizations do not permit discrimination [on the basis of disability]." Similarly, a college or university that "assists any agency, organization, or person in providing employment opportunities to any of its students shall assure itself that such employment opportunities, as a whole, are made available in a manner [that does not discriminate against students with disabilities]." Finally, a school that employs any of its students may not do so in a manner that discriminates against students with disabilities.

Notice and Documentation of Disability

Under the federal regulations, a student is responsible for identifying his or her disability to the college, requesting academic adjustments, and providing any necessary evidence of a disability-related need for the requested adjustment. In recent years, OCR and the courts have frequently found that a college did not violate Section 504 or ADA by denying a student academic adjustments in situations where the student failed to provide the necessary notification or documentation.

Generally, a school has no obligation to provide academic adjustment until it has received sufficient specific information to enable it to evaluate the student's needs and the school's ability to provide the needed academic adjustments. If the school has been provided sufficient notice from a qualified professional and then questions the diagnosis, description of limitations, and/or recommendations, the school can require that the student be evaluated by a professional of its choosing, and at its expense, before deciding what academic adjustments would be appropriate for the student. Following is a sample letter requesting accommodations:

Disabilities Services Office
Public University
123 New St.
Anytown, GA

Dear Sir/Madam:
I will be a freshman at Public University in the fall and am requesting accommodations for my attention deficit hyperactivity disorder (ADHD). I was first diagnosed with ADHD in grade school and have received accommodations throughout my academic career. As explained in the attached letters from Drs. [X] and [Y], my ADHD requires several accommodations—including a note-taker, alternative testing, and extended time for writing papers—so that I can compete on an equal basis with other students.
Please contact me at the address or phone number below so that we can discuss these accommodations.
Sincerely,
[Full name and phone number]

The frequency of tests and the qualifications of those giving them were at issue in *Guckenberger v. Boston University*, 974 F. Supp. 106

(D. Mass. 1997). Boston University (BU) required that students with learning disabilities be retested every three years and that they provide evaluations only by clinical or licensed psychologists or physicians. The court held that these requirements were unduly restrictive as applied to students required to be retested, because tests originally accepted by the university were later deemed to be conducted by unqualified individuals. However, the requirements were not unduly restrictive as applied to students who had not been tested prior to matriculation at the university. The court also found that these requirements were "necessary" to the process of accommodating students diagnosed with attention deficit disorder (ADD) and attention deficit hyperactivity disorder (ADHD).

Given the decision in *Guckenberger*, students applying to college should be prepared to provide recent test results (obtained within the last three years) by certified professionals to support their accommodation requests. In many cases, the IEP is not sufficient. Students who do not have the proper documentation will need to be evaluated in order to receive services. Accordingly, to ensure continuation of needed accommodations, students need to address the documentation issue *prior to* arriving at the postsecondary institution.

Retaliation

Section 504 and ADA Titles II and III all prohibit retaliation against individuals who have exercised their rights under those laws. To establish a basis for a retaliation claim, the student must show that (1) he or she was engaged in an activity protected by Section 504 or ADA, (2) he or she was subjected to some adverse action by the postsecondary educational institution, and (3) there is sufficient evidence of a connection between the protected activity and the adverse action to give rise to an inference of retaliation. Once this basis is established, the school may offer a legitimate, nondiscriminatory explanation for the adverse action. The student then has an opportunity to show that the institution's proffered reason for the adverse action is a pretext for discrimination.

Hostile Learning Environment

A cause of action exists under ADA and Section 504 for an educational institution's creation of a hostile learning environment for students with disabilities [*see, e.g., Guckenberger v. Boston University,*

957 F. Supp. 306 (D. Mass. 1997)]. To state a cognizable claim for hostile learning environment harassment under ADA and the Rehabilitation Act, a plaintiff must allege (1) that she is a member of a protected group; (2) that she has been subject to unwelcome harassment; (3) that the harassment is based on a protected characteristic, her disability; (4) that the harassment is sufficiently severe or pervasive that it alters the conditions of her education and creates an abusive educational environment; and (5) that there is a basis for institutional liability.

Individuals with Learning Disabilities

Increasingly, postsecondary educational institutions are confronted with issues pertaining to applicants or students with learning disabilities. The Individuals with Disabilities Education Act mandates services for students who have a learning disability, which it defines as "a disorder in one or more of the basic psychological processes involved in understanding or in using language, spoken or written, which disorder may manifest itself in imperfect ability to listen, think, speak, read, write, spell, or do mathematical calculations." This is consistent with the definition used by psychiatrists and psychologists that is found in the *Diagnostic and Statistical Manual of Mental Disorders*, 4th ed. (DSM-IV). The DSM-IV states that a diagnosis of learning disorder is called for when a student's reading, math, or written-expression ability is substantially less than would be expected considering his or her age, intelligence, and education, and when this deficiency materially impedes his or her academic achievement or daily living.

Cases applying ADA and Section 504, however, use a *very differ - ent* definition of disability, and students moving into higher education should be on notice that this definition has often been interpreted as excluding students who have been diagnosed with and received accommodations for "learning disabilities" in the past. The ADA definition of disability requires plaintiffs to prove that they have (1) a physical or mental impairment that (2) impacts a major life activity, and (3) that the impairment *substantially limits* that major life activity. Courts have acknowledged that learning disabilities as traditionally defined are unquestionably impairments and that learning is considered a major life activity under ADA. In ADA, however, "substantial limits" means "*[s]ignificantly restricted* as to the condition, manner or duration under which an individual can perform a particular major life activity *as compared to* the condition, manner or duration under which *the average person in the general population* can perform that same major life activity" (emphasis added).

Courts using this definition have held that a person who has been diagnosed with a learning disability as traditionally defined is not necessarily disabled under ADA. What this means is that a person with a learning problem is considered disabled as defined by ADA (and therefore entitled to accommodation) only if the learning problem "significantly restrict[s] the condition, manner or duration of his learning ability as compared to the average person in the general population" [*Wong v. Regents of University of California*, 379 F.3d 1097 (9th Cir. 2004)]. In *Wong*, the court held that a medical student who was first identified as having learning disabilities while in kindergarten was not disabled under ADA because he was not substantially limited by his learning disability as a whole, for purposes of daily living, as compared to most people. Other courts have similarly concluded that individuals with learning disabilities were not disabled as defined by ADA when they had not exhibited a pattern of substantial academic difficulties [*see, e.g., Gonzales v. National Bd. of Medical Examiners*, 225 F.3d 620 (6th Cir. 2000)]. The same courts have rejected arguments that the proper comparison in determining whether the student's ability was substantially limited was to other persons with similar educational backgrounds and not to the general population.

Because individuals with learning problems often learn strategies to help them self-accommodate, they may attain scores on some testing measures that are close to those of the general population and perform well in school. Thus, in order to be covered under ADA and Section 504, a person with a learning problem will have to show specific evidence that it limits him or her as compared to the average person in the general public. For example, in *Bartlett v. New York State Bd. of Law Examiners* (2d. Cir. 2000), a woman who had been diagnosed with a learning impairment (dyslexia) sued the New York State Board of Law Examiners after it refused to grant her the accommodations she requested on the bar exam. She claimed that her impairment limited her with respect to the major life activities of learning, reading, writing, studying, test-taking, and working. The parties, however, focused primarily on the life activity of reading, and the court concluded that it needed to assess the substantiality of Bartlett's limitation *after* taking into account her self-accommodations. When the case was sent back to a lower court, that court concluded that Bartlett was disabled in the major life activity of reading because, even after she self-accommodates, she reads very slowly as compared to the average reader and suffers fatigue caused by her inability to read with automaticity [*Bartlett v. New York State Bd. of Law Examiners*, 2001 WL 930792 (S.D.N.Y. Aug. 15, 2001)].

The *Bartlett* case is unusual because the plaintiff was able to show specific evidence that her learning problem limited her abilities as compared to the average person in the general public. Students who have been diagnosed with learning disabilities in the past should be prepared to show similar information when they move into higher education. Specifically, it is critical that such students (or their parents) discuss the distinction between IDEA's and DSM-IV's definitions of learning disability and ADA's definition of disability with the person providing documentation to support the student's request for accommodation. The supporting documentation should, like Bartlett's, identify how the individual's abilities compare with the general population.

Admissions

In the admissions process, the question that often arises is whether an individual with a learning disability is qualified for admission to a given program. As discussed earlier, colleges and universities may not ask an applicant if he or she has a disability, but an applicant may always identify a disability and ask that it be considered as a relevant factor in the admissions determination. In such cases, the institution should evaluate the applicant's *entire* file. A learning disability, for example, may serve as evidence of reasons for poor performance in high school or on standardized tests such as the SAT. Indeed, if there is evidence that a learning disability has prevented an applicant from performing as well as the applicant is capable of, the admissions committee may look for other evidence of the applicant's ability, such as performance in courses and on standardized tests that were modified to accommodate the learning disability, employment or community experiences, or letters of recommendation from teachers or employers who know the applicant well. In addition, the admissions committee may consider whether there is evidence showing that the applicant is able to perform well when appropriate accommodations are provided.

Safety concerns may also be at issue for an applicant with a learning disability, as in the case of an applicant to nursing school who has a learning disability that causes him or her to transpose numbers or an applicant to veterinary school who has a learning disability that precludes him or her from being able to perform certain important mathematical computations. There may be legitimate concerns that the nursing school applicant would be unable to accurately enter or follow information about medications on patients' charts and that the veterinary school applicant might be unable to accurately prescribe or compile medications. Ultimately, what would have to be determined is whether accommodations or adjustments could be made to eliminate those safety concerns, such as by allowing the nursing student to dictate notes into a tape to be transcribed by a secretary.

Another situation that arises in the context of the admission of applicants with learning disabilities to postsecondary educational programs involves special learning disabilities programs. In *Halasz v. University of New England*, 816 F. Supp. 37 (D. Me. 1993), the university operated a special program for students with learning disabilities, pursuant to which it provided tutorial assistance by learning disability specialists, training in study skills, note-takers, books on tape, and other aids. A fee was charged for the program. The university agreed to admit some larning-disabled students with lower than the requisite SAT scores and GPAs on the condition that the students enroll in the special program. The court upheld the university's program.

The court in *Halasz* noted that colleges and universities are free to set their own standards and requirements for admission. The program at issue in this case concerned an expanded type of accommodation to assist students with learning disabilities who were not already succeeding independently in academic settings. Although a university may not typically charge a student with disabilities for the cost of reasonable accommodations, the court found that a fee was appropriate for this program because it went beyond the reasonable accommodation obligation. So long as the university provided requisite reasonable accommodations for a student with disabilities at no cost, the court indicated—without really deciding—that a fee may be charged for additional services that are beyond the university's obligation. Moreover, the court held that the university could permissibly limit the number of students who would be admitted to the special learning disabilities program as long as (1) it did not limit the number of students with learning disabilities admitted to the school, and (2) it provided reasonable accommodations (at no charge) to all admitted students with learning disabilities.

Accommodations for Accepted Students

Every learning disability is different. Thus, each individual with a learning disability may require a unique form of assistance or accommodation. And each postsecondary educational program will have different requirements and standards. As a result, it is not possible to devise a generic list of appropriate accommodations for students with learning disabilities in postsecondary educational programs. The issue in each case is fact specific. The basic issue is whether the requested accommodations would require the school to fundamentally alter its program or lower its standards. As discussed earlier in this chapter, courts generally have held that postsecondary institutions do not have to accommodate students by lowering required standards. Nor is a college required to waive math, language, or specific testing requirements if the school can show that the requirements are necessary to achieve specific educational purposes. Moreover, students themselves are responsible for identifying their disability to the college, requesting academic adjustments, and providing any necessary evidence of a disability-related need for the requested adjustment.

Accordingly, if they have not already done so during the admissions process, students with learning disabilities should contact their schools' disability services office once they are admitted to college. The sooner students contact this office, the better. That will allow the students to work closely with the professionals in the disability services office, and to obtain the required documentation for the accommodations they request, well before their classes begin.

Enforcement

Students who believe a college or university has failed to comply with ADA and/or the Rehabilitation Act have two formal options for remedying that violation: (1) file an administrative complaint with the Department of Education's Office for Civil Rights (OCR) or (2) file a private lawsuit.

Administrative Complaint
A description of the OCR complaint process can be found on its website at http://www.ed.gov/about/offices/list/ocr/complaintprocess.html. The procedures involved in this process mirror those described for administrative complaints under Title II, which are discussed later in this book.

The OCR website also has links for filing an online complaint and a complaint form that can be printed off and sent to the OCR enforcement office serving your state or territory. This enforcement office can be located by looking to the bottom of http://www.ed.gov/about/offices/list/ocr/docs/howto.html?src=rt#note or by searching http://wdcrobcolp01.ed.gov/CFAPPS/OCR/contactus.cfm. The enforcement office also can provide technical assistance on a problem or help resolve civil rights disputes.

A complaint filed with OCR should include the following information:

- your name and address (a telephone number where you may be reached during business hours is helpful, but not required)
- a general description of the person(s) or class of persons injured by the alleged discriminatory act(s) (the names of the injured person[s] are not required)
- the name and location of the institution that committed the alleged discriminatory act(s)
- a description of the alleged discriminatory act(s) in sufficient detail to enable OCR to understand what occurred, when it occurred, and the basis for the alleged discrimination

Private Lawsuits
Students can also file private lawsuits in cases involving disability discrimination in postsecondary education. These cases will use the remedies and procedures for enforcing the access to programs and services requirements of ADA and the Rehabilitation Act discussed in Chapter 5 of this book.

In addition, and as more fully discussed in Chapter 5, the doctrine of sovereign immunity may impact the viability of ADA actions against state universities. Some courts have applied sovereign immunity principles to conclude that Section 504 cannot be used to obtain monetary damages against a state entity [*see, e.g., Garcia v. S.U.N.Y. Health Sciences Center of Brooklyn*, 280 F.3d 98 (2d Cir. 2001)]. Most courts, however, have found that a state has waived that immunity under the Rehabilitation Act by accepting federal funds [*see, e.g., Garrett v. University of Alabama*, 344 F.3d 1288 (11th Cir. 2003)].

Self-Advocacy by Students with Disabilities

As noted in the first section of this chapter, the move from high school to postsecondary education involves a dramatic shift in the respective responsibilities of the school and the student in terms of identifying disabilities and making accommodations for them. Another dramatic shift affects students specifically: It is often now *their* responsibility, rather than their parents', to speak with disability service providers. Many students are not prepared for this role after having had their parents advocate for them all through elementary, middle, and high school. Accordingly, self-advocacy skills should be a primary focus of students and their parents in the transition to and progression through college.

The importance of students learning self-advocacy before going to college is illustrated in a story that appears on the website of The Advocacy Consortium for College Students with Disabilities, http://www.ggw.org/~advocacyconsortium. The story is told by Patricia W. Heggie, the mother of a child with learning disabilities (LD) and attention deficit disorder (ADD), who felt that her son was ready for college because every available support had been given to him through the educational system and private providers [http://www.ggw.org/~advocacyconsortium/mothers_story.htm]. Heggie says that she "never fully appreciated the importance of that little piece of paper titled, "The Individualized Transition Plan (ITP)," which she calls "a critical document that should never be taken lightly."

After starting college, Heggie's son was overwhelmed in his classes. He had self-reported his LD and ADD to his professors and academic counselor, and they asked him what accommodations they could make. He didn't know the answer, and, although his advisors and professors were sympathetic, they didn't know what to do either. None of the school's academic counselors had specialized training in treating LD or ADD.

Heggie pulled out her son's transition plan from high school, which was written in her son's handwriting and had three signatures: those of the special education teacher, her son, and Heggie herself. When she signed the plan, she had thought of it as just one more piece of red tape needed to obtain support services. "What I didn't realize was that this plan demonstrated my son's lack of self-awareness and self-advocacy skills. If I had only known that the ITP was my son's chance to identify and address all the issues that were creating doubts! I'm embarrassed by my ignorance. I'm angry and disappointed that the school system placed such little emphasis on the ITP."

Heggie now says that, in retrospect, there are several questions she should have asked in assessing the effectiveness of LD services and transition planning:

- Does my son truly understand how his brain works and how he learns?
- Can he clearly articulate his abilities and disabilities in a way that people without knowledge of LD and ADD can understand?
- Can he provide examples of how his learning disabilities affect his academic performance and his daily living?
- Does he have independent living skills?
- Is he aware that updated testing and documentation are needed for continued eligibility for LD/ADD accommodations?
- Does he understand what his legal rights are with regard to access and accommodations under the law?
- •Does he have any idea how his LD might affect him in a work situation? In daily living? In relationships?
- Does he understand what resources are available to him and how to access those resources?
- When he was applying for college, did he and I know how to evaluate colleges regarding their knowledge about LD and their LD support services?

Other parents (and students with disabilities themselves) should ask these same questions. It would be best if they could obtain the answers, and then address any concerns that have been identified, be - fore the students begin college. The same is true is for older students with disabilities who return to school later in life. If these concerns cannot be fully addressed before the student enrolls, it is essential that the parents and/or student set up a plan, perhaps in conjunction with the school's disability services offices, to ensure that the student can be an effective self-advocate within the first year or two of school. This process may make parents nervous, but it is necessary for the student's success in college and afterward.

Conclusion

Higher education is a very different world from K–12 education. The Individuals with Disabilities Education Act emphasizes transition planning for students to help them navigate the move from K–12 to higher education, but that transition planning is often ineffective. Hence, students often find themselves in the higher education arena without sufficient training to advocate for themselves. Many universities have excellent disability services offices, and we urge students to visit those offices and learn of the resources they offer as soon as they arrive on campus (if not earlier). Students with disabilities should also visit those offices during college trips in advance of accepting an offer to attend an institution. An office that is not receptive to incoming students is not likely to be receptive to admitted students.

Given the increasing competition for college students, some universities now see accommodating students with disabilities as good business. Although students with disabilities cannot count on higher education to be perfect, they should expect to receive reasonable services. We urge parents to work with their children before entering college so that they can accumulate the skills necessary to be effective self-advocates. The further development of those skills can be an important part of the higher education experience and will benefit them throughout their lives.

5

Access and Accommodation

The vast majority of lawsuits filed under the Americans with Disabilities Act (ADA) have involved employment discrimination claims, but ADA's most visible effects have been improvements in accessibility and accommodations. Because of ADA and other laws, many people with disabilities are able to enter and use private businesses such as stores, restaurants, and theaters that were once inaccessible. The same is true of state, city, and county buildings and facilities, which once excluded people with disabilities. Access and accommodation are still far from complete, however. Disability advocates will have to continue pushing businesses and governments to meet that goal.

Several laws require such access and accommodation. The first federal law intended to ensure a barrier-free environment for persons with disabilities was the Architectural Barriers Act (ABA), which was enacted in 1968. The coverage of the ABA, however, is limited to buildings directly used or funded by the federal government.

Section 504 of the Rehabilitation Act of 1973 expanded the accessibility requirement. It requires that entities that receive any form of federal funding make all their programs and activities accessible to people with disabilities. Title III of ADA extended that mandate further, covering certain private entities regardless of whether they receive federal funds. ADA Title II similarly requires that state and local governments make their programs and activities accessible. More specifically, ADA Titles II and III state that new facilities must be "readily accessible to and usable by individuals with disabilities" and require the removal of "architectural barriers . . . in existing facilities . . . where such removal is readily achievable." Government and private entities must also make "reasonable modifications in policies, practices, or procedures" and provide "auxiliary aids and services" to ensure access for people with disabilities.

Finally, Section 508 of the Rehabilitation Act, 29 U.S.C. § 794d, requires federal agencies to ensure, unless it would pose an undue burden to do so, that electronic and information technology (EIT) must be accessible to federal employees with disabilities and people with disabilities who are members of the public seeking information or services from the agencies.

This chapter provides an overview of the accessibility requirements under each of these laws, but with a primary focus on ADA Titles II and III. ADA's requirements were modeled after those found in the regulations interpreting Section 504, which applied only to entities receiving federal funds. Under ADA Titles II and III, the same rules on accessibility and accommodation now apply to certain private entities and all state and local governments regardless of whether they get federal funding.

For additional information about ADA accessibility requirements, check the Department of Justice's ADA home page at www.ada.gov or www.usdoj.gov/crt/ada/adahom1.htm, which has links to several ADA publications, technical assistance documents, and websites for other government agencies with ADA responsibilities. The Department of Justice (DOJ) also provides information through a toll-free ADA Information Line that permits businesses, state and local governments, and others to call and ask questions about general or specific ADA requirements, order free ADA materials, or obtain information about filing a complaint. As of April 2005, the numbers are 800-514-0301 (voice) and 800-514-0383 (telecommunication device for the deaf, or TDD). Automated service, which allows callers to listen to recorded information and to order publications for delivery by mail or fax, is available twenty-four hours a day, seven days a week. ADA specialists are available Monday through Friday from 9:30 A.M. until 5:30 P.M. (Eastern time), except on Thursday when the hours are 12:30 P.M. until 5:30 P.M. Spanish-language service is also available. More information can be found at www.usdoj.gov/crt/ada/infoline. htm.

Qualified Individual with a Disability

Individuals with disabilities are entitled to access and accommodations under ADA and/or the Rehabilitation Act only if they are "otherwise qualified" for the program or service that they seek to utilize. Courts have used a three-step analysis for the "otherwise qualified" requirement under the Rehabilitation Act and ADA:

1. The disabled individual must meet all of the essential eligibility requirements in spite of his or her disability.
2. The rule has an exception: If the disabled individual cannot meet all the essential eligibility requirements because of his or her disability, it must be determined if he or she can do so with reasonable accommodations.
3. There is an exception to the exception: An accommodation is not reasonable if it "fundamentally alters" the nature of the program or creates an undue burden.

As shown hereafter, these steps are interrelated and tend to collapse into each other as courts apply the "otherwise qualified" standard.

Eligibility Criteria

Under ADA Titles II and III and Section 504, entities may not impose or apply eligibility criteria that "screen out or *tend* to screen out an individual with a disability or any class of individuals with disabilities . . . *unless* such criteria can be shown to be necessary for the provision of the goods, services, facilities, privileges, advantages, or accommodations being offered" (emphasis added).

EXAMPLE: Willie uses a wheelchair and wants to coach his daughter's youth softball team. The league, however, has a policy prohibiting coaches in wheelchairs from being on the field, regardless of the coach's disability or the field or game conditions involved, because of a concern about players being injured. This policy screens out people with disabilities and will violate ADA *unless* the league can show that the severity of the risk and the likelihood that an injury could occur would make it unreasonable for Willie to be on the field in his wheelchair.

EXAMPLE: Willie goes to the local supermarket to buy groceries and wants to pay by check. The grocery store owner tells Willie that he must present a driver's license to pay by check. Like many people with disabilities, Willie does not have a driver's license because his disability prevents him from driving cars. The identification requirement violates federal antidiscrimination law because it *tends* to screen out individuals with disabilities.

The Supreme Court has ruled that the determination of whether a requirement is essential should be made only *after* the defendant has attempted to make accommodations for the individual's disability. The Court stated that if a rule could be modified without doing violence to its purposes, then it could not be essential to the nature of the program or activity, and refusing to modify the rule would violate ADA.

The Supreme Court adopted this approach in *PGA Tour, Inc. v. Martin*, 532 U.S. 661 (2001), where it refused to defer to the PGA Tour's statement that a rule was essential. Casey Martin was a talented golfer who had a degenerative circulatory disorder that obstructed the blood flow from his right leg back to his heart. The disease caused severe pain, had atrophied his right leg, and created a risk of Martin hemorrhaging, developing blood clots, and fracturing his tibia so badly that an amputation might be required.

Martin asked the PGA to waive its rule requiring players to walk the golf course during tournaments and allow him to use a golf cart. He supported his request with detailed medical records, but the PGA refused to review those records or to waive its walking rule. Its position was that all competitors should be subject to the same rules. The PGA argued that waiving the walking rule would violate this principle and therefore fundamentally alter the nature of its tournaments "*even if [Martin] were the only person in the world who has both the talent to compete in those elite events and a disability sufficiently serious that he cannot do so without using a cart*" (emphasis added).

The Court disagreed. It said that the PGA's "refusal to consider Martin's personal circumstances in deciding whether to accommodate his disability runs counter to the clear language and purpose of the ADA." The Court stated that the statute "requires an *individualized inquiry* must be made to determine whether a specific modification for a particular person's disability would be reasonable under the circumstances as well as necessary for that person, and yet at the same time not work a fundamental alteration [in the defendant's program]" (emphasis added). The requested golf cart exception was found to be reasonable under the circumstances.

Reasonable Accommodations/Modifications

In *Alexander v. Choate*, 469 U.S. 287 (1985), the Supreme Court interpreted Section 504 and held that "while [an entity] need not be required to make 'fundamental' or 'substantial' modification to accommodate the handicapped, it may be required to make 'reasonable' ones." ADA includes a similar balancing test. Title III requires that owners and operators of places of public accommodation make "reasonable modifications" in their practices, policies, or procedures *unless* such modifications would "fundamentally alter" the nature of the goods, services, facilities, or other benefits offered or would result in an "undue burden." The term *undue burden* is defined as encompassing "significant difficulty or expense." When determining whether an action would result in an undue burden, one needs to consider (1) the nature and cost of the required action; (2) the overall financial resources, type of operation, and employment demographics of the covered entity and any applicable parent entity; (3) the impact of the action upon the covered entity; and (4) any legitimate safety concerns. Similar requirements are found in ADA Title II regulations.

As noted above, in *PGA Tour, Inc. v. Martin*, the Supreme Court stated that ADA "requires an *individualized inquiry* must be made to determine whether a specific modification for a particular person's disability would be reasonable under the circumstances as well as necessary for that person, and yet at the same time not work a fundamental alteration [in the defendant's program]" (emphasis added). Similarly, the Court held that under ADA the undue burden test requires an individualized inquiry. It recognized that the administrative burdens resulting from reasonable accommodation requests could be avoided if an entity could simply apply general rules and policies to both able-bodied individuals and people with disabilities, but the Court said that ADA does not "limit the reasonable modification requirement only to requests that are easy to evaluate."

It is impossible to overstate the importance of the Supreme Court's requiring an "individualized inquiry" where people with disabilities challenge a policy that excludes them from services. What this means, in essence, is that public and private entities can no longer deny services to an individual with a disability and simply say: "We have a rule against that." They must now explain the reasons behind the rule *and* why it cannot be modified.

> EXAMPLE: Joshua is blind and travels with a service dog. When he arrives at the entrance to a hardware store, he is told that it has a "no pets" policy. Under federal nondiscrimination law, the store is required to modify that policy as a reasonable modification.

> EXAMPLE: Joshua travels to a hospital to visit a sick friend. The hospital says that pets are not allowed and refuses to make an exception for a service animal. If a physician is willing to testify that its service dog rule was necessary to serve specific safety interests, the hospital is not required to permit Joshua to bring his service dog into the establishment.

Litigation should not be the first choice, though, where an accommodation is denied because "[w]e have a rule against that." For example, a person who uses a service animal reported that she often confronts resistance to bringing the animal into a facility because of a "no animals" rule. She was able to overcome that resistance by asking that she be given the opportunity to demonstrate that her dog would not cause any disturbances. When she signed up for an exercise class at a local indoor pool, she was told there was no room in the small area around the pool for her dog. She asked to look at the pool area so that she could show the staff that there was room, explaining that a well-trained service dog should be able to stay anywhere. Her dog behaved as she said he would, and she was able to take the class.

When she left the pool area to take a shower after the class, she was told that her dog would have to lie down outside the restroom/changing room door. She looked inside and found there was a lot of room under the sink and in the corner near the sink. The staff asked if the dog would stay there while she was changing and showering, and she assured the staff that he would—and he did. After working with the pool staff, she thanked them and then sent a letter to their boss commenting on their willingness to work with her.

Other people with disabilities should consider a similar strategy. After being told that a rule cannot be modified or an accommodation cannot be granted, they should first attempt to educate the management personnel at the business, school, or other entity about how the accommodation can be granted without interfering with the policy behind that rule. Only if that is unsuccessful should an individual with a disability consider filing a complaint.

Safety Issues

Threat to Self. ADA does not mention the risk to anyone in its definition of qualified individual with a disability. Instead, it creates a defense to a charge of employment discrimination under Title I if a person with a disability poses a "direct threat to the health or safety *of other individuals* in the workplace," 42 U.S.C. § 12113(b) (emphasis added). There is no mention in the statute of persons who present a risk *to themselves.* Despite this language, a regulation interpreting ADA Title I's employment provisions defines a direct threat as "a significant risk of substantial harm to the health or safety *of the indi - vidual or others* that cannot be eliminated or reduced by reasonable accommodation." The Supreme Court upheld this regulation in *Chevron U.S.A. Inc. v. Echazabal*, 536 U.S. 73 (2002), and, thus, a person can be barred from employment if he poses a risk to himself.

Courts interpreting Section 504, however, were split on whether an entity could bar individuals from participating in an activity because they posed a risk *to themselves,* and the regulations for Titles II and III are not definitive on this issue. Unlike the Title I regulations, the Title III regulations do not mention persons who present a risk *to themselves.* The Title III regulations state only that a covered entity may bar a person from participating "when that individual poses a direct threat to the health or safety *of others.*" The regulations also provide, though, that "[a] public accommodation may impose legitimate safety requirements that are necessary for safe operation." For example, height requirements may be justifiable for certain amusement park rides, and in a recreational rafting expedition all participants may be required to meet a necessary level of swimming proficiency. No court has directly ruled on the threat-to-self issue under ADA Titles II and III, but in *Larsen v. Carnival Corp., Inc.*, 242 F.Supp.2d 1333 (S.D. Fla. 2003), the court held that a cruise line did not violate ADA where a ship's physician concluded that a passenger had to be disembarked for his own safety: The ventilator that the passenger used every night to treat his sleep apnea was not functioning, and the passenger had almost died on five prior occasions. Under the cruise line's universal eligibility criteria, sailing could not impose a critical risk to an individual's health, and the decision to disembark the passenger was based upon a reasonable concern for his safety, rather than on mere speculation, stereotypes, or generalizations about his disability.

Risk to Others. Entities covered under Titles II and III and Section 504 are not required to permit an individual with a disability to participate in or benefit from their goods, services, facilities, or privileges if the individual would pose a direct threat to the health or safety *of others*. A determination that an individual with a disability poses a direct health or safety threat must be made on a case-by-case basis, through consideration of four basic factors: (1) the duration of the risk, (2) the nature and severity of the potential harm, (3) the likelihood that the potential harm will occur, and (4) the imminence of the potential harm.

The case-by-case nature of direct threat cases is illustrated by cases dealing with HIV. Courts have held that a dentist who refuses to treat a person who is HIV-positive violates Title III because there is little risk that the disease can be transmitted during the course of dental care [*see, e.g., Abbott v. Bragdon*, 163 F.3d 87 (1st Cir. 1998); *D.B. v. Bloom*, 896 F. Supp. 166 (D.N.J. 1995)]. In *Montalvo v. Radcliffe*, 167 F.3d 873 (4th Cir. 1999), however, the court held that a traditional Japanese-style martial arts school did not violate Title III when it barred a student with HIV because he posed a significant risk to the health or safety of other students. It noted that HIV could be transmitted through contact with a carrier's blood and that the type of activity offered at the school often resulted in bloody injuries to students.

Yet, even where there is case law deciding a direct threat issue in their favor, it would be understandable if people with HIV choose to focus on getting the service they desire without the frustration and delay of litigation. For example, a person who is HIV-positive and needs dental treatment could contact the local AIDS hotline and find out which doctors in the community have a good reputation for treating AIDS patients.

ADA Title II: Access to State and Local Government Services

Title II of ADA requires public entities to ensure that, when viewed in their entirety, all of their programs and facilities are accessible to people with disabilities. The term *public entity* includes any state or local government or any department, agency, or other instrumentality of such government). This obligation covers all programs or activities involving general-public contact as part of a public entity's ongoing operations. Thus, for example, Title II requires that all events or activities at a public school be fully accessible to people with disabilities if they are open to parents or the public. This would include graduation ceremonies, plays, parent-teacher meetings, and adult education classes.

ADA Title II provides only for equality of opportunity; it does not guarantee equality of results. Persons with disabilities need only be provided with an "equally effective opportunity to participate in or benefit from a public entity's aids, benefits, and services." Further, a public entity is not required to provide services for people with disabilities that it does not provide for others.

EXAMPLE: Hillary uses a wheelchair and has a modified van that she uses to transport herself. However, she is not able to remove snow from her driveway to get onto the city streets. She contacts the city and asks it to plow her driveway. The city is *not* required to honor her request if it does not provide that service for nondisabled residents.

ADA Title III: Access to Private Entities

Places of Public Accommodation
Title III of ADA prohibits discrimination against individuals with disabilities by a place of public accommodation. The phrase *place of public accommodation* may be confusing at first glance because one might think that it encompasses public buildings such as courthouses and government offices. In fact, the opposite is true. Public accommodations refer only to *private* entities that fall within at least one of the twelve listed categories such as hotels, restaurants, theaters, stores, service establishments, museums, and schools. The term *public accommodation* is used to describe these entities because they are typically *open* to the public. The definition of places of public accommodation is not limited to entities of a certain size or to a certain number of employees. Thus, *all* places of public accommodation must comply with Title III's accessibility requirements. As noted earlier, government facilities are covered under ADA Title II.

There is considerable dispute about whether a place of public accommodation under Title III is limited to actual physical structures or can cover things like insurance policies and websites. Because the statute refers to *places* of public accommodation, some courts have held that it applies only to physical structures. Other courts, however, have noted that Title III bans discrimination in services that could be provided through nonphysical structures like telephone or Internet lines.

Commercial Facilities

Title III also covers commercial facilities such as factories, warehouses, office buildings, and other buildings where people work. As discussed later in this chapter, it requires that new or altered construction be accessible but imposes no requirements on nonaltered, existing structures. If accessibility problems exist at these latter facilities, they can often be handled under Title I if they are places where people work, because places of employment must be modified, as a reasonable accommodation, for an employee with a disability.

Private Clubs

Private clubs are exempt from Title III's requirements. However, if a private club makes its facilities available to the general public (e.g., if the club rents its facilities to a daycare center open to the public), the club then becomes subject to Title III's mandates. In that case, both the private club and the public accommodation (e.g., the daycare center) will be subject to Title III.

Religious Entities

Religious entities are also exempt from Title III. The term *religious entity* includes any religious organization or place of worship, including entities controlled by a religious organization. Thus, for example, even if a school or social service program operated by a religious organization is governed by a lay board, the school or social service remains exempt from Title III. Moreover, the exemption applies even if a religious organization conducts an activity that would otherwise make it a public accommodation (such as operating a daycare center or nursing home that is open to the public). The test with respect to the religious entity exemption is whether the public accommodation activity (the daycare center or nursing home, for example) is *operated* by the religious organization, not who benefits from the services provided. A public accommodation that leases space from a religious entity *is* subject to Title III's requirements, however, if it is not itself a religious organization and is not controlled by a religious organization.

> EXAMPLE: Joyland daycare center leases space from a local church to run its operations in the church's basement during the week. The daycare center is run by its owners with no substantive input from church management. The operation of this daycare center would therefore be subject to ADA Title III, and the center would have to be willing to modify its policies or procedures to accommodate a child with a disability. However, if the entrance to the building itself is not accessible, a parent could not bring suit to make that entrance accessible because the entrance is most likely operated by the church.

Accessibility of Buildings and Facilities

Contrary to a belief held by many business owners, there is no grandfather clause that exempts buildings constructed before the passage of ADA and other federal disability laws. Each of the federal disability laws does, however, make a distinction between the degree of accessibility required for newly constructed buildings and facilities, on the one hand, and structures built before the laws were passed, on the other.

Congress recognized that accessibility can be incorporated into the design of new buildings and facilities and, thus, would add little or no additional cost to the structure. With existing facilities, however, there *is* a cost—sometimes a high one—to create accessibility. Accordingly, the federal disability laws place different accessibility requirements on new construction and renovations (referred to in the statutes as "alterations") to existing facilities:

- In general, *all* new construction must be fully accessible.
- Alterations to existing facilities owned and operated by *private* individuals or companies need only be made accessible "to the maximum extent feasible"; there is a somewhat higher burden on governmental entities that renovate existing facilities.
- If no renovations are made, private entities are required to remove structural architecture and communication

barriers in existing facilities only where such removal is "readily achievable"; existing government facilities, however, must be made accessible to people with disabilities unless that would cause a "fundamental alteration" to the program or activity or constitute an "undue financial and administrative burden" to the entity.

Each of these requirements is discussed more fully in the following sections.

Accessibility of New Construction and Alterations to Existing Facilities

The Architectural Barriers Act: Newly Constructed or Altered Facilities Used or Funded by the Federal Government
The Architectural Barriers Act (ABA) requires that facilities used or funded by the federal government be accessible. The coverage of the ABA, however, is limited. In addition to covering the Washington, D.C., subway system, the ABA covers only three types of structures: (1) those that were constructed or altered by or on behalf of the federal government after 1968; (2) those that were leased by the United States between 1968 and 1976 after being constructed in accordance with federal plans and specifications, or were leased by the United States after January 1, 1977; or (3) those that receive a federal grant or loan for design, construction, or alteration, as in the case of some college buildings and hospitals. Government agencies have adopted Uniform Federal Accessibility Standards (UFAS) to govern the construction and alteration of buildings covered by the ABA. The UFAS are available online at http://www.access-board.gov/ufas/ufas-html/ufas.htm, as is a UFAS checklist: http://www.access-board.gov/ufas/UFASchecklist.txt. In addition, the Architectural and Transportation Barriers Compliance Board (or Access Board) has answers to frequently asked questions about the ABA on its website at http://www.access-board.gov/enforcement/faq.htm.

Enforcement of the Architectural Barriers Act
Individuals with disabilities who experience accessibility problems with buildings covered by the ABA may file a complaint with the Access

Board using an online complaint form that is available at http://
www.access-board.gov/enforcement/form-email.htm. The Board's
website, however, notes that it cannot ensure the confidentiality of information submitted over the Internet. If you wish to maintain confidentiality, an alternate complaint form is available at http://www.
access-board.gov/enforcement/form-mail.htm. You can print it out and
then mail your completed form to Access Board, Office of Compliance
and Enforcement, 1331 F St., N.W., Suite 1000, Washington, D.C.
20004-1111. The fax number is 202-272-0081. Complaints can also be
made by phone: 202-272-0080 or 800-872-2253. The TDD numbers are
202-272-0082 and 800-993-2822. For more information, check http://
www.access-board.gov/enforcement/ABA%20%20enforce.htm.

The person who files such a complaint is not a party to the proceeding as a matter of course, but any person, including the complainant, may petition for permission "to participate in the proceedings when he/she claims an interest in the proceedings and may
contribute materially to their proper disposition." The Access Board
is required to send copies of complaints to all interested agencies and
persons. It also must apprise those persons who might become a
party to the compliance proceeding and give them a reasonable opportunity to respond or submit relevant documents.

The Access Board must attempt to informally resolve all complaints within 180 days after all affected agencies and persons have
received the complaint. Within ten days after the termination of the
180-day period, the Executive Director must either issue a citation or
provide a written statement explaining why a citation is considered
unnecessary. Any citation issued must specify the relief necessary to
ensure compliance with the ABA. Within fifteen days of receiving a
citation, a respondent must file an answer admitting or denying the
allegations and attaching pertinent documents.

Hearings under the ABA are presided over by Administrative Law
Judges (ALJs). An ALJ may schedule a prehearing conference and
may enter a prehearing order. The parties are empowered to exchange
exhibits and are encouraged to engage in voluntary discovery procedures. Hearings are conducted only to resolve issues of fact. When no
issues of material fact are in dispute, the ALJ may vacate a previously
set hearing date. Once a hearing has been conducted, the ALJ is required to issue a decision within thirty days (or within thirty days after the filing of posthearing briefs). The ALJ's decision must contain
findings of fact, conclusions of law, and the reasons for all findings.

Rehabilitation Act: Newly Constructed
or Altered Facilities Operated by Entities
Receiving Federal Funding

Section 504 of the Rehabilitation Act of 1973 provides additional protection for persons with disabilities seeking to achieve a barrier-free society, because Section 504 requires the accessibility of *all* federally assisted activities and programs, regardless of whether such programs or activities are conducted in buildings covered by the ABA. Moreover, because Section 504 allows individuals to sue in federal court, but no such right exists under the ABA, a person with a disability may wish to file a claim under Section 504 rather than to file an administrative complaint with the Access Board. In this event, however, the plaintiff must be aware that the remedy under Section 504 may not encompass architectural changes if other, less obtrusive methods will achieve accessibility.

ADA Title III: Newly Constructed or Altered
Facilities Operated by Private Entities

Regardless of whether they receive federal funding, all newly constructed places of public accommodation *and* commercial facilities must be readily accessible to and usable by individuals with disabilities. Further, when altering their facilities or portions thereof, public accommodations and commercial facilities must make such alterations in a manner that, to the maximum extent feasible, renders the altered portions readily accessible to and usable by individuals with disabilities.

The Department of Justice's Title III regulations set forth detailed criteria to be followed when making newly constructed or altered facilities accessible (*see, generally,* 28 C.F.R. §§ 36.401–406). These include ADA Accessibility Guidelines for Buildings and Facilities (ADAAG), 28 C.F.R. Pt. 36, App. A. The ADAAG can be found in several places on the Internet, including http://www.access-board.gov/adaag/html/adaag.htm and http://www.usdoj.gov/crt/ada/stdspdf.htm. An ADAAG Checklist is available online in both text and PDF formats at http://www.access-board.gov/adaag/checklist/a16.html and http://www.access-board.gov/adaag/checklist/pdf/a16.pdf, respectively. As of April 2005, publications from the Access Board, including copies in alternate formats (Braille, large print, audiocassette, or disk), can also be ordered at pubs@access-board.gov or by calling 202-272-0080 or 800-872-2253. The TDD numbers are 202-272-0082 and 800-993-2822. For more information, check http://www.access-board.gov/indexes/pubsindex.htm. Given the often very technical nature of accessibility questions, we advise people with disabilities to obtain copies of these publications, as they can use them to show a public or private entity how to solve a barrier problem.

A few significant regulatory provisions deserve explanation. First, the requirement that a newly constructed facility be accessible applies to the *entire* facility, *including* work areas; it does not just apply to areas open to the public. However, employee work areas need only be designed and constructed so that individuals with disabilities can approach, enter, and exit them. The guidelines "do not require that any areas used only as work areas be constructed to permit maneuvering within the work area or be constructed or equipped (i.e., with racks or shelves) to be accessible." Nonetheless, if an entity hires an individual with a disability, that entity is subject to ADA Title I and may be required to redesign a workspace to make it more accessible. Thus, we have found that it is sometimes possible to convince companies that are building new structures to exceed the ADAAG requirements for new facilities by pointing out to them that it is cheaper to design an accessible facility than to retrofit it later when individuals with disabilities are hired.

Second, full compliance with the requirement that newly constructed places of public accommodation must be accessible is excused if the entity can demonstrate that it is "structurally impracticable" to meet accessibility requirements due to the "unique characteristics of [the] terrain." In such a case, the facility shall be made accessible to the extent that it is not structurally impracticable to do so. This problem is most likely to arise in very hilly areas where it is impossible to build an entrance that complies with all the slope requirements.

Third, elevators are *not* required to be installed in a newly constructed or altered facility that has fewer than three stories *or* less than 3,000 square feet per story. This exemption does not apply, however, if the facility is a professional office of a health care provider; a shopping center or a shopping mall; a terminal, depot, or other station used for specified public transportation; or an airport passenger terminal.

Fourth, where a public accommodation or commercial facility is undertaking an alteration that affects, or could affect, the usability of or access to an area of a facility that contains a "primary function" (i.e., "a major activity for which the area is intended"), the entity must ensure that, to the maximum extent feasible, "the path of travel to the altered area and the bathrooms, telephones, and drinking fountains serving the altered area" are readily accessible to and usable by individuals with disabilities. An entity does not have to comply with this rule, however, if "the cost and scope of such alteration is *dispro - portionate* to the cost of the overall alteration."

Alterations will be deemed disproportionate when the cost to provide an accessible path to the altered area is greater than 20 percent of the cost of the alteration to the primary function area. When the costs are found to be disproportionate, the path of travel must be made accessible to the extent that can be accomplished without incurring disproportionate costs. In such a case, when choosing which accessible elements to provide, the regulations state that the order of priority should be in providing

1. an accessible entrance;
2. an accessible route to the altered area;
3. at least one accessible restroom for each sex or a single unisex restroom;
4. accessible telephones;
5. accessible drinking fountains; and,
6. when possible, additional accessible elements such as parking, storage, and alarms.

EXAMPLE: A private university renovates the classrooms in a two-story building. Teaching is a primary function of a university, so the classroom renovation triggers the accessibility requirements. The university should make sure that the building's entrance is accessible, that there is at least one accessible restroom for each sex, and that the telephones, drinking fountains, and parking area are accessible. But the university need not install an elevator; the elevator exemption applies because the building has fewer than three stories

ADA Title II: Newly Constructed or Altered Facilities
Operated by State and Local Government Entities
Public entities are required to follow regulations with respect to new construction and alteration of existing buildings that are similar, but

not identical, to those under Title III. The most significant difference between the Title II and Title III requirements is that public entities under Title II are not entitled to the elevator exemption extended to private entities under Title III. Further, the Title II regulations provide that state and local government entities may follow either the Uniform Federal Accessibility Standards or the ADA Accessibility Guidelines for Buildings and Facilities, which were discussed earlier. There are significant differences between the two standards concerning issues such as text telephones for hearing-impaired people, Brailled elevator car control buttons, requirements relating to seating and assistive listening systems in assembly areas, and the number of accessible checkout areas in stores.

> EXAMPLE: A public university renovates the classrooms in a two-story building similar to the one discussed in the previous example. Like the private school, the public university should make sure that the building's entrance is accessible, that there is at least one accessible restroom for each sex, and that the telephones, drinking fountains, and parking areas are accessible. In the case of the public university, however, an elevator must be installed because public entities under Title II are not entitled to the elevator exemption extended to private entities under Title III.

Removal of Barriers from Existing Facilities

ADA Title III: Barrier Removal by Private Entities
Public Accommodations. Public accommodations owned or operated by private entities are required to remove structural architecture and communication barriers in existing facilities where such removal is "readily achievable." The readily achievable standard is much lower than the undue burden or undue hardship standards, and means "easily accomplishable and able to be carried out without much difficulty or expense." Factors to be considered when determining whether barrier removal is readily achievable include (1) the nature and cost of the action needed; (2) the financial resources of, and the number of persons employed at, the facility; (3) the effect of the action on the entity's expenses or resources; (4) the impact of the action upon the operation of the facility; and (5) the size, nature, type, and financial resources of the covered entity. An ADA Checklist for Readily Achievable Barrier Removal can be found at http://

www.usdoj.gov/crt/ada/racheck.pdf and http://www.usdoj.gov/crt/ada/checktxt.htm.

ADA recognizes that retrofitting existing facilities can be very costly and applies a less rigorous degree of accessibility to them than it does to new facilities where accessibility fixtures can be economically incorporated. Accordingly, to the extent that compliance with ADA's technical requirements is *not* readily achievable, a private entity may use other readily achievable measures that do not fully comply to achieve accessibility if those measures do not pose a significant health or safety risk.

The obligation of public accommodations to remove barriers in existing facilities includes the obligation to remove structural communication barriers such as permanent signage and alarm systems, to render sound buffers adequate, and to avoid the presence of physical partitions that hamper the passage of sound waves between employees and customers. This category also includes barriers caused by temporary or movable structures, such as furniture, equipment, or display racks. To make premises accessible to persons who use wheelchairs, for example, restaurants may need to rearrange tables and chairs and stores may need to reconfigure display racks and shelves. The latter actions are not readily achievable, however, to the extent that they would result "in a significant loss of selling or serving space." In such situations, a public accommodation must make its goods or services available to people with disabilities through alternative measures that are readily achievable.

Because entities subject to Title III may lack the resources to remove all existing barriers at a given time, the regulations recommend that public accommodations follow specified priorities for removing barriers in existing facilities: (1) Provide access to places of public accommodation (such as by installing entrance ramps, widening entrances, and providing accessible parking); (2) provide access to areas where goods and services are made available to the public (such as by adjusting the layout of display racks, rearranging tables, widening doors, providing Brailled and raised signage and visual alarms, and installing ramps); (3) provide access to restroom facilities (such as by removing obstructing furniture or vending machines, widening doors, installing ramps, providing accessible signage, widening toilet stalls, and installing grab bars); and (4) take any other steps necessary to provide access to the goods, services, facilities, or other benefits provided.

The obligation to engage in readily achievable barrier removal is continuing. Barrier removal that was initially not readily achievable may, as a result of changed circumstances, become readily achievable.

Title III creates an exception for historic properties. To the extent that barrier removal would alter the historic nature of a property, such barrier removal is not required.

> EXAMPLE: Java Coffee Shop is located in a shopping plaza. It is connected to the plaza by a hallway. The shop puts chairs and tables in the hallway along with an easel sign advertising its business. In addition, there are chairs and tables within the coffee shop. Most of the business is carryout, but some customers do occasionally sit at one of the tables and drink their coffee. The hallway sign and the tables and chairs in the hallway impede access for individuals who use wheelchairs and pose a safety hazard for visually impaired patrons. The chairs and tables within the coffee shop are so close together that they provide no path of travel for wheelchair users who seek to place an order. Changing the seating arrangement removing the tables and chairs, as well as sign, from the hallway are readily achievable. Nonetheless, the coffee shop would be entitled to maintain enough seating within its facilities to serve its customers.

Commercial Facilities. ADA Title III does not impose any barrier-removal requirements on nonaltered, existing structures that fit into the category of commercial facilities such as factories, warehouses, office buildings, and other buildings where people work. If accessibility problems exist at these facilities, they can often be handled under Title I if they are places where people work because places of employment must be modified, as a reasonable accommodation, for an employee with a disability.

ADA Title II: Barrier Removal by State and Local Governments

The standards for accessibility for state and local government entities covered under ADA Title II are higher than the standards for places of public accommodations under Title III. Under Title III, existing facilities must be made accessible only to the extent that accessibility is "readily achievable." Under Title II, however, the programs or activities of public entities must be made accessible to people with disabilities unless doing so would cause a "fundamental alteration" to the program or activity or constitute an "undue financial and administrative burden" to the entity. The latter exception is much narrower. Individuals with disabilities should have access to government services and facilities in all but extraordinary circumstances. Thus, if one action would result in a fundamental alteration or undue burden, the public entity must take other actions that would not have such a result.

Title II requires that the services, programs, and activities of a public entity must be readily accessible to and usable by individuals with disabilities *when viewed in their entirety;* it does not necessarily require public entities to make *each* of their existing facilities accessible. Structural changes are not required if other methods would provide effective accessibility, and public entities are not required to ensure program accessibility for a historic property if the result would be to threaten or destroy its historic significance. Where an accommodation is not required because it would threaten or destroy the historic significance of such a property, alternative methods of achieving accessibility must be provided (such as via use of audiovisual materials and devices, guides, or other methods).

EXAMPLE: The county has a public services office where people can pay local taxes and other fees as well as have meetings with county officials. The building is a historic structure and does not have an elevator. It would be impossible to install an elevator without destroying the historical character of the facility. Nonetheless, the county has been able to make the first-floor entrance to the facility accessible. The county should also make sure that first-floor meeting places are accessible and offer to provide services at that location, upon request, to individuals with disabilities who cannot travel to the other floors of the facility.

New ADA and ABA Guidelines

On July 23, 2004, the Access Board issued updated accessibility guidelines for new or altered facilities covered by ADA and ABA. These guidelines address a wide range of facilities in the private and public sectors but are not mandatory. Instead, they serve as the baseline for enforceable standards maintained by other federal agencies and are not required to be followed except as adopted by an enforcing authority. Later in 2005, these agencies will update their ADA and ABA standards based on the new guidelines, and they will indicate when the new standards are to be followed. Until then, the current standards remain in effect. The new guidelines are available at http://www.access-board.gov/ada-aba/Blue%20HTML/ADA-ABA%20Guidelines%20 Blue.htm and http://www.access-board.gov/ada-aba/final.pdf.

Landlords and Tenants

The nondiscrimination mandate of Title III applies to "any person who owns, *leases (or leases to)*, or operates a place of public accommodation." The DOJ regulations explain that responsibility for accessibility will be allocated among landlords and tenants and that the allocation may be determined by lease or contract. The regulations reflect the principles that (1) both landlords and tenants are covered by the public accommodation requirements of Title III and (2) Title III is not intended to change existing responsibilities between landlords and tenants as set forth in leasing agreements.

The parties to a lease are free to allocate responsibilities in any way they choose. Any allocation made in a lease or other contract, however, is effective only *as between the landlord and tenant*. Both the landlord and tenant remain fully liable in a lawsuit brought by an individual who alleges the facility is not in compliance with ADA provisions relating to that place of public accommodation.

> EXAMPLE: A landlord and a tenant are both sued by an individual who alleges that a facility is not accessible. The landlord argues that it cannot be held liable because the lease agreement shifted all responsibility for ADA compliance to the tenant. Despite this agreement, both the landlord and the tenant remain fully liable to the individual who encountered the accessibility problem. The lease could, however, require the tenant to compensate the landlord for all losses caused by the tenant's failure to comply with its obligations under the lease. Any dispute over this provision would be solely between the landlord and the tenant; it would not affect their liability for having an inaccessible building.

An entity that is not itself a public accommodation (e.g., a trade association or a performing artist) that leases space for a conference, performance, or the like at a place of public accommodation may thereby become a public accommodation subject to ADA. This rule, however, applies *only* when the entity at issue gives some form of payment in cash or services to lease the space. Similarly, a private club that would not otherwise be covered by ADA becomes subject to Title III if it rents its facilities to a trade association for a conference, inasmuch as the private club becomes a public accommodation when it leases space for the purpose of holding a conference.

EXAMPLE: The American Bar Association rents some facilities at a local hotel to hold a continuing legal education conference. Although the ABA is not normally covered by ADA, because it is a membership organization it becomes subject to ADA when it rents this facility for the purpose of holding a conference.

Auxiliary Aids and Services

ADA Title III: Provision of Auxiliary Aids and Services by Private Entities

Owners and operators of places of public accommodation must provide necessary auxiliary aids and services for individuals with disabilities unless doing so would constitute an undue burden or result in a fundamental alteration. The term *auxiliary aids and services* includes, for example, providing qualified interpreters or readers for hearing- or vision-impaired persons, acquiring or modifying equipment or devices, or other similar services and actions. However, a public accommodation is not required to provide services of a personal nature such as assistance with toileting, eating, or dressing.

The auxiliary aid requirement is flexible, and public accommodations are "strongly encouraged" to consult with the disabled individual before providing a particular aid or service. A public accommodation can choose among various alternatives so long as the result is *effective*, and it is *not* required to give primary consideration to the request of an individual with a disability with respect to which aid or service to provide. For example, a restaurant need not provide Braille menus for patrons who are blind if it provides a waiter or other employee to read the menu.

The DOJ regulations require that, if a public accommodation customarily offers its customers, clients, or participants the opportunity to make outgoing telephone calls on more than an incidental basis, it must make a TDD available to an individual with impaired hearing or speech. Hotels and motels must possess a TDD or similar device at the front desk to permit receipt of calls from guests who use TDDs in their rooms. And public accommodations that provide verbal information or videos, films, or the like must make such information available to people with hearing impairments, such as via captioning or written scripts.

With the exception of a few specifically mandated accommodations, however, whether a particular auxiliary aid or service must be provided will depend upon whether the fundamental alteration or undue burden tests are satisfied. If provision of one auxiliary aid or service would result in a fundamental alteration or undue burden, the public accommodation must provide an alternative aid or service that would *not* result in a fundamental alteration or undue burden to the extent that such an accommodation is possible.

> EXAMPLE: The local department store has a ladies' clothing department. It also has changing rooms for patrons to try on clothing. At least one of those changing rooms should be accessible, and the aisles of the department store should be configured so that people who use wheelchairs can look at clothing. Further, store personnel should offer to assist individuals who cannot reach certain clothes from racks. But store personnel would not be expected to go into a fitting room and help someone change because that would be a service of a personal nature.

ADA Title II: Provision of Auxiliary Aids and Services by State and Local Governments

State and local government entities have an affirmative obligation to ensure effective communication with disabled individuals. When an auxiliary aid or service is required under Title II, a public entity must allow the individual with a disability to request the accommodation of his or her choice and must give *primary consideration* to that choice. Primary consideration means that the public entity must honor that choice, unless it can demonstrate that another equally effective means of accommodation is available or that use of the individual's choice would result in a fundamental alteration or undue burden.

> EXAMPLE: Due to a shortage of sign language interpreters, a university developed alternatives to interpretation for students with hearing impairments, including real-time stenocaptioning, taped lectures and transcription by a stenocaptioner at a later date, taped lectures and interpretation at a later date, use of an oral interpreter, or two note-takers

in addition to the use of a Communication Assistant (i.e., a trained note-taker not enrolled in the class). The school would be in compliance with ADA because it (1) has legitimate nondiscriminatory reasons for its failure to hire adequate sign language interpreters to cover all the classroom needs of hearing-impaired students and (2) offered an array of second-best alternatives when signers were unavailable.

When a public entity "communicates by telephone with applicants and beneficiaries," the entity must provide a TDD or "equally effective telecommunication system" to communicate with individuals who are hearing- or speech-impaired. All telephone emergency services, including 911 services, must provide direct access to individuals who use TDDs or computer modems. Public entities must provide adequate information and signage to ensure that all interested persons, including persons with impaired hearing or vision, can obtain information as to the existence and location of accessible services, activities, and facilities.

A public entity may not impose a surcharge on persons with disabilities in order to cover the costs of accommodations or auxiliary aids. And, as under Title III, public entities are not required to provide personal devices or services of a personal nature.

Enforcement and Remedies Against State and Local Governments

Persons who believe a state or local government has failed to comply with ADA Title II and/or the Rehabilitation Act have three formal options for remedying that violation:

1. file a complaint with the Office of Civil Rights within the federal agency that provided the funding to the program at issue or that has been designated to investigate disability-related discrimination complaints against state and local government programs under Title II;
2. file a complaint with the Department of Justice for referral to the proper agency; or
3. file a private lawsuit against the state or local government.

Each of these options is discussed in the following sections.

Administrative Enforcement Through a
Federal Agency's Office of Civil Rights
As noted in the previous section, the first option for enforcing ADA
Title II and the Rehabilitation Act is to file a complaint with the Office of Civil Rights (OCR) of the federal agency that provided the
program's funding or that has been designated to investigate disability-related discrimination complaints against state and local government programs. A list of designated agencies with their addresses can
be found at http://www.usdoj.gov/crt/ada/investag.htm. The procedures the agencies must follow when they receive the complaint are
discussed in the second paragraph hereafter.

Filing a Complaint with the Department of
Justice for Referral to the Proper Agency
The second option under ADA Title II and the Rehabilitation Act is
to file a complaint with the Department of Justice for referral to the
proper agency. A Title II complaint form is available in English at
http://www.usdoj.gov/crt/ada/t2cmpfrm.htm and in Spanish at
http://www.usdoj.gov/crt/ada/t2compfm_esp.htm. Alternatively,
one can write to the U.S. Department of Justice, Civil Rights Division, Disability Rights Section, 950 Pennsylvania Avenue, N.W.,
Washington, DC 20530. One may also wish to call the ADA Information Line to ask about filing a complaint with the Department of
Justice and to order forms that can assist one in providing information about the violation. As of April 2005, the numbers are 800-514-
0301 (voice) and 800-514-0383 (TDD).

When a federal agency receives a complaint—either directly or
through the Department of Justice—and determines that it has jurisdiction over the matter, it must either resolve the complaint or issue a
"letter of findings" that describes the findings of fact, conclusions of
law, and remedies for each violation found. The administrative procedures do not allow individual complainants to participate in the administrative hearings. The only parties to such proceedings are the
state or local government and the federal agency responsible for enforcing Section 504 and Title II. To resolve the complaint, the agency
should attempt to negotiate a voluntary agreement with the state or local government. If that effort fails, the agency must refer the complaint

to the DOJ for further action, which may include institution of a civil suit. The DOJ's Disability Rights Section, however, has only a small number of lawyers to bring actions to enforce ADA and Section 504. In fact, a recent report from the U.S. Commission on Civil Rights found that in fiscal 2002 the Disability Rights Section initiated 701 investigations and filed 28 cases—figures that, respectively, are 181 and 9 fewer than in fiscal 2001.

Private Lawsuits by Individuals with Disabilities

Given the immensity of the task of ensuring accessibility, DOJ's role will at best be a small one in directly enforcing the ADA itself. Accordingly, such individuals should consider filing suit in federal court against a public entity to enforce ADA Title II and Section 504's provisions on services and program accessibility. In most cases, it is not necessary to undergo a federal agency's administrative procedures before filing such an action. However, when an individual with a disability brings a Section 504 or ADA Title II claim in conjunction with a claim under another federal law that *does* require administrative remedies to be used before suit is filed, the individual must exhaust the administrative steps prescribed by the second law. For example, if an individual with a disability files an action claiming educational discrimination under both Section 504 and the Individuals with Disabilities Education Act (discussed in Chapter 3 of this book), the administrative procedures prescribed under IDEA must be followed before filing a lawsuit.

Sovereign Immunity Issues

Sovereign Immunity and Suits Seeking Monetary Damages Under ADA Title II. One issue likely to be faced in a lawsuit against a *state* government is whether it has "sovereign immunity." The principle of sovereign immunity generally means that a private individual cannot sue a sovereign (government) without its consent: The sovereign is immune from suit. In practice, sovereign immunity is far more complicated. State governments, for example, have been historically considered to have more immunity than local governments.

There have already been two U.S. Supreme Court decisions on whether states are immune from suit under ADA. In *Board of Trustees of University of Alabama v. Garrett*, 531 U.S. 356 (2001), the

Court held that state government employers have immunity from suits for *money damages* under the *employment provisions* of Title I of ADA. The Court left open the question of whether monetary damages are permitted for access and accommodation violations under ADA Title II. It answered that question to some extent in *Tennessee v. Lane*, 541 U.S. 509 (2004), when it held that in enacting Title II Congress had validly revoked states' sovereign immunity "as it applies to the class of cases implicating the fundamental right of access to the courts." This is a very narrow ruling, however. The Court still left open the question of whether individuals with disabilities can bring private suits for *money damages* against states for failing to provide reasonable access in a situation that does not impact a fundamental constitutional right. When the Supreme Court will address this broader question is unknown, and lower courts will continue to struggle with the issue until it does.

Sovereign Immunity and Suits Seeking Monetary Damages Under Section 504 of the Rehabilitation Act. Lower courts may also continue to struggle with the issue of whether states have waived their sovereign immunity by accepting federal funds. In *Atascadero State Hospital v. Scanlon*, 473 U.S. 234 (1985), the Supreme Court held that, in enacting Section 504, Congress did not intend to overturn the states' immunity from suit. In response to the resulting public outcry over the decision, Congress amended the Rehabilitation Act to say that a state shall not be immune from suit in federal court for a violation of Section 504. The law is currently unsettled, however, on whether this provision actually means that states no longer have sovereign immunity from Section 504 claims; but the vast majority of courts have held that states have waived such immunity as a condition of receiving federal funds, especially for any new monies they are accepting.

Sovereign Immunity and Suits Seeking Accessibility or to Change Future Conduct. No matter how the Court ultimately decides the sovereign immunity issues under ADA Title II and Section 504, it will affect only suits for *money damages*. In *Garrett*, the Court suggested in a footnote that individuals with disabilities can still bring suits against state officials in their official capacities for *injunctive and declaratory relief* under ADA Title II. Injunctive and declaratory relief is *prospective* relief in which one asks the state official to refrain from certain future conduct or for the court to make a declaration about the unlawfulness of certain conduct. For example, one might request that a building entrance be made accessible in the future or that the state official refuse to engage in certain conduct in the future. The principle of sovereign immunity does *not* apply to requests for injunctive and declaratory relief. Accordingly, it is now clear that injunctive relief is available against state defendants.

> EXAMPLE: Sheila, who uses a wheelchair, receives a letter from the state informing her that she has been called for jury service. When she arrives at the courthouse for jury service, she learns that the jury boxes are not handicapped accessible and, thus, that she is not eligible for jury service. However, she wants to fulfill her civic duty of making herself available for jury service. Although she has suffered no monetary harm, she can sue the state for a failure to make jury boxes accessible and seek, as a form of relief, an injunction to require them to make jury boxes accessible in the future.

Sovereign Immunity and Local Governments. The Supreme Court's ultimate resolution of the question of sovereign immunity for *state governments* under ADA and Section 504 also will not affect the ability of individuals with disabilities to sue *municipal or local governments*. The principle of sovereign immunity applies to states, not to local government. Hence, dozens of lawsuits have been filed against local government for a failure to install curb ramps. Those lawsuits are not jeopardized by the sovereign immunity decisions.

Availability of Monetary Damages Against State, Local, and Federal Governments

Even where courts have recognized the availability of money damage claims in accessibility suits against state and local governments, however, they have limited them to cases involving *intentional* discrimination. This is a very high standard and is seldom met. Moreover, in *Barnes v. Gorman*, 536 U.S. 181 (2002), the Supreme Court held that *punitive* damages are *not* available under Section 504 and Title II of ADA. The Supreme Court has also held that monetary damages are not available against the *federal* government for violations of the Rehabilitation Act's prohibition of discrimination on the basis of disability "under any program or activity conducted by any Executive agency" [*Lane v. Pena*, 518 U.S. 187 (1996)].

Attorney Fees

ADA does provide that courts and agencies may award attorney fees and litigation expenses (including the cost of expert witnesses) to prevailing parties. This is critical because, as shown in previous sections, obtaining money damages against a state or local government is difficult. Accordingly, the only real monetary incentive for lawyers to comply with ADA and Section 504 is the fact that they will be required to pay the other side's attorney fees if they lose a case. Many lawyers, however, are not inclined to get involved in disability discrimination issues (and there are few nonprofit organizations that handle these kinds of cases). Nonetheless, because accessibility violations are often flagrant, some attorneys do make a living by seeking to enforce the standards involved. People in your local disability community should know the identity of these lawyers.

Self-Advocacy by People with Disabilities

Given the limited remedies and legal help available, many people with disabilities have found that the best way to get a state or local government to comply with ADA is to engage in informed self-advocacy. To do that, people with disabilities need to educate first themselves and then others regarding ADA's requirements. As noted above, given the often very technical nature of accessibility questions, we advise people with disabilities to obtain copies of publications from DOJ and the Access Board. They can then use these publications to show a public or private entity specifically how to address a barrier they have confronted.

For example, Professor Milani knows a group that educated itself and then used the media and political pressure to get an accessibility problem fixed. The group was concerned that the curb ramps installed when a city repaved its streets were not flush with the pavement; wheelchair users could not roll their front wheels over the high lip at the edge of the curb ramps. The group researched ADA rules on curb ramps and found that they state that "[t]ransitions from ramps to . . . streets shall be flush and free of abrupt changes." Members then contacted both the mayor's office and the media about the issue. A TV report showing the difficulty wheelchair users had with the ramps—including video of one of them tipping over backward while trying to jump the lip of a ramp—helped prompt the city government to tear out the curb ramps and install new ones that complied with ADA guidelines.

An advocate in Florida also uses the media to get the police to enforce the parking laws for accessible parking spaces. He notifies the press in advance before he addresses a city council, city commission, or county commission on this matter. The press can then make the issue a news story. Indeed, the advocate reports that, as a result of his efforts, more than a couple police chiefs have been called into the mayor's or city manager's office and told that all officers are to ticket any and all vehicles parked illegally in accessible parking spaces. Two cities even did sweeps of public parking lots looking for people using parking permits that were not their own (i.e., people who were not disabled using a permit issued to a different person).

Use of the media is, of course, not always an option. Another, more straightforward form of self-advocacy is to write a complaint letter (which may also be helpful in a future lawsuit as evidence that you notified the state or local government of the problem and tried to resolve it without filing suit). A sample complaint letter follows:

Chief Administrator
State or Local Agency
123 New St.
Anytown, GA

Dear Sir/Madam:
    I am a quadriplegic and use a wheelchair for mobility. I also have a service dog, Satin, who helps to pull my wheelchair, open doors, and retrieve dropped items. On [date] I tried to enter the Anytown Auditorium with Satin to attend a concert. Satin was wearing a vest that identified him as a service dog, but a security officer stopped me and said that pets were not allowed in the auditorium. I told the officer that Satin was a service dog, and he asked what the dog was trained to do. I explained and presented K-9 credentials to both the initial officer and his supervisor who had been called regarding my dog. Despite my explanation, the officers denied me entry onto the premises.
    Before I left, I requested the names and badge numbers of the security officers. They are [Name] (Badge # 1234) and [Name] (Badge # 2345).
    The officers' action violated Title II of the Americans with Disabilities Act and Section 504 of the Rehabilitation Act of 1973, and I fear that I will be unable to attend future events at the Anytown Auditorium unless the no-pets policy is changed to allow people with dis-

abilities to be accompanied by their service animals. Please contact me at the address or phone number below so we can discuss this problem.
Sincerely,
[*Name, address, and phone number*]

Enforcement and Remedies Against Private Entities

ADA Title III may be enforced both privately by an individual plaintiff and publicly by the U.S. Attorney General.

Suits by Individuals with Disabilities
Individuals with disabilities may file suit under ADA when they have been subjected to discrimination on the basis of disability in violation of Title III or have "reasonable grounds" for believing that they are "about to be subjected to discrimination" in violation of the provisions relating to the construction or alteration of places of public accommodation. Remedies are limited to injunctive relief. For violations of the provisions requiring newly constructed or altered facilities to be accessible, injunctive relief includes an order that facilities be made readily accessible. Moreover, ADA provides that "[w]here appropriate, injunctive relief shall also include requiring the provision of an auxiliary aid or service, modification of a policy, or provision of alternative methods, to the extent required by [Title III]."

Damages are *not* available in private actions brought under ADA Title III. As with ADA Title II, though, courts and agencies may award attorney fees and litigation expenses. Accordingly, the only real monetary incentive for public accommodations to comply with ADA is having to pay the other side's attorney fees if they lose a case.

Suits by the Attorney General
The Attorney General has authority to file suit when there is reasonable cause to believe that a person or group of persons is engaged in a "pattern or practice" of discriminating against individuals with disabilities or when the alleged discrimination "raises an issue of general public importance." Information on how to file a Title III complaint with the Department of Justice is available at http://www.usdoj.gov/crt/ada/t3compfm.htm. The complaint should include

- full name, address, and telephone number, and the name of the party discriminated against;
- the name of the business, organization, or institution that one believe has discriminated;
- a description of the act or acts of discrimination, the date or dates of the discriminatory acts, and the name or names of the individuals whom one believes discriminated;
- other information that one believes is necessary to support your complaint; and
- copies of relevant documents. (Do not send original documents; rather, keep these in a file that one can locate easily.)

Sign and send the letter to the U.S. Department of Justice, Civil Rights Division, Disability Rights Section, 950 Pennsylvania Avenue, N.W., Washington, D.C. 20530. One may also call the ADA Information Line to ask about filing a complaint with the Department of Justice and to order forms that can assist you in providing information about the violation. As of April 2005, the numbers are 800-514-0301 (voice) and 800-514-0383 (TDD).

Officials at the Disability Rights Section will investigate the complaint and begin litigation if they believe there is a pattern or practice of discrimination or if the complaint raises an issue of general public importance. They will then attempt to negotiate a settlement of the matter or bring an action in U.S. District Court on behalf of the Unites States. The Disability Rights Section does not act as an attorney for, or representative of, the individual who filed the complaint.

Monetary damages, while not recoverable in private suits, *are* recoverable in suits filed by the Attorney General. Further, the court has discretion in actions filed by the Attorney General to vindicate the public interest by assessing penalties of up to $50,000 for a first violation and $100,000 for subsequent violations. In determining the amount of any such penalty, however, the court must consider "any good faith effort or attempt to comply with this Act by the entity." Punitive damages are not available under Title III.

Self-Advocacy by People with Disabilities

Before filing a lawsuit or a complaint with the Department of Justice, individuals with disabilities should consider first writing a complaint letter to the public accommodation that they believe has violated

ADA Title III. This may be a quicker way to resolve the problem. Even if it isn't, such a letter may be helpful in a future lawsuit as evidence that one notified the defendant of the problem and tried to resolve it without filing suit. A second sample complaint letter follows:

Chief Administrator
Public Accommodation
123 New St.
Anytown, GA

Dear Sir/Madam:
    I am a paraplegic and use a wheelchair for mobility. On [date] I visited the Taco Barn restaurant located at 234 Main St. During my visit I encountered accessibility problems with the (1) parking lot, (2) entrance, (3) condiment and drink dispenser, (4) dining room, and (5) restroom.
    These accessibility problems violate Title III of the Americans with Disabilities Act and prevent me from having full and equal enjoyment of the goods, services, facilities, privileges, advantages, and accommodations of the Taco Barn. Please contact me at the address or phone number below so we can discuss these problems.
    Sincerely,
    [*Name, address, and phone number*]

The media also can be used to advocate for changes by private businesses. For example, Professor Colker assisted Willie, an individual with brain damage who was having problems attending music and sporting events. Because of his injuries, Willie is nonverbal and needs an attendant 24/7. The attendant has to face him while assisting him to move his breathing tube or some other apparatus when necessary. Willie cannot attend music and sporting events alone, and, if an event extends over a shift change, he also may need a complicated change in shift workers. Over the years, he has been able to purchase an accessible seat but has been required to pay for two seats so that his attendant could also attend the event. This gets pretty expensive!
    Willie came to Professor Colker to discuss the problem, and she got him in touch with a pro bono attorney. The attorney approached various vendors in the city to see if they might work out an amicable arrangement. A local TV station also agreed to cover the story. Professor Colker then contacted some of the vendors and said she would

be happy to give them positive publicity during her interview for the segment if they worked out an accommodation for Willie. In the end, Willie avoided litigation, received some favorable publicity, and got a few entertainment establishments to change their policy. It was not a perfect victory, but it certainly improved Willie's situation somewhat at no expense to Willie or his family.

Electronic and Information Technology Used by Federal Agencies

In 1998, Congress amended Section 508 of the Rehabilitation Act, 29 U.S.C. § 794d, to require federal agencies to ensure, unless it would pose an undue burden to do so, that electronic and information technology (EIT) be accessible to federal employees with disabilities and people with disabilities who are members of the public seeking information or services from the agencies. Section 508 expressly applies only to federal government agencies; the Attorney General has stated that it does not require private companies that market technologies to the federal government to modify EIT products used by company employees or to make their Internet sites accessible to people with disabilities (see *Information Technology and People with Disabilities: The Current State of Federal Accessibility—Executive Summary and Recommendations*, http://www.usdoj.gov/crt/508/report/exec.htm). In 1999, however, a letter issued by the Department of Education indicated that it interpreted the statute to apply to state entities such as colleges and universities. (To date, no court has adopted this administrative interpretation.)

The Architectural and Transportation Barriers Compliance Board (or Access Board) has issued standards for EIT. Federal agencies procuring an EIT product must ensure that it complies with the regulations "when such products are available in the commercial marketplace or when such products are developed in response to a Government solicitation." If no product in the marketplace meets all the standards, the agency must procure the product that best meets the standards. If compliance with the standards imposes an undue burden, the agency must provide the information and data involved by an alternative means, and the agency's documentation supporting the procurement must explain why, and to what extent, compliance with each standard creates an undue burden. The Section 508 standards do not require a fundamental alteration in the nature of a product or its components, the installation of specific accessibility-related software, or the attachment of an assistive technology device at a federal employee's workstation if he or she is not an individual with a disability. The standards do not require that an agency's EIT be available for access and use by individuals with disabilities at a location other than that at which it is provided to the public. And, finally, the standards do not apply to systems critical to the direct fulfillment of military or intelligence missions.

The Section 508 regulations include specific standards for several different types of EIT that are too detailed to discuss in this book. Accordingly, readers are encouraged to visit the government website dedicated to the law's implementation: http://www.section508.gov.

Conclusion

Making our society universally accessible is a monumental challenge. When Congress enacted ADA, it thought that new construction and major alterations would ultimately get rid of most accessibility issues. Unfortunately, it underestimated the difficulty involved in making preexisting structures accessible, and individuals with disabilities still often struggle to use many facilities that are open to the public.

The Department of Justice, however, has been very active in promulgating regulations and guidelines for facilities to follow in making themselves more accessible. These guidelines have good pictures and diagrams and can be readily understood by most people. Professor Colker trains her law students to read those guidelines and conduct an accessibility audit. Armed with a tape measure and an instrument to measure slope, they are able to prepare very helpful reports that can be used as a basis to effectuate change. Indeed, over the years her students have succeeded in getting entities to make many changes to improve their accessibility. Their success derives, in part, from the fact that they try to think of low-cost solutions to accessibility problems that entities are often happy to employ—moving obstructions in hallways, changing door handles, adjusting door hinges, adding Braille signage, and creating modified rules and policies. The rest of us, too, can take little steps in our daily lives—such as suggesting that easel signs in hallways that impede access are moved—to help make our society somewhat more accessible.

Nonetheless, more dramatic efforts are sometimes necessary through litigation. Accessibility litigation can be relatively inexpensive, because the lawyers often need to engage in little discovery other than to document accessibility problems. And the lawyers can often retool in order to become sufficiently expert in handling this kind of straightforward litigation. We urge our readers to suggest to lawyers in the community that they acquire the knowledge necessary to handle this kind of litigation because, unfortunately, flagrant accessibility violations are still occurring all around us.

6

Transportation

At the time ADA was passed, individuals with disabilities faced enormous transportation problems. Despite their disproportionately heavy reliance on public transportation, it was rarely accessible. ADA and the Rehabilitation Act now require that such transportation be accessible and usable by individuals with disabilities. Specifically, the Rehabilitation Act covers all transportation providers (whether government or private) that receive federal funds. ADA Title II covers public transportation (other than by air travel) provided by *public en -tities.* The term *public entity* includes any state or local government (or any department, agency, or other instrumentality of such government), the National Railroad Passenger Corporation (Amtrak), and any commuter rail authority. Finally, ADA Title III applies to ground transportation provided by *private entities*, and there are many similarities (as well as some significant differences) between the rules governing them and those for public entities.

The Department of Transportation (DOT) has a website that includes links to the full ADA and Rehabilitation Act regulations governing transportation provided by public and private entities at http://www.fta.dot.gov/transit_data_info/ad. Information resources that relate to specific kinds of transportation are mentioned in the sections that follow.

Ground Transportation Provided by Public Entities

ADA Title II requires that entities providing public transportation not discriminate against people with disabilities. Accordingly, all new buses or rail vehicles used on fixed-route systems (systems with set routes and fixed schedules) must be accessible to individuals with disabilities, including individuals who use wheelchairs. This means that new buses and rail systems must be fitted with lifts or ramps and foldup seats or other wheelchair spaces with appropriate securement devices. A public entity may apply for an exemption from this rule, but any exemption granted will be temporary, limited to a specified date. The requirements of this part do *not* apply to public school transportation.

Regarding used vehicles, public entities must demonstrate good-faith efforts to purchase or lease a used vehicle that is accessible. Similarly, a public entity that remanufactures a vehicle to extend its life for five years, or purchases or leases a remanufactured vehicle, must ensure that, "to the maximum extent feasible," the vehicle is accessible. An exception is made for "historic vehicles" if altering such vehicles would significantly alter their historic character.

The regulations also include specific rules on issues such as announcing stops, service animals, and securement devices. These topics are discussed separately in the sections that follow. For a good overview of the rules that apply to city bus systems, see http://www.adainfonet.org/ada-infonet/documents/transportation/city-bus-systems.asp.

Paratransit Services

One of the largest sources of frustration for many people with disabilities is paratransit. ADA Title II requires that, if a public transportation provider's fixed-route system is not accessible to certain people with disabilities, the public entity must provide paratransit or other special transportation services that pick people up at a requested location and drop them off at another. The paratransit service can be by van, taxi, car, or other vehicle and must provide a level of services to people with disabilities and their companions comparable to that provided to nondisabled persons. This requirement does not cover a commuter bus service (fixed-route bus service predominantly in one direction during peak periods, usually between the central business district and outlying suburbs). Further, paratransit services need to be provided only in the service area where a public entity operates a fixed-route service and not where the entity provides only commuter bus service. Public airport shuttle or connector systems and public university transport systems are also not required to provide paratransit services.

Among the most frequent complaints of paratransit users is the difficulty of scheduling rides. Many report that when they call to reserve a time they are told that they cannot do so because (1) they did not give the paratransit provider enough notice, (2) all available rides are already booked, or (3) paratransit is available only for trips to the doctor and the like. Regulations issued by the Department of Transportation, however, prohibit providers from denying rides for such reasons, and paratransit riders would be wise to be familiar with these regulations. Among other things, the regulations state that

- riders with disabilities may be required to reserve rides at least *one day* in advance;
- restrictions or priorities based on trip purpose are prohibited;
- paratransit services must be available during the same days and hours of operation as fixed-route services;
- capacity constraints (such as restrictions on the number of trips available to an individual, waiting lists, untimely pickups or a substantial number of trips with excessive trip lengths) are prohibited;
- the fare may not exceed twice the fare that would be charged in the entity's fixed-route system; and
- the requirement that paratransit services be provided to people with disabilities and their companions is limited to *one* companion of the individual; other companions will be permitted to ride with the person with a disability to the extent that space is available.

A good overview of the rules regarding paratransit services can be found at http://www.ada-infonet.org/documents/transportation/paratransit-service.asp.

In providing paratransit services, public entities must respond to requests from persons with disabilities only "to the extent practicable" to meet the comparable level of services provided to individuals without disabilities [42 U.S.C. §12143(a)]. Further, paratransit services must be provided in only three circumstances: (1) when an individual's disability prevents boarding, riding, or disembarking onto or from accessible transportation vehicles without assistance; (2) when an individual with a disability requires transportation during the fixed-route system's hours of operation but that system does not provide an accessible vehicle during the time the individual needs it; or (3) when an individual's disability prevents him or her from traveling to a bus or rail stop. For a good overview of eligibility for paratransit services, see http://www.ada-infonet.org/documents/transportation/ paratransit-eligibility.asp. In addition, some local paratransit providers have websites for their riders. Examples in large cities include Chicago at http://www.rtachicago.com/infocenter/paratransit.asp and New York at http://www.mta.nyc.ny.us/mta/ada/paratransit. htm, but websites are also available from providers in numerous medium-sized and even smaller communities. However, individuals who prefer to ride regular transportation, and are able to do so, cannot be denied access to regular transportation.

> EXAMPLE: Steven, who is visually impaired, is waiting at the bus stop to ride regular transportation. He is with his service dog. When the bus pulls up, the driver informs Steven that he will have to use paratransit if he wants to travel with his service dog. The bus driver, however, is in error. Steven is entitled to use regular transportation because, with his service dog, he is able to use that system. The city needs to accommodate his disability by permitting use of the service dog and verbally informing him when he has arrived at his destination.

> EXAMPLE: John, who has Tourette's syndrome, prefers to use public transportation. He cannot be denied use of public transportation merely because he might make loud noises.

There are several ways to remedy problems with paratransit, including filing formal complaints with the federal government and bringing the lawsuits described later in this chapter; however, it is often best to try to work with the paratransit provider first. No matter which route an individual has chosen, it is critical to have specific information about the problem the individual has faced, including (1) what happened (refusal to schedule a ride, broken lift, late arrival, etc.); (2) the date, time, and location of the event in question; (3) the person with whom the individual spoke at the paratransit provider and what he or she said (make sure to ask for the person's full name); and (4) the names and phone numbers of anyone else who witnessed the problem.

If an individual with a disability decides to proceed on his or her own, the information mentioned above should be included in the complaint letter sent to the paratransit agency or the Department of Transportation. A sample complaint letter follows:

Paratransit Provider
123 New St.
Anytown, GA

Dear Sir/Madam:

I use the [*name of paratransit system*], and I was recently refused transportation because I was told all rides were booked up [*or other specific complaint*]. I called at [*specific time*] on February 12, 2004, to schedule a ride for February 15. The woman I spoke to told me her first name was Ann but refused to give me her last name. She wanted to know why I wanted to know her last name, and I told her just in case I called back I would know whom to ask for. She informed me that she was not the one who usually answered the phones.

I missed two important meetings because I could not get a ride on February 15. I had to waste another day making up these meetings.

I am aware that the regulations governing paratransit state that riders with disabilities may be required to reserve rides at least one day in advance. I called on February 12 for a ride on February 15—three days in advance—and, thus, the refusal to schedule a ride violated the regulations. Please contact me at the address or phone number below so we can discuss this problem.

Sincerely,
[*Name, address, and phone number*]

If one knows of other people having problems with paratransit, however, consider joining forces. For example, Professor Milani worked with a local independent living center to create a log book of complaints. Clients were told to get the information mentioned earlier as soon as they had a paratransit problem and then to call the receptionist at the center, where the information was recorded in the log book kept at the desk. After three years, it contained more than ninety complaints and showed that people were experiencing the same problems on a repeated basis.

Gathering information like this can be invaluable in negotiating with paratransit providers for better service. Individuals with disabilities who inform transportation authorities of problems they've experienced are often told that their difficulties were isolated incidents. A complaint log book can be used to refute that statement if a copy of it is sent in advance of, or presented at, a meeting between a group of paratransit riders and the head of the local transportation authority. Another advantage to creating a complaint log is that showing repeated problems will likely be required in a lawsuit concerning paratransit.

> EXAMPLE: A group of individuals with disabilities kept a log book of service denials. They showed denials of 37 of the 130 rides requested four days in advance, 38 of the 105 rides requested three days in advance, 67 of the 180 rides requested two days in advance, and 92 of the 161 rides requested for the next day. They were able to prevail in a lawsuit concerning lack of service because the court found a "substantial" rate of service denial [*Anderson v. Rochester-Genesee Re - gional Transp. Authority*, 337 F.3d 201 (2d Cir. 2003)].

Demand-Responsive Systems

If a public entity operates a demand-responsive system (any system other than a fixed-route system that provides designated transportation) for the general public, all of the vehicles it purchases or leases must be accessible. An exception can be made if the entity demonstrates that its system, when viewed in its entirety, provides services to disabled persons that are equivalent to those provided to nondisabled persons. This provision applies to public vanpool systems—voluntary commuter ridesharing arrangements using a van that seats more than seven persons, including the driver.

Lift Maintenance and Repair

Public entities must establish a system of regular and frequent maintenance checks of lifts. When a lift is not working, the vehicle must be taken out of service before its next service and be repaired before it is returned to service. If there is no spare vehicle available and taking it out of service will reduce the transportation provided, the vehicle with an inoperable lift may be kept in service for no more than three days. If a vehicle with an inoperable lift is operating on a fixed route and the wait for the next accessible vehicle on the route exceeds thirty minutes, the entity shall promptly provide alternative transportation to individuals with disabilities who are unable to use the vehicle because its lift does not work.

A person who experiences a lift problem should record the same information discussed in the section on paratransit above. And joining forces with others who have had similar problems would again be wise, inasmuch as at least one court has found that a public transportation authority violated ADA where there was a pattern of wheelchair lift breakdowns that left passengers stranded.

> EXAMPLE: Approximately 40 percent of a transportation authority's buses are 1990-model buses that have wheelchair lifts. These lifts use a hydraulic, electronic, and mechanical system that is hard to maintain and is easily damaged. If the system does not operate, the lift cannot be operated manually. Several witnesses have testified that they experienced "numerous," "many," or "several" instances of inoperable wheelchair lifts, often had to wait extended periods of time for another accessible bus, and were never provided with alternative transportation. A court found in favor of the plaintiffs "due to a widespread and systemic problem of inoperable wheelchair lifts on [the] fixed route bus system [*Martin v. Metropolitan Atlanta Rapid Transit Authority*, 225 F. Supp. 2d 1362 (N.D. Ga. 2002)].

Transportation Facilities

All new facilities used to provide public transportation services must be accessible. Alterations to existing facilities or parts of existing facilities must be made so that, to the maximum extent feasible, the altered portions are accessible. Where alterations are made to a facility's primary function areas (e.g., waiting areas, ticket purchase and collection areas, train or bus platforms, baggage checking and return areas, and employment areas), they must be done in such a way that the path of travel to the altered area is readily accessible. The term *path of travel* includes sidewalks, curb ramps, parking areas, entrances, and clear floor paths through corridors, waiting areas, and other improved areas. It also includes the restrooms, telephones, and drinking fountains serving the altered area. However, an entity is not required to make altered areas accessible if the cost of making alterations to the path of travel and to drinking fountains, telephones, and restrooms along that path is disproportionate to the cost of the overall alteration. Alterations will be deemed disproportionate to the overall alteration "when the cost exceeds 20 percent of the cost of the alteration to the primary function area."

Key Stations
The key stations for rapid-rail, light-rail, and commuter rail systems were to be made accessible by July 26, 1993. (A key station is one that has been so designated by a light- or rapid-rail operator through planning and public participation processes.) However, the period in which to comply may be extended up to 2020 for stations that need "extraordinarily expensive structural changes." By 2010, at least two-thirds of all key stations for light- or rapid-rail systems (but not commuter rail systems) must be readily accessible.

Light- or Rapid-Rail Systems
When a public entity operates a light- or rapid-rail train containing two or more cars, at least one vehicle per train must be accessible. There is an exception, however, for historic vehicles used on a segment of a light- or rapid-rail system that is on the National Register of Historic Places if rendering the train accessible would significantly alter its historic character. An overview of the regulations governing such systems is available at http://www.ada-infonet.org/ada-infonet/documents/transportation/rapid-rail-systems.asp.

Commuter Rail Services and Amtrak
Commuter rail services and intercity rail services provided by the National Railroad Passenger Corporation (Amtrak) must have at least one passenger car per train that is accessible. Newly purchased rail passenger cars must also be accessible. Specifically, coach cars must allow an individual in a wheelchair to (1) enter, (2) have space to park and secure the wheelchair, (3) have a seat to which he or she can transfer from the wheelchair, and (4) have access to a restroom equipped for wheelchair users. However, an exception for new cars purchased for use in *commuter rail* transportation states that they are *not* required to have (1) a restroom usable by an individual who uses a wheelchair if no restroom is provided in such car for any passenger, (2) space in which to fold and store a wheelchair, or (3) a seat to which a passenger who uses a wheelchair can transfer. In addition, dining cars are generally not

required to be wheelchair accessible from the station, but single-level dining cars must be accessible from within the train.

When purchasing used cars, Amtrak and commuter rail operators must make "demonstrated good-faith efforts" to obtain accessible ones. If a rail passenger car is remanufactured so as to extend its life for ten years, it must be made readily accessible to the maximum extent feasible.

New Amtrak or commuter rail stations must also be accessible. Existing stations must be made accessible "as soon as practicable" but in no event later than 2011. Existing key stations used in commuter rail transportation systems were required to be accessible by 1994, but the Secretary of Transportation may extend this time limit up to 2010 "in a case where the raising of the entire passenger platform is the only means available of attaining accessibility or where other extraordinarily expensive structural changes are necessary to attain accessibility."

Alterations to existing stations or parts thereof used by Amtrak or a commuter rail provider must be made in such a way as to ensure that, to the maximum extent feasible, the altered portions are accessible. The DOT regulations set forth a mechanism for determining who bears the legal and financial responsibility for accessibility modifications to such stations. Basically, the regulations authorize—and encourage—all covered parties to come to their own agreement regarding the allocation of responsibility.

Transportation Provided by Private Entities

Title III of ADA covers transportation (other than by air travel) provided by private entities. There are different sets of standards for private entities whose primary business is transporting people and those that provide transportation as only part of their services. The requirements of this part do *not* apply to transportation provided to schoolchildren to and from a private elementary or secondary school and its school-related activities if the school is providing transportation service to students with disabilities equivalent to that provided to students without disabilities.

Buses and Vans: Private Entities That Focus on Transportation
Companies that focus on transportation cannot discriminate based on disability. Accordingly, they must purchase new vehicles that are read-

ily accessible. There are exceptions, however, for automobiles, vans with a seating capacity of fewer than eight passengers, and over-the-road buses, or OTRBs (i.e., buses that have elevated passenger decks over baggage compartments). Private taxi services are subject to this nondiscrimination standard but are not required to purchase or lease accessible automobiles. When a taxi service purchases or leases a vehicle other than an automobile, the vehicle is required to be accessible unless the taxi service can demonstrate it provides equivalent services to persons with disabilities as those provided to nondisabled persons.

Buses and Vans: Private Entities That Provide Transportation as Only Part of Their Services

Private entities not primarily engaged in the business of transporting people are subject to different regulations than those that are. If those entities operate a fixed-route system, they must ensure that any vehicle they purchase or lease with a seating capacity in excess of sixteen passengers (including the driver) is accessible. The same requirement applies for vehicles with smaller seating capacities unless the entity can show that, when viewed in its entirety, its fixed-route and/or demand-responsive system provides disabled individuals with service equivalent to that provided to nondisabled individuals.

Rail Vehicles: Private Entities That Focus on Transportation

All new rail passenger cars used to provide specified public transportation must be accessible. Passenger cars remanufactured so as to extend their life for ten years or more must, to the maximum extent feasible, be readily accessible.

Over-the-Road Buses

The regulations for over-the-road buses are a prime example of the impact that disability advocates can have on government policy. Both before and after ADA was passed, a group known as American Disabled for Accessible Public Transit (ADAPT) held protests and blocked buses in cities across the United States to demonstrate the need for access to public transit. ADAPT members from around the country also protested at busing industry meetings and appeared at congressional and Department of Transportation hearings. Many went to jail for the right to ride.

Finally, after a several-year delay, ADA regulations became effective for large-OTRB operators beginning October 30, 2000, and for small-OTRB operators beginning October 29, 2001. All OTRB operators must comply with the accessibility requirements described later in this chapter and also may not

- use or request the use of persons (e.g., family members or traveling companions of a passenger with a disability, or medical or public safety personnel) other than the operator's employees for routine boarding or other assistance unless the passenger requests or consents to such assistance;
- require or request a passenger with a disability to reschedule his or her trip, or to travel at a time other than the time the passenger has requested; or
- fail to provide reservation services to passengers with disabilities equivalent to those provided other passengers.

Large operators of fixed-route systems are required to ensure that any new OTRB they purchase or lease is accessible. These operators must ensure that no less than 50 percent of its buses are accessible by October 30, 2006, and that 100 percent are accessible by October 29, 2012. An operator may, however, apply to the Secretary of Transportation for an extension of the fleet accessibility deadlines. Small operators and private entities not primarily in the business of transporting people that operate fixed-route systems may comply with the law by doing the same or by providing equivalent service to individuals with disabilities.

Until complete accessibility is reached, both large and small operators must ensure that any individual with a disability who requests service in an accessible OTRB receives such service. For example:

- Operators may require that a rider provide up to forty-eight hours' notice of the need for an accessible bus; if such notice is not given, the operator still must provide the service if it can do so by making a reasonable effort.
- A small operator does not need to satisfy this rule, however, if it is providing service equivalent to its fixed-route service.

The ADA regulations also recognize that some small fixed-route operators who exclusively or primarily purchase or lease used buses may never have a fleet of 100 percent–accessible buses. Such operators must continue to comply with the regulations for any service not provided entirely via accessible buses.

If the general public can purchase a ticket with one operator for a fixed-route trip of two or more stages where two or more operators provide service, (1) the first operator must arrange for an accessible bus or equivalent service to be provided for each stage of the trip, (2) each operator is responsible for providing the required transportation for its portion of the trip, and (3) all fixed-route operators involved in interline service must be capable of receiving communications at all times concerning interline service for passengers with disabilities.

Entities that provide *demand-responsive* OTRB service are not required to purchase or lease accessible buses except as needed to meet the following requirements. First, any individual with a disability who requests service on an accessible OTRB must receive such service. Second, operators may require up to forty-eight hours' notice; if such notice is not provided, the operator still must provide the service if it can do so by making a reasonable effort. Finally, an operator is not required to fundamentally alter its normal reservation policies or to displace another passenger who has reserved a seat on the bus.

When an OTRB makes an intermediate or rest stop, passengers with disabilities, including wheelchair users, shall be permitted to leave and return to the bus like other passengers. Accordingly, operators must provide assistance to passengers with disabilities such as operating the lift and assisting with securement. If an OTRB operator owns, leases, or controls the facility where the stop is made (or contracts with the person who owns, leases, or controls such a facility), the operator shall ensure that the facility is fully compliant with applicable ADA requirements.

If an OTRB with an inaccessible restroom is making an express run of three hours or more without a rest stop, it must make a good-faith effort to accommodate a request for an unscheduled rest stop by a passenger with a disability who is unable to use the inaccessible restroom. The operator is not required to make the stop, but it must explain to the passenger the reason for its decision not to do so.

In February 2001, the Department of Justice (DOJ) entered into a settlement with Greyhound Lines, which details its obligations and plans for compliance with ADA. This agreement can be found on the

DOJ website at http://www.usdoj.gov/crt/ada/greyhnd.htm. The agreement documented several problems faced by riders, including the following:

- Gerald DiPaolo alleged that he was not offered transfer assistance during his trip from Hollywood, Florida, to Lamar, Arkansas, in July 1998. In his complaint Mr. DiPaolo stated that assistance was necessary to accommodate his mobility impairment. Greyhound sent the customer an apology letter and a voucher for free travel.
- Melvin Henderson alleged that Greyhound employees refused to provide boarding assistance during several trips he took between Mariana, Florida, and Fort Myer, Florida, in July 1996; that he had to be carried by other passengers; and that he was dropped.
- Leon Bryant alleged that, during his trip from Oxnard, California, to Jacksonville, Florida, in May 1998, he was verbally harassed by the driver and was refused seating in the area designated for passengers with disabilities. The cramped seating exacerbated his mobility impairment (causing pain and swelling) and required use of his pain medication. Also, when Mr. Bryant asked to file a complaint, he was refused assistance.
- Katia Dich alleged that, upon arriving in Key West, Florida, from Miami, Florida, in April 1998, the driver refused to assist her exit from the bus or to provide other customer assistance and verbally harassed her. Ultimately, a police officer had to assist her.
- Darlene Brazie alleged that drivers and other employees of Greyhound refused to provide her boarding assistance while she was a passenger with Greyhound from Marietta, Georgia, to Wickenburg, Arizona, in April 1993, despite her physical disabilities associated with polio. Ms. Brazie also asserted that a Greyhound driver verbally harassed her during her trip. Greyhound stated that this driver was subsequently terminated.
- Elizabeth Schultz alleged that drivers or other employees of Greyhound improperly carried her onto a bus in Holland, Michigan, in June 1993, almost dropped her during a transfer in Grand Rapids, Michigan, and improperly carried her off a bus in Lansing, Michigan, while she was a passenger with Greyhound. Ms. Schultz also alleged that the driver treated her in a condescending manner during the last portion of her trip to Lansing, Michigan. In her complaint she stated that she has

physical disabilities associated with cerebral palsy and multiple sclerosis, which made walking impossible. Greyhound sent the customer an apology letter and a voucher for free travel.

- Shirley Guy alleged that Greyhound employees refused to sell her a ticket from New York City to Manchester, Vermont, in September 1995 and May 1996, because she was accompanied by a service animal. Ms. Guy further alleged that, on her second trip, the driver verbally harassed her and initially refused to allow her to board with her service dog, and that after the driver was told by his supervisor to allow her on board, she was told to sit in the back of the bus.

- T. D. Childs, a blind Greyhound passenger who was traveling from Huntington, West Virginia, to Little Rock, Arkansas, in May 1997, alleged that Greyhound employees refused to provide assistance to him as he was boarding a Greyhound bus and at transfer stations, and that this refusal caused him to almost miss a connection. Mr. Childs also alleged that Greyhound employees refused to provide assistance on his return trip.

- Erica Maitland alleged that she tried to board a bus in Roanoke, Virginia, to New York City with her son in June 1997, and that on her first visit, Greyhound employees refused to sell her a ticket but sold other nondisabled passengers tickets to the same destination following her request. The following day, she was allowed to buy a ticket. The driver allegedly yelled at her son and told him that he was responsible for boarding and deboarding Ms. Maitland from the bus. Ms. Maitland alleged that her son had a hernia and would be unable to carry his mother.

- Ernest Means alleged that, despite notifying Greyhound three days in advance of his trip, he was denied boarding assistance throughout his trip from Zanesville, Ohio, to Wilmington, Delaware, in December 1996. As a consequence, he was repeatedly forced to call upon the assistance of other passengers or friends to assist him. Mr. Means uses a wheelchair.

- Towanda Redman alleged that Greyhound employees refused to assist her in carrying and stowing her luggage onboard a bus in Salt Lake City, Utah, when she was traveling to Burley, Idaho, in January 1997. Ms. Redman, who uses a wheelchair, states that Greyhound employees ultimately helped her only after her sister contacted the Greyhound Customer Service department in Dallas, Texas. Ms. Redman also stated that, when she arrived in Burley, Idaho, a manager of the station refused to assist her after the bus driver left her and her luggage at the locked bus depot. Ultimately, Ms. Redman was driven home by the police.

As a result of these and other complaints, the Department of Justice entered into a successful resolution with Greyhound. Although DOJ has limited resources with which to enforce disability laws throughout the country, it can be particularly helpful when major carriers are engaging in a pattern or practice of lack of accessibility. Again, careful documentation can help persuade DOJ to intervene in such matters.

In its resolution with DOJ, Greyhound agreed to several procedures, including the following:

1. Maintaining a toll-free hotline to accept calls from individuals with disabilities who require assistance or who believe that they have experienced discriminatory treatment. As of April 2005, the number for the Customers with Disabilities Travel Assistance Line was 1-800-752-4841. Other helpful numbers are 1-800-345-3109 (Deaf/Hard of Hearing/TTY/TDD) and 1-800-755-2357 (ADA Compliance Corporate Office).
2. Fully investigating and attempting to resolve any complaints that passengers file within sixty days of an action that a passenger alleges (1) was discrimination on the basis of disability or (2) caused a physical injury resulting from treatment by any Greyhound employee. Greyhound will attempt to resolve the complaint within ninety days of being notified and, if successful, promptly provide a written verification of the resolution to the customer. For any complaints that are received after sixty days from the alleged discrimination and that do not allege physical injury by any Greyhound employee, Greyhound shall provide the passenger with a copy of a brochure explaining its ADA policies.

More information on Greyhound's current services for travelers with disabilities can be found at http://www.greyhound.com/travel_information/disabilities.shtml.

Accessibility Requirements for Vehicles Operated by Public and Private Entities

The regulations provide minimum guidelines and requirements for the accessibility of transportation vehicles covered under ADA Titles

II and III, 49 C.F.R. Part 38. The accessibility provisions are detailed and technical and include requirements with respect to mobility-aid accessibility (such as boarding devices, vehicle lifts, securement devices, and platform configurations); doors, steps, and thresholds; priority seating signs; interior circulation; handrails and stanchions; lighting; fare boxes; public information systems; stop requests; and destination and route signs. The following sections highlight the regulations in the areas that are the most frequent sources of problems for people with disabilities.

Securement Systems, Lifts, and Ramps

An entity may require that an individual permit his or her wheelchair to be secured and is not required to permit wheelchair users to ride in places other than designated securement locations in the vehicle. However, the entity may not deny transportation to a wheelchair or its user because it cannot be secured or restrained satisfactorily by the vehicle's securement system. An entity may recommend that a wheelchair user transfer to a vehicle seat but may not require him or her to do so. Where necessary or upon request, transportation personnel shall assist individuals with disabilities with the use of securement systems, ramps, and lifts. Individuals with disabilities who do not use wheelchairs, including standees, may use a vehicle's lift or ramp to enter the vehicle.

Information About Stops and Services

The DOT regulations include several specific service requirements for entities providing ground transportation. On fixed-route systems, stops must be announced "at least at transfer points with other fixed routes, other major intersections and destination points, and intervals along a route sufficient to permit individuals with visual impairments or other disabilities to be oriented to their location" [49 C.F.R. § 37.167]. Where vehicles for more than one route serve the same stop, "the entity shall provide a means by which an individual with a visual impairment or other disability can identify the proper vehicle to enter or be identified to the vehicle operator as a person seeking a ride on a particular route" *Id.* The entity must make adequate information concerning transportation services available to individuals with disabilities including using accessible formats and technology, to enable users to obtain information and schedule service.

Service Animals

Service animals may accompany individuals with disabilities in vehicles and facilities, and the entity must allow a person with a disability to travel with a respirator or portable oxygen supply if it is consistent with applicable DOT rules regarding the transportation of hazardous materials.

Use of Lifts and Wheelchair Seating

A transportation provider may not refuse to use a lift to allow a passenger to exit a vehicle at a bus or rail stop unless (1) the lift cannot be deployed or will be damaged if it is or (2) temporary conditions, not under the entity's control, prevent all passengers from using the stop safely. Adequate time must be allowed for individuals with disabilities to board or exit the vehicle.

When an individual with a disability needs to sit in a seat or occupy a wheelchair securement location, the entity shall ask the following persons to move: (1) individuals other than those with a disability or elderly persons sitting in a priority seating location for those groups (or other seat as necessary); (2) individuals sitting in a fold-down or other movable seat in a wheelchair securement location. Signage designating wheelchair securement areas or priority seating areas for elderly persons and persons with disabilities must include language informing persons that they should comply with requests to move to make room for an individual with a disability, but the entity is not required to force other passengers to move.

Miscellaneous Regulatory Provisions

The regulations also provide that

- providers of transportation services may not charge people with disabilities for the provision of reasonable accommodations;
- even if it provides special services for individuals with disabilities, an entity may not deny an individual with a disability the

opportunity to use services provided to the general public if the individual is capable of using such services;

- an entity may not require that an individual with a disability be accompanied by an attendant or use designated priority seats if the individual chooses not to do so; and
- an entity may refuse service to an individual with a disability who engages in "violent, seriously disruptive or illegal conduct," but it may not refuse to provide service to such an individual "solely because the individual's disability results in appearance or involuntary behavior that may offend, annoy, or inconvenience employees of the entity or other persons" [49 C.F.R. § 37.5(h)].

Toll-Free ADA Assistance Line

The DOT operates a toll-free Federal Transit Administration (FTA) Americans with Disabilities Act Assistance Line, which, as of April 2005, can be reached at 1-888-446-4511 (voice) or through the Federal Information Relay Service at 1-800-877-8339. Questions and concerns will be addressed by the FTA's ADA Officer of the Day. Riders who require specific technical assistance will be directed to the appropriate FTA program office. The DOT can also be reached by electronic mail at ada.assistance@fta.dot.gov, and the FTA website is located at http://www.fta.dot.gov/transit_data_info/ada. This website has links to ADA regulations governing public transportation.

Administrative Enforcement Actions by the Federal Transit Administration

The FTA website also has a rider complaint form that can be filled out and sent to the FTA to start an administrative enforcement action against both public entities and private entities receiving federal funds. This form can be used to file an administrative complaint with the FTA's Office for Civil Rights (OCR), which investigates the complaint and, if a violation is found, attempts to enter into a conciliation agreement with the entity. The procedures used in such an investigation mirror those described for administrative complaints under ADA Title II, which are discussed in Chapter 5 of this book.

At the close of an investigation, the OCR will issue a Letter of Finding that sets forth the agency's determination regarding an issue involving a specific factual situation. Past letters are available on the FTA website at http://www.fta.dot.gov/transit_data_info/ada. Such letters may be helpful to others when dealing with the same issue involving similar facts.

Lawsuits by Private Individuals

An individual with a disability may file a private suit against *public entities* that provide transportation under ADA Title II and/or the Rehabilitation Act in state or federal court. The procedures for and possible limits of such an action are discussed in Chapter 5 of this book.

Alternatively, lawsuits against *private* transportation providers are authorized under ADA Title III. The procedures for and possible limits of such an action are also discussed in Chapter 5.

Airline Transportation

Congress enacted the Air Carrier Access Act of 1986 (ACAA) to prohibit air carriers, including certain foreign air carriers, from discriminating against otherwise qualified individuals with disabilities. The Department of Transportation has issued regulations interpreting the ACAA, which can be found at http://airconsumer.ost.dot.gov/rules/382SHORT.htm. An overview of the ACAA and its regulations is available on the Federal Aviation Administration's (FAA) website at http://www.faa.gov/passengers/Disabilities.cfm. A more detailed discussion is available on the DOT's website at http://airconsumer.ost.dot.gov/ACAAcomplaint.htm. The DOT website also provides helpful information in its publications *New Horizons for the Air Trav - eller with a Disability* and *Passengers with Disabilities*, which are available online at http://airconsumer.ost.dot.gov/publications/horizons.htm and http://airconsumer.ost.dot.gov/publications/disabled.htm, respectively.

The most significant provisions of the regulations are as follows:

- (1) Newly purchased aircraft having 30 or more passenger seats must have moveable aisle armrests on at least half the aisle seats, (2) those with 100 or more passenger seats must have space in the cabin to store at least one folding wheelchair, (3) and aircraft with more than one aisle in which restrooms are provided must contain at least one accessible restroom. Air carriers are not required to retrofit existing aircraft, but accessibility features are required to be added as existing planes are refurbished.

- Airport facilities (terminal facilities, including parking and ground transportation facilities) must be accessible.
- Air carriers may not refuse transportation to a qualified individual with a disability on the basis of his or her disability or because "the person's disability results in appearance or involuntary behavior that may offend, annoy, or inconvenience crewmembers or other passengers." Carriers may not limit the number of persons with disabilities who may travel on a given flight.
- Air carriers *may* refuse to provide transportation to any passenger "on the basis of safety" or to any passenger whose transport would violate FAA regulations. A carrier that refuses to provide transportation to any individual on the basis of disability must set forth reasons for that decision in writing within ten days.
- Air carriers *may* require up to forty-eight hours notice and one hour advance check-in for a passenger who wishes to receive (1) medical oxygen for use on board the flight, (2) carriage of an incubator, (3) hook-up of a respirator, (4) accommodation of a passenger on a stretcher, (5) transportation of an electric wheelchair when the aircraft has fewer than 60 seats, (6) provision of hazardous materials packaging for a battery for a wheelchair, (7) accommodation for a group of ten or more qualified individuals with a disability who make reservations and travel as a group, and (8) provision of an on-board wheelchair on an aircraft that does not have an accessible restroom. If a passenger does not meet the notice or check-in requirements, the carrier must still provide the service, equipment, or accommodation if it can do so by making a reasonable effort and without delaying the flight.
- Air carriers may require that a passenger with a disability be accompanied by an attendant *only* when the passenger is (1) traveling on a stretcher or in an incubator, (2) mentally disabled to such an extent that he or she is unable to comprehend or respond appropriately to safety instructions, (3) so severely mobility-impaired that he or she is unable to assist in his or her own evacuation of the aircraft, or (4) both severely visually impaired *and* severely hearing-impaired *and* unable to establish "*some* means of communication with carrier personnel." If the carrier deter-

mines that a passenger with a disability must be accompanied by an attendant for one of the foregoing reasons, but the passenger disagrees, the carrier may not charge for the transportation of the attendant.

- Air carriers may restrict the seating of passengers with disabilities to comply only with the FAA's exit-seating regulations, or only when necessary (1) to mitigate safety concerns resulting from a passenger's disability that causes involuntary active behavior or (2) to accommodate a service animal (e.g., seeing-eye dog or hearing dog). The FAA's exit-seating regulations provide that a person seated in a row next to an emergency door must be able to (1) "locate the door and quickly follow the instructions, written and oral, for its use"; (2) "physically . . . open the door"; (3) "determine when to open the door"; (4) "go quickly through the open exit"; and (5) "devote full attention to his or her emergency task." Thus, persons with severe visual or hearing impairments are precluded from sitting in exit rows, as are persons who are unable to perform one or more of the specific physical tasks without assistance.

- Air carriers must accommodate passengers with hearing impairments by (1) providing timely access to routine information such as that concerning ticketing, flight delays, schedule changes, connections, and gate assignments; (2) maintaining a telecommunication device for the deaf (TDD) reservation and information service; and (3) ensuring that video instructions are captioned or contain an inset for a sign-language interpreter.

- Air carriers must provide assistance to persons with disabilities in entering and leaving aircraft, in moving to and from seats, in preparing meals (such as by opening packages or identifying food), in moving to and from the lavatory (when the passenger is semi-ambulatory or the plane contains an onboard wheelchair), and in loading and retrieving carry-on items. Air carriers are *not* required to provide assistance with actual eating, to provide restroom assistance, or to provide medical services.

- Air carriers are prohibited from (1) requiring an individual with a disability "to accept special services (including, but not limited to, preboarding) not requested by the passenger"; (2) excluding a qualified person with a disability from services that are available to nondisabled persons "even if there are separate or different services available" to persons with disabilities, except when specifically permitted by the regulations; and (3) taking action against an individual because he or she has asserted rights protected by the ACAA.

- Qualified individuals with a disability must undergo security screening in the same manner as other passengers, and use of an aid for independent travel shall not subject the person or the aid to special screening procedures if the person clears the security system without activating it. Information about the Transportation Security Administration (TSA) Screening of Persons with Disabilities Program developed after the terrorist attacks on September 11, 2001, can be accessed at http://www.tsa.gov/public/display?theme=156.

Complaints Resolution Official

Each air carrier must have at least one Complaints Resolution Official (CRO), who has the authority to resolve complaints on the air carrier's behalf, available at each airport during its scheduled operations time. The CRO can be made available by telephone. If the complaint is received before the disputed action by the carrier's personnel has resulted in violation of the ACAA, the CRO must take action to ensure compliance with the rule. The CRO, however, does not have the authority to overturn a safety-based decision made by the pilot-in-command of an aircraft.

If the CRO agrees with the passenger that an ACAA violation has occurred, he or she must provide the passenger with a written statement summarizing the facts and what steps, if any, the carrier proposes to take in response to the violation. If, however, the CRO determines that there has been no violation, he or she must provide the passenger with a written statement summarizing the facts and reasons for this decision or conclusion. The statement must inform the passenger of his or her right to pursue DOT enforcement action and, if possible, be given to the passenger at the airport; otherwise, it shall be sent to the passenger within ten days of the incident.

Carriers must also establish a procedure for resolving written complaints alleging ACAA violations. A passenger's written complaint must be postmarked within forty-five days of the alleged violation, should note whether he or she contacted the CRO at the time of the alleged violation, and include the CRO's name and the date of contact, if available. It should also include any written response received from the CRO. Carriers must respond to a written complaint within thirty days after receiving it. The response must state the airline's position on the alleged violation and may also state whether and why no violation occurred or what the airline plans to do about the problem. The carrier must also inform the passenger of his or her right to pursue DOT enforcement action.

Toll-Free Hotline for Air Travelers with Disabilities

The Department of Transportation has established a toll-free hotline to provide consumers with general information about the rights of air travelers with disabilities, respond to requests for printed consumer information, and assist air travelers with time-sensitive disability-related issues that need to be addressed in real time. The line is staffed from 7 A.M. to 11 P.M. Eastern time, seven days a week, and can be reached at 1-800-778-4838 (voice) or 1-800-455-9880 (TTD).

Administrative Enforcement Actions by the DOT

Individuals who believe they have been discriminated against by an airline may submit a complaint to the DOT's Aviation Consumer Protection Division (ACPD). The complaint may be made in a letter or filed on the disability complaint form that can be found at http://airconsumer.ost.dot.gov/forms/382form.pdf. In addition, it can either be filed by e-mail to airconsumer@ost.dot.gov or mailed to Aviation Consumer Protection Division, Attn: C-75-D, U.S. Department of Transportation, 400 7th Street, S.W., Washington, D.C. 20590.

In recent years, ACPD and the Office of the Assistant General Counsel for Aviation Enforcement and Proceedings (Enforcement Office) have pursued enforcement actions in situations where the number of complaints received show a pattern or practice of discrimination. Specifically, the Enforcement Office has analyzed noncompliance with ACAA regulations, including in-depth investigations of several major air carriers for violations relating to boarding and wheelchair assistance based on formal and informal complaints. Airlines have been directed to cease and desist from further ACAA violations and fined as much as $1.35 million. The DOT typically cuts the fine, though, if the carrier agrees to spend money on better service for the disabled. For example, Delta Air Lines agreed to a $1.35 million civil penalty but will pay the DOT only $100,000 if it reduces complaints from passengers and spends at least $1.25 million to improve service.

Private Suits by Individuals with Disabilities: Federal Suits under the ACAA

Administrative enforcement actions may be the only legal remedy available to people who have encountered ACAA violations because courts are divided on whether individuals with disabilities can file private suits to enforce the ACAA. Some courts have allowed such actions, but others have held that Congress did not specifically authorize actions by private individuals when it enacted the statute. What this means is that people in some areas of the country (where courts have recognized private suits) can sue an airline directly, but people in other areas (where courts have rejected them) cannot do so and are instead limited to filing administrative actions with the DOT. The only way for individuals to determine whether they can bring a private claim is through careful legal research.

Given the limits of filing a complaint with the DOT and the possible lack of a private action, passengers should consider attempting to resolve a problem with an airline on their own. In Professor Milani's case, for example, one airline failed to load his power wheelchair on the plane, forcing him to use a loaner chair (which he could not propel himself) until his own chair arrived. Because damages are not available under the ACAA, he has requested compensation in the form of a travel voucher for his next flight on the airline. This is a sample letter that passengers can use if they have a similar experience:

Big Airline
123 New St.
Anytown, GA

cc: Aviation Consumer Protection Division
ATTN: C-75-D
U.S. Department of Transportation
400 7th Street, S.W.
Washington, D.C. 20590

Dear Sir/Madam:

Your airline recently lost my wheelchair and caused me to experience significant delay and frustration. I was booked on Flight # __ on [*date*] from [*city*] to [*city*] and checked my chair at the gate. When I arrived in [*city*], the gate agent, _____, [*get the person's full name and the names of anyone else you spoke with*] told me the chair had not been placed on my flight. Accordingly, I was placed in a loaner chair that I could not propel myself and [*fill in remaining details about the prob - lems experienced*].

This delay and frustration was worth far more to me than the amount I paid for the ticket, and accordingly, I request a travel voucher for my next flight on your airline [*or other remedy*].

Please contact me at the address or phone number below so we can discuss this problem.

Sincerely,

[*Name, address, and phone number*]

Private Suits by Individuals with Disabilities: Personal Injury Suits

Courts are also divided on whether individuals with disabilities can file personal injury suits under state law if they believe they were injured through an airline's negligence. Some courts have held that the Airline Deregulation Act of 1978 preempts state law claims for an airline's failure to provide accommodations under the theory that allowing an action under state law would interfere with the federal government's regulation of airline travel. Courts rejecting the preemption argument reason that allowing personal injury claims does not interfere with the Deregulation Act's purpose of barring states from regulating airlines. The only way for individuals to determine whether they can bring a person injury claim is through careful legal research.

Self-Advocacy by People with Disabilities

Avoiding travel problems altogether is, of course, preferable to filing a complaint after the fact, and, toward this end (as noted hereafter), there are several websites that include tips for travelers with disabilities. For example, it would be wise to inform your travel agent or the carrier of the following details when you make reservations:

- the type of disability you have and the equipment you use for mobility, such as crutches or a wheelchair
- the form of assistance that you will need while flying and at the airport
- your need for a manual or electric wheelchair to be stored and brought to the airplane door/gate upon arrival
- your special diet requirements

A particularly helpful website is the one for the Society for Accessible Travel and Hospitality (SATH), http://www.sath.org/. SATH is a nonprofit educational organization that has actively represented travelers with disabilities since 1976. It provides links to the access information for several airlines: http://www.sath.org/index.html?section=Travel%20Tips%20and%20Access%20Information. The airline sites usually provide contact numbers and recommendations for requesting accommodations. Other helpful sites include http://www.access-able.com/, which has specific travel tips at http://www.access-able.com/tips/air.htm, and http://www.mossresourcenet.org/travel.htm. Reviewing these sites before calling the airline directly could save valuable time and identify issues that disabled travelers might not have thought of on their own.

When calling an airline, travelers with disabilities must be provided information upon request concerning facilities and services available to them. When feasible, this information will pertain to the specific aircraft scheduled for a specific flight, including (1) any limitations concerning the ability of the aircraft to accommodate an individual with a disability (the carrier shall provide this information to any passenger who states that he or she uses a wheelchair for boarding, even if the passenger does not explicitly request the information); (2) the location of seats (if any) with movable aisle armrests, and of seats that the carrier does not make available to an individual with a disability (e.g., exit rows); (3) any limitations on the availability of storage facilities in the cabin or cargo bay for mobility aids or other equipment commonly used by an individual with a disability; and (4) whether the aircraft has an accessible lavatory. Any carrier that provides telephone service for the purpose of making reservations or offering general information must provide comparable services for hearing-impaired individuals, utilizing telecommunications devices for the deaf (TDDs).

Travelers with hearing impairments face special challenges, as one of our colleagues can attest. Indeed, she has shared a story with us that might be of some help to others with auditory impairments. She can't hear when gate changes are made at the airport—a problem that is aggravated by the fact that gate changes are often announced over the PA system rather than noted immediately on a screen (assuming there is even a nearby screen). When this colleague checks into her gate, she always informs the gate attendant that she is hearing impaired, tells the attendant where she will be sitting, and then asks the attendant to inform her personally if any important announcements are made about her flight. It's not a foolproof strategy; our colleague has missed flights because attendants did not comply with her request. But an attempt to avoid the problem before it occurs is worthwhile.

Conclusion

Although Congress placed considerable emphasis on transportation issues when it was enacting the Americans with Disabilities Act, we have a long way to go before transportation is fully accessible for individuals with disabilities. In many cases, the technology is in place in terms of wheelchair lifts on buses and the availability of paratransit. Yet, broken equipment and overburdened transportation systems can make these services meaningfully unavailable for many disabled individuals. When Professor Milani engages in air travel, he has to consider the consequences if his powered chair is lost or broken. In fact, he frequently drives long distances in his wheelchair-equipped van to avoid air transportation for that reason. Realistically speaking, individuals with disabilities often do not have the same range of options as nondisabled individuals due to the unreliability of handicapped accessibility. Unfortunately, in our society, many people face serious inconveniences when they use public transportation—and individuals with disabilities face a disproportionate amount of that inconvenience. Greater investment in public transportation by our society would benefit all of us, particularly individuals with disabilities. For now, such individuals need to be vigilant and document consistent accessibility problems so that they can bring those problems to the attention of transportation officials or, if necessary, the courts.

7

Housing

The Fair Housing Amendments Act of 1988 (FHAA) extended the Fair Housing Act (FHA) to prohibit discrimination against people with disabilities. The FHAA uses the same definition of *individual with a disability* as that found in the Rehabilitation Act of 1973 and the Americans with Disabilities Act (ADA): an individual who (1) has a physical or mental impairment that substantially limits one or more of the individual's major life activities; (2) has a record of such impairment (e.g., someone with a history of cancer); or (3) is regarded as having such an impairment (e.g., an individual who has been misclassified as disabled or who is treated as being disabled when in fact he or she is not disabled). Thus, Rehabilitation Act and ADA case law on that definition, which is discussed in Chapter 2 of this book, will also impact people who are covered under the FHAA.

The Department of Housing and Urban Development (HUD) has issued regulations interpreting the FHAA. These regulations prohibit discrimination on the basis of disability by a "person in the business of selling or renting dwellings," which includes private owners as well as real estate agents and brokers. Private owners of single-family dwellings, however, are not subject to any provision of the FHA, with *one exception:* They are subject to the nondiscriminatory advertising provision if (a) they own three or fewer single-family homes and (b) the dwellings at issue are being sold or rented without the use of a realtor. The same limitation applies where the dwelling contains four or fewer separate living quarters and the owner occupies one of the living quarters as his or her residence.

The FHA also does not cover religious organizations or private clubs that restrict housing to their members. This exemption applies to the dwellings that those entities own or operate "for other than a commercial purpose."

HUD provides information on housing issues in a number of ways, including a website specifically designed for people with disabilities, http://www.hud.gov/groups/disabilities.cfm, which provides links to housing and accessibility resources as well as links to the Fair Housing laws. HUD's Fair Housing Information Clearinghouse offers technical assistance on accessibility questions and provides information and materials about federal Fair Housing laws and HUD Fair Housing programs and initiatives.

Discrimination in the Rental or Sale of Housing

Sale/Rental of Dwellings

It is illegal under the FHAA to discriminate in the sale or rental of a dwelling, or to "otherwise make unavailable or deny" a dwelling, because of the disability of (a) the buyer or renter, (b) a person who will reside in the dwelling after it is sold or rented, or (c) any person associated with the buyer or renter. The FHAA also bars discrimination with respect to the "terms, conditions, or privileges of sale or rental of a dwelling," or with respect to "the provision of services or facilities in connection with such dwelling," due to the disability of any of the above-named persons. Discrimination includes

- the refusal to allow an individual with a disability to make reasonable modifications of existing premises at his or her own expense;
- the refusal to make reasonable accommodations in rules, practices, or services when necessary to allow a person with a disability equal use and enjoyment of the premises; and
- the failure to design and construct multifamily dwellings so that such dwellings are accessible to people with disabilities.

It is *not* illegal, however, to refuse to rent or sell housing to an individual, with or without a disability, "whose tenancy would constitute a direct threat to the health or safety of other individuals or whose tenancy would result in substantial physical damage to the property of others."

The FHAA requires that landlords allow renters with disabilities to make modifications to increase the accessibility of a rental property. Such modifications, however, must be done at the renter's expense, and the landlord may, under reasonable circumstances, require the renter to restore the premises to their premodified condition. The landlord may not refuse to allow the modification unless he or she shows that the change would be unreasonable [42 U.S.C. § 3604(f)(3)(A)].

EXAMPLE: Regina Freer, a wheelchair user, asked a trailer park for permission to install, at her own cost, a wheelchair ramp that wrapped around the side and front of her trailer and partially protruded into her driveway. The park refused, claiming that the ramp would impede trailer removal and shorten the tenant's driveway so that parked cars would obstruct the trailer park's access road. The park proposed an alternative ramp design that the tenant rejected as unsuitable to her needs. Her request was reasonable under the FHAA because it could be disassembled within three hours (and this process would not impede trailer removal). Further, a photograph of the driveway cast substantial doubt on the claim that the tenant's ramp design would impede traffic in the driveway and on the access road.

The FHAA also provides that landlords may not increase the required security deposit when renting to a person with a disability, but the landlord may require as part of the restoration agreement that the tenant set aside reasonable funds in an interest-bearing escrow account. Moreover, a landlord may require the tenant to provide reasonable descriptions of proposed modifications plus "reasonable assurances that the work will be done in a workmanlike manner and that any required building permits will be obtained."

Professor Milani has a friend who modified several apartments to accommodate his needs as a wheelchair user. The most costly of these modifications has been a roll-in shower. Before he moves in, this wheelchair user discusses the design and cost of the roll-in shower with the apartment complex's management. He then signs an agreement that says that he will restore the apartment to its premodification condition when he moves out. Sometimes the work is hired out and sometimes it is done by the apartment complex's own maintenance personnel.

Before any modifications can be made, of course, the tenant must decide on the most efficient way to make the property accessible. There are several resources on universal design principles that can help identify such modifications. A good place to start is the Center for Universal Design, a national research, information, and technical assistance center that evaluates, develops, and promotes universal design in housing, public and commercial facilities, and related products. Among the publications available on its website, http://www. design.ncsu.edu/cud/pubs/center/pubslist.htm, is a *Tenant's Guide to Apartment Modifications: An Idea Source Pamphlet to Simple, Low-Cost Modifications to Increase Accessibility in Apartments.* Other helpful websites include http://www.extension.iastate.edu/Pages/housing/uni-design.html, http://www.aarp.org/life/homedesign/, http://www.makoa.org/accessable-design.htm, and http://www.abledata.com/Site_2/accessib.htm.

For an overview of the rights of tenants with disabilities from the Disabilities Law Project, see http://www.dlp-pa.org/pubs/manuals/TR_2003.pdf. Two related websites are http://www.povertylaw.org/legalresearch/articles/free/trafford.htm and http://www.oradvocacy.org/pubs/housingfacts1.htm.

Multifamily Dwellings

Multifamily dwellings built for first occupancy after March 13, 1991, must be designed so that (1) the public and common-use portions are accessible to people with disabilities; (2) all doors are wide enough to allow wheelchair passage; and (3) all premises within such dwellings contain accessible routes into and through the dwelling, accessible light switches and environmental controls, reinforcements in bathroom walls to allow later installation of grab bars, and kitchens and bathrooms that allow an individual in a wheelchair to adequately maneuver. All covered multifamily dwellings must have one building entrance on an accessible route unless it is impractical to do so because of the terrain or unusual characteristics of the site. The term *multifamily dwellings* is defined as (1) buildings consisting of four or more units if such buildings have one or more elevators and (2) ground-floor units in other buildings consisting of four or more units.

The HUD website, http://www.hud.gov/offices/hsg/mfh/hto/

inventorysurvey.cfm, includes an inventory designed to assist prospective applicants with locating units in HUD-insured and HUD-subsidized multifamily properties that serve the elderly and/or persons with disabilities. The website also includes links to services in HUD-assisted project areas such as creating Neighborhood Network Centers in rental projects, insuring rental housing, and providing Housing Counseling. For these links, go to http://www.hud.gov/offices/hsg/mfh/hsgrent.cfm.

The fact that an apartment is identified as accessible, however, does not mean that it works for *all* people with disabilities. For example, Professor Colker had a student who was very diminutive and used a walker. She qualified for subsidized HUD, handicapped-accessible, rental housing. All the HUD units, however, were designed according to specifications for wheelchair users (higher toilets, sinks, and so forth), which were disastrous for her. Although these units were technically in compliance with the design guidelines, the student brought this problem to HUD's attention while it was renovating the units and convinced HUD that it needed to modify one unit for her. Parents of disabled children might face this problem as well, so they may wish to consider making a similar proposal.

Representations and Advertisements

It is illegal under the FHA to (1) represent to people with disabilities that "any dwelling is not available for inspection, sale, or rental when such dwelling is in fact so available" or (2) "[f]or profit, to induce or attempt to induce any person to sell or rent any dwelling by representations regarding the entry or prospective entry into the neighborhood" of persons with disabilities [42 U.S.C. § 3604(d), (e)]. The HUD regulations detail specific practices that are illegal under these provisions [*see, generally,* 24 C.F.R. §§ 100.80 and 100.85].

The section of the FHA dealing with discrimination in the rental or sale of housing also prohibits discriminatory advertising practices—namely, the indication of "preference, limitation or discrimination" based on any of the protected categories, including disability. Thus, for example, owners of apartment houses or developers of housing projects may not advertise in such a manner that would appear to exclude people with disabilities or to reflect a bias against people with disabilities.

Reasonable Accommodations

Under the FHAA, discrimination includes "a refusal to make reasonable accommodations in rules, policies, practices, or services, when such accommodations may be necessary to afford [a] person [with a disability] equal opportunity to use and enjoy a dwelling." Courts interpreting this language have incorporated the concept, developed under Section 504 of the Rehabilitation Act of 1973, that an accommodation need not be made where it would constitute a "fundamental alteration" of or place an "undue burden" on a housing program.

> EXAMPLE: A landlord has a policy of requiring tenants to pay their rent in person at the rental office. Sharon has a mental disability that makes her afraid to leave her unit. The landlord should provide her with a reasonable accommodation such as permitting her to mail her rent or to have a friend deliver it in person for her.

> EXAMPLE: A landlord has a policy of providing parking spaces to tenants. These parking spots are unassigned—whoever gets to the spot first may take it—and most people try to park as close to the building as possible. Louis has a mobility impairment that makes it difficult for him to get from the rear of the lot to the building. He requests an assigned space near the front of the lot as a reasonable accommodation for his disability. The landlord should provide him with the spot.

A person with a disability may ask for reasonable accommodations at any time during the housing application process, during the time he or she is a tenant, or even during eviction proceedings. There is no limit on the number of reasonable accommodations requests an individual with a disability can make, and a housing provider must consider each request on its own merits. The joint statement on *Reasonable Accommodations Under the Fair Housing Act* issued by the Department of Justice and HUD on May 17, 2004—available online at http://www.usdoj.gov/crt/housing/jointstatement_ra.htm—provides several examples of such accommodations in a question and answer format. Other helpful websites include http://www.povertylaw.org/legalresearch/articles/free/trafford.htm and http://www.vlpnet.org/legalresources/LandlordTenantLaw/HandBook/chapter3.htm.

Housing providers can ask a person requesting a reasonable accommodation to provide documentation that it (1) is necessary because of a disability and (2) will allow the disabled individual to use the housing unit and any services included with the rental in a manner equal to other tenants' use and/or will comply with the housing provider's rules for tenant conduct. The housing provider may not, however, ask about the nature or extent of the disability or require an applicant or tenant to release his or her medical records.

An individual with disability seeking such an accommodation should consider putting the request in writing and including a letter from an appropriate professional (a doctor, counselor, social service provider, pastor, or other reliable professional source) who is familiar with the individual and his or her disability-related needs. This statement should (1) explain that the individual's disability results in one or more functional limitations (such as inability to climb stairs, blindness, or difficulty in maintaining emotional stability) and (2) describe how the requested accommodation relates to the individual's functional limitations and will allow the individual to have equal access to the housing. The individual should seek a reasonable accommodation that will permit him or her to make full and equal use of the facility; but that request should not appear to be for special treatment.

> EXAMPLE: Joseph has multiple sclerosis and needs a parking space near his condominium unit in order to be able to use his car. The condo unit has assigned spaces that come with each unit. Joseph documents his MS and requests that he be assigned a space closer to his unit. The condo manager agrees to provide him with a closer space but asks Joseph to relinquish his current space in exchange for the closer space. Joseph refuses to relinquish his other space, saying that his relatives would use it when they visit. The condo manager may deny Joseph's request because he is arguably requesting special treatment (through two parking spaces) rather than equal treatment (through one accessible parking space).

Here is a suggested format for a reasonable accommodations request from the North Dakota Fair Housing Council (http://www.ndfhc.org/fair_housing/reasonable_accommodations.htm):

- Indicate that you qualify as a person with a disability as defined by civil rights laws.
- State where you live and who is responsible for the building.

- Describe the policy, rule, or architectural barrier that is problematic and how it interferes with your needs, rights, or enjoyment of your housing.
- Describe the change you are seeking in the policy, rule, or barrier.
- Cite the applicable law that protects your rights.
- Ask for a written response within a certain amount of time.
- Sign and date the request and keep a copy for your files.

A sample complaint letter is provided later in this chapter.

Service Animals

Courts have held that providing reasonable accommodations to people with disabilities includes allowing them to keep service animals in no-pet buildings, whether publicly or privately owned. In order to be protected by the FHAA with regard to service animals, (1) the person must have a disability, (2) the animal must serve a function directly related to the person's disability, and (3) the request to have the service animal must be reasonable. Courts have rejected the argument that a service animal must be professionally trained or certified and note that there is no requirement in the federal regulations as to the amount or type of work a service animal must provide for the benefit of the disabled person. The service animal is not limited to the traditional seeing-eye dog. For example, individuals who are deaf often live with service animals who can alert them to different sounds, such as knocks at the door, a smoke detector, a ringing telephone, or cars coming up a driveway.

The Doris Day Animal League publishes a very thorough pamphlet called *Best Friends for Life,* which discusses the rights of people with disabilities to have service animals in rental housing. The pamphlet is available on the organization's website, http://www.ddal.org/pdf/bffl.pdf; it can also be ordered either from there at http://www.ddal.org/pubs/bestfriends or by phone at 202-546-1761. Another website, http://www.deltasociety.org/dsz102.htm, provides an overview of the federal laws dealing with service animals in rental housing. Finally, responses to frequently asked questions about service animals in rental housing can be found at http://www.metrokc.gov/dias/ocre/animals.htm.

Here is a sample letter requesting a waiver of a no-pets policy:

Danny Thomas
Building Manager
123456 North Divide
Bismarck, ND 58501

Dear Mr. Thomas:

I, Jim Olson, qualify as a person with a disability as defined by the Fair Housing Act Amendments of 1988. I live at 123456 North Divide in unit #205. This building is managed by you, Danny Thomas, and owned by Jane Anderson.

Our building's rules state a no-pets policy. Because of my disability, a doctor has prescribed a service animal to assist in my daily living. The note from my doctor is attached.

I am requesting that you make a reasonable accommodation in the building's rules to permit me to have a service animal.

Under the Fair Housing Act Amendments, 42 U.S.C. 3604)(f)(3)(B), it is unlawful discrimination for a management company to deny a person with a disability a reasonable accommodation of an existing building rule or policy if such an accommodation may be necessary to afford such person full enjoyment of the premises.

Please respond in writing to my request for a reasonable accommodation within ten days of the date of this letter. I look forward to your response and appreciate your attention to this critical matter.

Sincerely,

[*Name and address*]

Direct Threat Defense

Like the Rehabilitation Act and ADA, the FHAA includes a direct threat defense to disability discrimination claims: "Nothing in this subchapter requires that a dwelling be made available to an individual whose tenancy would constitute *a direct threat to the health or safety of other individuals* or whose tenancy would result in substantial physical damages to the property of others." Courts have required, however, that apartment complexes that attempt to exclude tenants with mental disorders and a history of threatening behavior must first show that there was no reasonable accommodation that would have allowed those tenants to live there safely. They have also required the landlord to base his or her decision on objective evidence rather than on conjecture and stereotype.

An information sheet from the Bazelon Center for Mental Health Law, available online at http://www.bazelon.org/issues/housing/info sheets/fhinfosheet8.html, explores what constitutes a direct threat to others not requiring a reasonable accommodation, what kinds of behavior have triggered the exclusion in the past, and, finally, what circumstances will require a reasonable accommodation despite a tenant's admittedly threatening behavior. The Bazelon Center for Mental Health Law also has an information sheet that discusses the applicability of reasonable accommodations in the context of eviction, including situations in which the eviction is prompted by complaints from other tenants of aggressive or disturbing behavior by a tenant with mental illness; for this you can go to http://www.bazelon.org/issues/housing/infosheets/fhinfosheet4.html. Other websites with information on this issue include http://www.metrokc.gov/dias/ocre/FHFAQTRR.htm# odd and the section on the direct threat defense in the DOJ and HUD joint statement on *Reasonable Accommodations Under the Fair Housing Act* at http://www.usdoj.gov/crt/housing/jointstatement_ra.htm.

EXAMPLE: A landlord requires that all persons applying to rent an apartment complete an application that includes information on their current place of residence. Richard disclosed that he currently resides at Oxford House, which is a group home for men receiving treatment for alcoholism. Based solely on the stereotype that recovering alcoholics are violent, the landlord excludes Richard. Such an action violates the FHAA.

EXAMPLE: The fact pattern is the same as above except that, this time, the landlord contacts Richard's references and learns that Richard has posed a direct threat to persons or property in the recent past and that his alcoholism treatment has been unsuccessful. The landlord would now have a lawful basis for denying housing to Richard.

Discrimination in Residential Real Estate–Related Transactions

The FHA prohibits discrimination in residential real estate–related transactions based on race, color, religion, sex, handicap, familial status, or national origin. The term *residential real estate–related transaction* refers to the construction, improvement, or maintenance of a dwelling, the "making or purchasing of loans or providing other financial assistance" with respect to the purchase, and to the "selling, brokering or appraising of residential real property." Again, the HUD regulations list detailed practices that are considered to violate this provision (*see, generally,* 24 C.F.R. §§ 100.120-100.35).

Discrimination in Provision of Brokerage Services

The FHA also prohibits discrimination in the **provision of** brokerage services. Prohibited actions include, but are not limited to, setting different fees for membership in a multiple-listing service; denying or limiting benefits accruing to members in a real estate brokers' organization; or establishing geographic boundaries, office location, or residence requirements for access to, or membership in, any real estate–related organization based on an individual's membership in any of the statutorily protected categories.

Interference or Coercion

The FHA makes it unlawful to coerce, intimidate, threaten, or interfere with any person in the exercise or enjoyment of any right granted under or protected by the statute. Violence or physical coercion is not required for a retaliation claim, but the conduct complained about must be of sufficient magnitude to permit a finding of intimidation, coercion, threats, or interference. It is unclear, however, whether the ability to bring an interference or coercion claim depends upon the validity of a claim alleging discrimination in the sale or rental of housing when the plaintiff files under both sections. Some courts have stated that there must be a violation of the discrimination provision for an interference claim to succeed [*see, e.g., Congdon v. Strine*, 854 F. Supp. 355 (E.D. Pa. 1994)].

> EXAMPLE: Leonard claims that the other condominium owners shunned him after he complained about some accessibility problems at the condominium complex. He alleges no violence or physical coercion. He also alleges no intimidation or coercion. A mere failure to be sociable is unlikely to rise to the level of a FHAA violation.

> EXAMPLE: Jeffrey, Vincent, David, and Sherman are recovering alcoholics and drug users who reside in a group rental home for recovering substance abusers. The residents are self-sufficient, house conflicts

are resolved democratically, and any resident who relapses is ejected from the house by the other residents. They run the group home as a single-family dwelling unit. None of the individual rooms have locks on the doors, and each of the tenants has an undivided right to occupy the entire unit. The home has been the subject of repeated police harassment and unfavorable zoning rulings. The police allegedly made comments such as "If you think we are going to let those people stay in this town, you've got another thing coming." This pattern of activity is likely to constitute harassment under the FHAA even though there is no allegation of violence or physical coercion.

Zoning

The FHAA states that it does not limit "the applicability of any reasonable local, state, or federal restrictions regarding the maximum number of occupants permitted to occupy a dwelling." The legislative history to the statute, however, indicates that this proviso is not intended to permit zoning regulations that discriminate against persons with disabilities. Thus, a vast number of courts have granted relief to plaintiffs with disabilities who sought (1) to receive special exemptions under applicable zoning regulations or (2) to have zoning regulations interpreted in a manner that would provide persons with disabilities equal access to housing. These courts have recognized that if persons with disabilities are to have equal access to housing in residential areas, zoning regulations regarding single-family residences must be modified to allow small groups of persons with disabilities to live together in one residential home.

For example, the U.S. Supreme Court ruled in *City of Edmonds v. Oxford House, Inc.*, 514 U.S. 725 (1995), that a single-family zoning provision did not fall within the FHAA's exemption for "any reasonable local, state, or federal restrictions *regarding the maximum number of occupants* permitted to occupy a dwelling" (emphasis added.) In that case, the city issued a citation to Oxford House, a group home for ten to twelve adults recovering from alcoholism and drug addiction, alleging that it had violated a zoning regulation by operating in neighborhood zoned for single-family housing. The regulation defined *family* as persons related by genetics, adoption, or marriage or a group of five or fewer unrelated persons. Oxford House claimed that the city violated the FHAA by refusing to make a reasonable accommodation to allow its residents to remain in the single-family dwelling at issue. The city contended that the single-family zoning provision was exempt from the FHAA. The Supreme Court agreed with Oxford House, holding that the zoning provision specified who could compose a family unit, not the maximum number of occupants that a dwelling unit could house, and thus did not fall within the FHAA's exemption for total-occupancy limits.

Zoning for group homes for people with disabilities is still a frequent source of litigation, however. These suits are usually brought by organizations, both not-for-profit and for-profit, that are seeking to build or expand such homes. The Department of Justice and HUD issued a joint statement in 1999 on group homes, local land use, and the FHA that includes answers to a number of frequently asked questions; this is available online at http://www.usdoj.gov/crt/housing/final8_1.htm. A number of other websites also provide information on issues related to group homes for people with disabilities, including http://www.oxfordhouse.org/fairhouse.html, http://www.advocacyinc.org/HS2_text.htm, and http://www.ci.mesa.az.us/citymgt/mayorcc/FAQ'sD1.asp. Some of these websites offer information that is specific to a certain state, but all of them provide information on the relevant federal rules.

EXAMPLE: Although aware that local zoning laws do not permit groups of four or more unrelated people to live together in a single-family neighborhood, a group-home operator decides to run a home for four adults with disabilities in the neighborhood. Some neighbors testify that they are opposed to the group home on the grounds that it will create parking problems in the neighborhood. If the group-home operator submits a plan to provide whatever off-street parking is needed, then the zoning board cannot use that complaint as a legitimate basis to deny the zoning variance.

EXAMPLE: The fact pattern is the same as above except that, this time, the home is for four adults with mental retardation who do not have driver's licenses. Such a group home is unlikely to have a greater impact on parking, traffic, noise, or utility use when compared with an "ordinary" family. There would be no need for the home operator to have a plan for additional off-street parking irrespective of the testimony of neighborhood residents.

FHA: Enforcement and Remedies

Responsibility for enforcing the Fair Housing Act lies with the Secretary of HUD. A private individual who is an aggrieved person may also sue directly under the act, however. The FHA defines an aggrieved person as one who either has been injured by a discriminatory housing practice or believes that he or she will be "injured by a discriminatory housing practice that is about to occur." This term has been broadly interpreted by the courts.

Administrative Enforcement

An aggrieved party may file an administrative complaint with HUD within one year of the alleged discriminatory conduct. If the complainant is within the jurisdiction of a state or local agency that operates under a Fair Housing law that HUD has certified as being the "substantial equivalent" of the FHA, HUD will refer the complaint to that agency for proceedings in accordance with state law. HUD may take no further action without the consent of such certified agency unless the certified agency fails to institute proceedings within 30 days or fails to carry forward proceedings with reasonable promptness, or unless the Secretary of HUD determines that the certified agency no longer qualifies for certification. If that agency does not institute proceedings (or if there is no certified agency), HUD must administratively proceed with the complaint.

Information about filing a complaint can be found at http://www.hud.gov/complaints/housediscrim.cfm. From that site, you can file a complaint online or print a complaint form, fill it out, and drop it off at your local HUD office or mail it to the Office of Fair Housing and Equal Opportunity, Department of Housing and Urban Development, 451 Seventh St. S.W., Room 5204, Washington, DC 20410-2000. Alternatively, you may wish to mail it to the Fair Housing hub closest to you, which can be identified through links on the website. In addition, HUD has a Complaint Line: 1-800-669-9777. A final option is to write a letter with

- name and address
- the name and address of the person complaint is about
- the address of the house or apartment one was trying to rent or buy

- the date when this incident occurred
- a short description of what happened

Then simply mail the letter to the Fair Housing hub closest to you.

A primary advantage of administrative proceedings is speedy resolution. HUD is required to complete an investigation within 100 days and to make a determination as to whether "reasonable cause exists to believe that a discriminatory housing practice has occurred or is about to occur, unless it is impracticable to do so, or unless the Secretary has approved a conciliation agreement with respect to the complaint." If it is unable to complete the investigation within the 100-day period, HUD will notify the aggrieved person and the respondent, by mail, of the reasons for the delay.

The Assistant Secretary for Fair Housing and Equal Opportunity is to dismiss all cases in which he or she has determined that no reasonable cause to believe that a discriminatory housing practice has occurred or is about to occur. Only those cases in which reasonable cause has been found by the Assistant Secretary will be sent to the General Counsel for review. Findings of no violation are communicated immediately to the complainant, whereas findings of violation must be submitted to the General Counsel for approval.

If the investigation leads to a finding of reasonable cause that the Fair Housing Act has been violated, HUD must immediately charge the respondent and begin prosecution. If reasonable cause is not found, HUD will dismiss the action. HUD has taken the position that the statute does not contemplate a right of appeal from an agency finding that no reasonable cause exists to find that an FHAA violation has occurred; the complainant's only recourse is to file a private civil action. HUD's opinion has not been tested in the courts, however.

When HUD files a charge, the aggrieved person, the respondent, or HUD has 20 days to elect to have the matter resolved in federal court (to preserve the right to a jury trial). If an election is made to go to court, the Attorney General must commence the action in federal district court within 30 days. If no election is made, the matter will be heard at an administrative hearing, during which the parties have the rights to be represented by counsel, to present evidence and cross-examine witnesses, and to issue subpoenas. The administrative hearing must be commenced within 120 days of the issuance of the charge, and a decision must be issued within 60 days of the hearing's conclusion.

The Administrative Law Judge (ALJ) has the power to award money damages and/or injunctive relief such as ordering the housing provider to refrain from certain future conduct or declaration that certain conduct is unlawful. For example, the ALJ may order that an entrance be made accessible in the future or that the housing provider refuse to engage in certain conduct in the future. The ALJ may also award attorney fees to the prevailing party and assess civil penalties against the violators. The ALJ may *not* award punitive damages. Further, the Fair Housing Act Amendments do not provide that an ALJ may furnish "such affirmative action as may be appropriate," although such a provision *is* included in the relief available from a federal court.

The ALJ's decision may be reviewed by the Secretary of HUD within thirty days after the final order of the ALJ is entered, regardless of whether the party has filed a complaint with HUD. If the defendant does not comply with the ALJ's order, HUD may petition for enforcement in a court of appeals within sixty days. A flowchart of the HUD complaint process is available at http://www.fhosc.org/discrimination/hud_chart.html.

At any time after filing a charge, HUD may authorize the Attorney General to bring a civil action for temporary relief. The Attorney General must "promptly" commence the action. The filing of a civil action for temporary relief will not affect the continuation of the administrative proceedings.

Private Enforcement

An aggrieved party may also sue directly in federal court (without going through the administrative process) within two years of the allegedly discriminatory action. The two-year limitations period does not include the time during which HUD administrative proceedings were pending. But an aggrieved party is barred from filing an action if he or she has consented to a conciliation agreement, or if an ALJ has commenced a hearing on the record with respect to the same or a similar charge. If the defendant is found to have violated the Fair Housing Act, the court may award actual and punitive damages, as well as equitable relief—such as injunctive relief or the ordering of such affirmative action as may be appropriate. In addition, the court may award the prevailing party reasonable attorney fees and costs. Further, the FHA provides that "[t]he United States shall be liable for such fees and costs to the same extent as a private person."

Self-Advocacy by People with Disabilities
Before filing a lawsuit or a complaint with HUD, individuals with disabilities should consider first writing a complaint letter to the entity that they believe has violated the FHAA. This may be a quicker way to resolve the problem. Even if not, such a letter may be helpful in a future lawsuit as evidence that the aggrieved party notified the defendant of the problem and tried to resolve it without filing suit. A sample complaint letter follows:

Chief Administrator
Carman Towers
123 New St.
Anytown, GA

Dear Sir/Madam:
    I am a resident of apartment #123 in the Carman Towers apartment complex that you manage and that is owned by the Carman Real Estate Investment Trust. I would like to obtain a parking space close to my building to accommodate my disability. I was diagnosed with multiple sclerosis (MS) three years ago and qualify as a person with a disability as defined by the Federal Fair Housing Act Amendments of 1988. My MS has caused physical weakness, difficulty in walking, loss of balance and coordination, visual disturbance, fatigue, loss of stamina, and severe headaches. Due to my MS, it has become increasingly difficult for me to walk from my car to my apartment, and my doctor has advised that this poses a danger to my health. A letter from my doctor explaining this is attached.
    As you know, parking in this section of Anytown is extremely scarce, and it is especially hard to find a parking spot near the Carman Towers. I am aware, however, that Carman Towers owns two parking garages near the buildings. I also know there has been a first-come/first-served policy when allocating parking spaces in them.
    I believe that it would be a reasonable accommodation, as required under the Fair Housing Amendments Act of 1988, to make a parking spot available to me immediately on account of my disability. Under the FHAA, 42 U.S.C. 3604)(f)(3)(B), it is unlawful discrimination for a management company to deny a person with a disability a reasonable accommodation of an existing building rule or policy if such an accommodation may be necessary to afford such person full enjoyment of the premises.

Please respond in writing to my request for a reasonable accommodation within ten days of the date of this letter. I look forward to your response and appreciate your attention to this critical matter.

Sincerely,

[*Name and address*]

Section 504

As noted above, Congress based the FHAA's antidiscrimination provisions on regulations and case law under the Rehabilitation Act. Plaintiffs with disabilities often bring claims based on discriminatory housing practices under Section 504 and ADA in addition to the FHAA. Several courts have held that Section 504 precludes a recipient of federal financial assistance from discriminating against individuals with disabilities with respect to the provision of housing. A plaintiff with a disability may not, however, utilize Section 504 to circumvent the requirements of federal statutes relating to the provision of federally subsidized housing. In other words, Section 504 does not eliminate the requirement that individuals with disabilities must fall within the class of individuals eligible to participate in housing programs funded pursuant to laws such as the one that provides for supportive housing for the elderly. For example, in *Knutzen v. Eben Ezer Lutheran Housing Center,* 815 F.2d 1343 (10th Cir. 1987), the court held that excluding nonelderly mentally impaired and developmentally disabled individuals from a federally funded housing project for the elderly and mobility-impaired did not violate Section 504. Accordingly, before filing a complaint alleging discrimination in federally funded housing, people with disabilities should first determine whether they fall within the scope of the federal program. If they do not, there is no discrimination under Section 504.

Conclusion

The Fair Housing Act Amendments provide a broad set of strong remedies for individuals who can prove that they are victims of disability-related discrimination. Much of the disability-related litigation under the FHAA has involved the act's effect on the ability of local governments to exercise control over group-living arrangements. Many individuals with disabilities find that living in a group home is an economical way to avoid expensive nursing-home care while still living independently. We can expect that, based on biased ideas about group-home residents, neighbors will continue to object to such homes in their backyard; but the FHAA does provide an effective set of remedies to prevent local zoning boards from incorporating such prejudice and stereotypes into their decisionmaking process. Many people are still unaware that the FHAA was amended in 1988 to include disability-related discrimination. By being aware of their rights, individuals with disabilities can help achieve more effective enforcement of that landmark federal statute.

8
Voting

The right to vote is basic to our democratic way of life. Most Americans take for granted that they can vote in a confidential manner at their local polling place. However, polling data from both the 1996 and 2000 presidential elections suggest that individuals with disabilities are far less likely to vote than other adults. In 1996, 31 percent of adults with disabilities voted, compared to 49 percent of all adults. In 2000, the figures were 41 and 51 percent, respectively. The Government Accounting Office (GAO), after controlling for demographic and other factors related to voting, estimated in 2001 that individuals with disabilities are about 15 percent less likely to vote than those without disabilities.[1] Estimates indicate that if individuals with disabilities had voted in 2000 with the same turnout as the rest of the adult population, Vice-President Gore would have won the popular vote by between 1 million and 1.5 million votes and, moreover, that he would easily have won Florida and the electoral vote. Indeed, according to the American Association of People with Disabilities, 40.5 percent of Florida voters with disabilities voted in the 2000 presidential election, with an estimated 1.8 million disabled Floridians not voting. Two problems that contribute to this low turnout are voter disenfranchisement and the inaccessibility of polling places.

Even those disabled individuals who can get to polling places are sometimes unable to vote confidentially, because many voting machines are inaccessible to voters with manual or visual disabilities. The secret ballot was developed in the United States to avoid problems of harassment and intimidation that otherwise occurred at polling places: "American history is replete with stories of polling places as 'scenes of battle, murder, and sudden death,' and sham battles designed to frighten away elderly and timid voters."[2] Although Congress has taken some steps to correct this problem, it is still a source of major frustration for many individuals with disabilities.

The 2004 Election

Although the U.S. Department of Justice has issued guidelines for accessible polling places (see http://www.usdoj.gov/crt/ada/votingck. htm), those guidelines do not speak to *how* elections are conducted. Accessibility complaints from the 2004 election were numerous. Some individuals complained that they could not physically stand for the several hours necessary to wait to vote. No folding chairs were available for people to rest. Further, there was no signage indicating that people with disabilities could request accommodations providing relief from the long lines.

At some polling places, although accommodations were made for individuals with disabilities, there was no uniform procedure for ensuring that such accommodations were being offered. Individuals with hidden disabilities were often challenged to provide documentation that proved their disability status. Even individuals with obvious disabilities were sometimes harassed when they sought accommodations. For example, when a disabled voter carrying oxygen sought to vote in Broward County with assistance, he was required to present proof of disability. And in Delaware County, Pennsylvania, a voter who used a wheelchair was reportedly told that she had to get out of the wheelchair in the booth if she wanted to vote (*see* http://www. electionprotection2004.org/edaynews.htm).

Because of the length of the lines, some polling places enforced time limits for voting. After waiting for several hours, some individuals with disabilities found themselves unable to vote in the five or fewer minutes that they were allocated to vote. In one polling place, voters were reportedly limited to two minutes to cast their vote.

Some individuals with disabilities need assistance when voting, but polling places were inconsistent in terms of how they allowed individuals to access assistance. Indeed, some polling places insisted that only a family member or legal guardian could assist disabled individuals even if they had no family members living in the state who could offer such assistance. One voter reported that poll workers called the police when she sought to assist her sight-impaired neighbor.

Although the Help America Vote Act (discussed in the following section) requires that curbside voting be made available to voters who cannot get to their polling sites due to accessibility problems, that requirement is frequently not met. Both poll workers and voters complained that this requirement was often not met during the 2004 election.

Solving many of these kinds of problems is relatively simple and inexpensive. Clear signage indicating how people can request assistance or accommodations would streamline the process. Consistent rules across polling places would ensure that all voters with disabilities are given an equal chance to vote, irrespective of their polling place location. States could liberalize their rules about voting assistance so that voters with disabilities can choose whom they trust to assist them with voting. And early voting could be made easier for all voters, including those with disabilities.

Voters with disabilities may have been the decisive factor in President Bush's popular vote plurality over Senator Kerry. According to polls conducted by the National Organization on Disability, Al Gore carried the disability vote 56 to 38 percent in 2000, whereas in 2004 Bush reportedly carried the disability vote 52.5 percent to 46 percent (http://www.aapd-dc.org/dvpmain/preparation/voteproblems.html). Given the volatile nature of the disability vote, both parties should be vying for that vote in the next presidential election. Bipartisan efforts to make voting more accessible for this key constituency could have a big impact on that next election.

Although this chapter identifies legal channels that can be explored to make voting more accessible to individuals with disabilities, it is important to recognize the power of the disability vote in seeking reforms.

Voter Disenfranchisement

Voter disenfranchisement results from state constitutional or statutory provisions that bar persons from voting if they fit such "descriptors" as *under guardianship or conservatorship, idiot, insane, lunatic, mentally incompetent, mentally incapacitated, unsound mind,* and *not quiet and peaceable.*[3] Forty-four states have such laws or regulations, which bar many individuals with mental disabilities from voting—even those who are fully competent in terms of their capability to vote because they are under guardianship procedures that ensure that they are monitored and receiving treatment. Because the elderly are placed into guardianship in disproportionately high numbers, such laws often directly, and negatively, affect them in particular.

Ironically, these laws disenfranchise individuals who are competent to vote because the guardianship procedures make sure that they are monitored and receiving treatment. These same laws, however, do not bar from voting those people who are incompetent to do so because of untreated, serious mental illness but who escape attention because they are not under guardianship. As Justice Kennedy himself noted, "It is a common phenomenon that a patient functions well with medication, yet, because of the mental illness itself, lacks the discipline or capacity to follow the regime the medication requires" [*Olmstead v. L. C.*, 527 U.S. 581, 610 (1999) (Kennedy, J., concurring)]. In practice, these rules often exclude only those with traditional psychiatric disorders from voting, while permitting incapacitated persons diagnosed with mental retardation or senility to vote as they choose.

Recent cases in Missouri and Maine have tried to challenge restrictive state definitions of competence. The Missouri case was filed in October 2004 by Steven Prye, a 52-year-old Harvard-educated lawyer who was diagnosed as having schizoaffective disorder and being in need of a guardian. At the time of the initial guardianship decision, he was living in Illinois and was allowed to vote; upon moving to Missouri, however, he learned that state law precluded him from voting due to his incompetent status. His lawyer described Prye as "more engaged and better informed than many voters I know." Prye's lawsuit alleged violations of the Fourteenth Amendment, ADA, and Section 504 of the Rehabilitation Act. He sought an injunction to allow him to register and vote in Missouri as well as a declaratory judgment that the state's prohibition violated federal law and the U.S. Constitution. However, his suit in federal court was unsuccessful; the court ruled that he needed to pursue remedies in state court by reopening his guardianship status.

Similar litigation was successful in Maine in 2001 [*see Doe v. Rowe*, 156 F. Supp.2d 35 (D. Me. 2001)]. Pursuant to Maine's constitution and a relevant implementing statute, persons who are "under guardianship for reasons of mental illness" are prohibited from registering to vote and from voting in any election. For example, when "Jane Doe" was placed under full guardianship due to a bipolar disorder diagnosis in 1993, she did not specifically ask whether she would continue to have the right to vote. Through a court order on October 31, 2000, shortly before the 2000 presidential election, she was able to get her guardianship order modified to state explicitly that she was eligible to vote in the November 2000 election. Similarly, when "Jill Doe" was found to be incapacitated due to bipolar disorder in 1996, no one raised the issue of her capacity to vote before placing her under full guardianship; and, like Jane, Jill sought to have her guardianship amended to clarify that she should be able to vote. However, Jill's request was summarily denied despite an affidavit from her attending psychiatrist saying that she had the mental capacity to understand the nature and effect of voting. Like Jane and Jill, "June Doe" also was under full guardianship and thereby lost her right to vote even though that issue had never been discussed at her guardianship hearing. But because she was hospitalized during the 2000 election, she was not able to seek an order modifying her guardianship at the time of the election, even though her treating psychiatrist indicated that she was competent to vote.

Following the 2000 election, the Maine federal district court concluded that Maine's disenfranchisement rules violated the Fourteenth Amendment's due process and equal-protection clauses, as well as ADA Title II and Section 504 of the Rehabilitation Act.

Although litigation may be successful in these fact situations, it may be "too little, too late." Of the three women involved in the Maine litigation, only Jane was able to vote in the 2000 presidential election because she successfully petitioned the court that was overseeing her guardianship to reopen her status to explicitly state that she could vote. In the future, people involved in guardianship decisions should try to think about voting rights at the time of the initial guardianship decision. If competence to vote is correctly decided at that time, future problems may be avoided.

Given the overwhelming number of states that have state laws precluding individuals with full guardianships from voting, statutory reform is an important step in nearly all the states. Few states have engaged in statutory reform despite the prevalence of this problem. Rather than develop new rules following litigation, Maine simply repealed its previous rule.

The challenge for states following litigation such as that in Maine and Missouri is to develop new rules that properly exclude incompetent voters while not disenfranchising large groups of individuals with mental illness who are competent. Two types of reforms are needed to solve this problem. First, (a) the question of whether individuals who are considered to require full guardianship are competent to vote should be discussed at the guardianship hearing, and (b) a procedure should exist for reopening that decision in the event that a person becomes more competent as a result of regularly taking medication. Second, states need to update their definition of competence. Antiquated words like *idiot* and *lunatic* should not be the basis of determining competency. Many states, like Maine and Ohio, include these terms in their constitutions—and such terms are difficult to remove from state constitutions. (Attempts to do so were unsuccessful in Maine in November 1997 and November 2000.) State officials therefore face state constitutional barriers against creating modern statutes and regulations defining competence. Litigation like that in Maine and Missouri can help to invalidate sections of some state constitutions. In the meantime, however, voting officials have a lot of work ahead of them to define competence meaningfully.

Surprisingly, even the eight states that focus on the "capacity to vote" provide judges with little or no guidance. Ohio is typical of those states. In a provision adopted in 1851, Ohio's constitution says: "No idiot, or insane person, shall be entitled to the privileges of an elector" (Article V, Constitution of the State of Ohio). Two state provisions enforce this rule. Section 3503.18 of Baldwin's Ohio Revised Code, Title XXXV, requires that: "[a]t least once each month the probate judge shall file with the board [of elections] the names and residences of all persons over eighteen years of age who have been adjudicated incompetent for the purpose of voting, as provided in section 5122.301 of the Revised Code." Likewise, section 5122.301 generally provides that no person judged incompetent loses his or her civil right to vote unless there is an adjudication of incompetence with respect to voting. Despite the language of the state constitution, these rules therefore require a specific determination of incompetence before someone loses the right to vote. But there are no state standards to guide a judge in determining what constitutes competency to vote. An 1869 decision by the Ohio Supreme Court distinguishes between those who are a "lunatic or an idiot" and those who are merely "enfeebled by age," but such a distinction can hardly act as guidance in a modern court proceeding [see *Sinks v. Reese*, 19 Ohio St. 306 (1869)].

Guardianship can be an effective way to protect the health and safety of an individual with mental illness. It can improve the competency of an individual by ensuring that he or she starts taking medication regularly and receives improved nutrition. Yet, historically, courts have not considered the impact of their guardianship decisions on voting even though the overwhelming majority of states routinely disenfranchise individuals under full guardianship. In the 2000 election, we learned that "every vote counts," especially in states like Florida with large numbers of senior citizens who may be under guardianship or living in assisted living settings. Indeed, judges should consider the impact of guardianship on voting when making initial guardianship decisions, and state lawmakers should rethink their system of penalizing individuals for taking steps to protect their health and safety. As the population ages, the disenfranchisement of people under guardianship may increase. New policies thus need to be put in place immediately to deal with this serious problem of disenfranchisement.

Accessibility Problems

Individuals with disabilities frequently face one of two types of problems if they have manual or visual impairments: (1) They are denied the right to a secret ballot, or (2) they are not able to vote at a polling place. Both problems often come into play when individuals with disabilities use absentee ballots. Individuals with disabilities are denied a secret ballot when they must seek third-party assistance in order to vote. Not only is their ballot no longer private, but they also have to worry whether the person assisting them will cast the ballot they intended.

EXAMPLE: One voter explained: "Once, after my wife cast my ballot, she said to me: 'Jim, I know you love me. Now I know that you trust me, because you think I'm marking this ballot for that idiot.' Twice in Massachusetts and once in California, while relying on a poll worker to cast my ballot, the poll worker attempted to change my mind about whom I was voting for. I held firm, but to this day I really do not know if they cast my ballot according to my wishes. To voters with disabilities, there is always some level of uncertainty when another person marks your ballot for you."[4]

Congress has repeatedly sought to protect the rights of disabled individuals who vote, yet little real progress has occurred. The Government Accounting Office studied the accessibility of polling places during the 2000 presidential election. In the context of accessibility, *path of travel* is usually considered to be fundamental. In other words, if one cannot get from the parking lot to the facility, then it is inaccessible. The GAO found that 56 percent of polling places have one or more potential impediments but offer curbside voting, and that 28 percent have one or more potential impediments and do *not* offer curbside voting. It also found that, inside the voting room, *none* of the polling places surveyed have special ballots or voting equipment adapted for blind voters.

Although curbside voting is sometimes made available to individuals with disabilities, this is a controversial solution because it is often difficult to get the attention of poll workers to make curbside voting possible. Plus, the experience can feel intimidating to the voter.

EXAMPLE: Fred Shotz explains: "The sign offering curbside voting to people with disabilities said to speak to the poll deputy but there was nobody outside the polling place. After the deputy came outside a few minutes later I asked him how a person with a disability was supposed to request curbside voting and he stated that I should have pulled up in front of the door and blown my horn. He couldn't answer why there was no sign providing those directions. I sat for quite some time waiting for an opportunity to vote. Three or four times a poll worker came out to tell me that all of the machines were in use plus there were people in line. A voting machine was finally brought out. As the poll worker carrying the machine came out of the door a uniformed Broward Sheriff Deputy came walking up. He stood about 6 feet from the driver's door of my van staring at me. I was not comfortable voting and … I felt like I was in Bosnia with an armed officer just feet from me as I tried to cast a private ballot."[5]

Accessibility problems at polling places include door thresholds that are higher than a half-inch, which wheelchairs cannot traverse; ramps that are too steep to be in ADA compliance; entryways that are too narrow for wheelchair users; and doors that are heavier than compliance standards permit. (This last problem is especially commonplace at places of worship that are used as polling places.) Exterior door handles that require excessive twisting or turning are also not ADA compliant. Inside the facility, steps, narrow interior doorways, and improper door handles are barriers to access. And of course voting stations that are designed for people to stand while voting are not accessible to people who use wheelchairs.

Congress did respond to these problems, in part, with the Help America Vote Act of 2002, 42 U.S.C. § 15301 *et seq.*, which we discuss hereafter. But there is little reason to believe that much has changed since the GAO conducted its survey in 2001. Hence, individuals with disabilities should presume that their polling place will have accessibility problems when they seek to vote. They should try to deal with these problems *in advance of* Election Day in order to guarantee their right to vote independently and privately. Once voters arrive at a polling place on Election Day, they will find it difficult to remedy the accessibility problems that confront them there. But if they know in advance of voting that an accessibility problem exists, they can avail themselves of several potential solutions.

Let us assume, for example, that Mary uses a wheelchair and is assigned to the nearby church for her polling place. As noted in Chapter 5 of this book, churches are exempted from the accessibility requirements of ADA Title III, and they often have accessibility problems. Mary visits the local church and discovers that there is no ramp from the parking lot to the front door. Moreover, she finds that the interior path of travel is too narrow for her wheelchair to enter the room in which voting will take place. Although she could request a temporary ramp to solve the exterior accessibility problem, she realizes that there is no easy solution to the interior accessibility problem.

Mary has three potential options that she could discuss with her local board of elections. First, she can inquire as to whether *curbside* voting will be possible at her polling place. Second, she can inquire whether another polling place has been designated as complying with federal accessibility standards and ask to be transferred to that polling place. Third, she can inquire about voting by absentee ballot.

None of these solutions is ideal, but each is available if she makes an inquiry *in advance of* the election. Curbside voting may seem less private than regular voting and being isolated from other voters may make Mary feel uncomfortable. An alternative polling place may be farther from her house and harder for her to travel to, especially if the weather is poor. And absentee balloting may force her to make her voting decisions well in advance of the election. Nonetheless, each of these options should allow her to vote privately and independently.

By contrast, if she waits until the day of the election to determine that an accessibility problem exists, she may find it difficult to correct the problem. On Election Day, she may need to get the attention of a poll worker to assist her in finding a way to vote. The poll worker may not be qualified to assist her and may not be aware of her options. And if Mary chooses to vote late in the day, the voting period might end before her problem is solved. (Members of the military are allowed to complete their absentee ballots on the day of the election, but few states allow other voters to do likewise.) Mary's only option, then, may be to get permission to vote at another polling place that is accessible, and this would work only if the logistics of entering her name at the other polling place can be quickly solved. Further, Mary would need to find a way to travel to the other location.

Unfortunately, there are few good options for Mary on Election Day. Hence, we urge her to know her rights and exercise them *in ad-vance of* Election Day so that she can cast her ballot privately and independently.

Early Statutory Protections

Congress has been tackling the problem of voting rights for individuals with disabilities since 1965. The 1965 Voting Rights Act contains a provision stating that "[a]ny voter who requires assistance to vote by reason of blindness, disability, or inability to read or write may be given assistance by a person of the voter's choice" (*see* Voting Rights Act of 1965, 42 U.S.C. § 1973 [amended 1984]). The 1965 statute did nothing to correct the problem of access to polling places. It simply eliminated the secret-ballot requirement for individuals with disabilities.

Voting Accessibility for the Elderly and Handicapped Act

In 1984, Congress focused more specifically on the problem of access to polling places with enactment of the Voting Accessibility for the Elderly and Handicapped Act (VAEHA), 42 U.S.C. § 1973ee-1(b). The purpose of this act is "to promote the fundamental right to vote by improving access for handicapped and elderly individuals to registration facilities and polling places for federal elections."

Voter Registration

The VAEHA, which applies only to *federal elections*, contains provisions on registering to vote and voting. With respect to voter registration, the act requires that each state make available

- instructions, printed in large type, conspicuously displayed at each permanent registration facility and each polling place; and
- information by telecommunication devices for the deaf.

Absentee Balloting

The VAEHA also requires that states permit disabled voters to vote by absentee ballot *without* notarization or medical certification, *unless* the individual desires

- to automatically receive an application or a ballot on a continuing basis, or
- to apply for an absentee ballot after the deadline has passed.

The act defines *an individual with a disability* broadly as including anyone who has "a temporary or permanent physical disability." A temporary broken leg is therefore a disability under the VAEHA, even though it is not a disability under ADA. Absentee voting may not be the desirable or preferable option for an individual with a disability, but the 1984 act does provide that it must be an option for disabled voters.

The VAEHA also contains provisions designed to improve the accessibility of polling places. On the one hand, it provides that each political subdivision responsible for conducting elections must ensure that *all* polling places for federal elections are accessible to disabled voters. On the other hand, it provides that disabled voters may make an advance request to be assigned to an accessible polling place or be provided with an alternate means of casting a ballot on the day of the election if they have been assigned to an inaccessible polling place. Despite requiring that all polling places be accessible, Congress apparently contemplated that this requirement would not be met. It therefore mandated that voters have the option of requesting an accessible polling place or an alternative method of voting. Curbside voting is often the alternate method made available when polling places are inaccessible.

Enforcement

Although the VAEHA has some good provisions, its enforcement mechanism is extremely weak. The U.S. Attorney General or a person who is personally aggrieved by noncompliance may bring an action for declaratory or injunctive relief in federal court, but only if the person first provides forty-five days' notice to the chief election officer of the state in which the noncompliance has occurred. Further, no award of attorney fees may be made with respect to an enforcement action under this section of the VAEHA.

In practice, this enforcement scheme means that few will use the judicial system to redress noncompliance with the act. If an individual with a disability discovers on Election Day that he or she is unable to vote due to an inaccessible facility, it won't do much good to give the state forty-five days' notice and then bring suit. The opportunity to vote during that election has already been lost. Further, it will be very difficult to find a lawyer to bring such an action because few voters can afford to pay a lawyer an hourly rate for such an action, and the lawyer cannot collect attorney fees from the state if the action is successful. Public interest organizations might bring such an action, but they have many potential lawsuits competing for their time. And although the U.S. Attorney General could possibly bring an enforcement action, the forty-five-day rule also applies to the Attorney General.

Nevertheless, disabled voters may wish to pursue judicial action. If so, they can file a complaint with the U.S. Attorney General. The Attorney General's contact information is Voting Section, Civil Rights Division, U.S. Department of Justice, P.O. Box 66128, Washington, D.C. 20035-6128; 800-253-3931 (voice/relay); www.usdoj. gov/crt/voting.

Voluntary Compliance

Given the limited judicial remedies available under the 1984 act, voluntary compliance is a very important mechanism for voting by individuals with disabilities. As discussed earlier, one requirement of the VAEHA is that states make available an alternative polling place when an individual's regular polling place is inaccessible. But to take advantage of this rule, voters need to learn of the accessibility problem in advance of the election. Many states have an easy process for requesting an accessible means of voting. In Pennsylvania, for example, disabled voters can obtain a form that allows them to request an alternative means for casting a ballot. This form requires that they identify the nature of their disability. It must be received *seven days before* Election Day. The seven-day rule, however, can be waived "where circumstances arise unexpectedly." Upon receipt of the written request, the County Board of Elections provides an individual with an alternative ballot that may be returned to the County Board of Elections any time before Election Day or returned to an accessible location designated by the County Board of Elections between the hours of 7 A.M. and 8 P.M. on Election Day. Though similar to an absentee ballot, this method allows an individual to vote as late as Election Day itself.

As in many states, Pennsylvania's means of seeking an alternative ballot presumes that an individual can complete a form and sign it. Interestingly, the application for an alternative ballot form does ask whether the individual needs assistance to complete the alternative ballot. Of course, many people who need assistance in completing an alternative ballot would also need assistance with completing the application for an alternative ballot. Presumably, accommodations are made upon request when an individual cannot complete the alternative ballot application.

Americans with Disabilities Act

In theory, the enactment of the Americans with Disabilities Act in 1990 should have helped create additional remedies for disabled voters. ADA Title II, which covers public entities—a category that includes state government—requires accessibility to programs, services, and activities offered by such entities. Since voting and elections are covered programs, state as well as federal elections are covered by this statute.

The Federal Election Commission has adopted voluntary guidelines for state election officials that would result in ADA compliance. Schools and other public facilities covered by ADA Title II are also required to be accessible to the public, irrespective of whether they are polling places. Those general accessibility requirements, however, do not apply to the method of polling. They apply only to access to the building itself.

Bear in mind that one advantage of using ADA to attain polling place access is that a broader set of remedies may be available. Attorney fees are available to the prevailing party making pro bono litigation more feasible. And unlike the VAEHA, which requires forty-five days' notice, ADA contains no procedural requirements to bring suit. Nonetheless, it is likely that the only relief available under ADA Title II, as with the various voting rights statutes, would be injunctive relief—*prospective* relief in which one asks a state official to refrain from certain future conduct or for the court to make a declaration about the unlawfulness of certain conduct. ADA Title II is therefore not a much more potent weapon than the specific statutes written to cover voting issues. The major importance of ADA Title II is that it covers *state* elections, not just federal elections like the VAEHA.

Some important and successful litigation has gone forward under ADA Title II. In 2000, the New York Attorney General brought a suit on behalf of disabled voters to require several counties to make their polling places compliant with ADA. This suit resulted in injunctive relief and set the important precedent that a state Attorney General could sue on behalf of disabled voters [*see People of New York ex rel. Spitzer v. County of Delaware*, 82 F. Supp.2d 12 (N.D. N.Y. 2000)]. But as with most voting rights litigation, the relief was fairly limited. The county was required to make elections accessible to the extent that such compliance was feasible by Election Day.

Of course, in situations where counties are not complying with ADA accessibility requirements, voters should consider petitioning their state Attorney General for a lawsuit on their behalf.

Help America Vote Act

President George W. Bush signed the Help America Vote Act (HAVA), 42 U.S.C. § 15301 *et seq.*, into law on October 29, 2002. HAVA gives states significant financial incentives to implement accessibility, but it does not provide specific standards or guidelines on the definition of accessibility. Instead, it simply reaffirms the applicability of existing standards such as those found under ADA and VAEHA. The only new substantive standard is that, by January 1, 2006, every polling place in the county must have at least one voting system that is accessible to individuals with disabilities. Given that the VAEHA had already mandated that all polling places be accessible, this was not much of a new requirement.

HAVA is stronger than previous laws in specifying that individuals are to have access to secret and independent voting opportunities. It states that voting systems shall be "accessible for individuals with disabilities, including nonvisual accessibility for the blind and visually impaired, in a manner that provides the same opportunity for access and participation (including privacy and independence) as for other voters" [42 U.S.C. § 15481(a)(3)]. There are limited options, however, to enforce this right. The Attorney General may bring an enforcement action or an individual can pursue state-created administrative processes (42 U.S.C. §§ 15511 and 15522). HAVA provides for no private right of action.

As of April 2005, many states are making decisions about what voting technology to purchase to comply with HAVA. Individuals with disabilities need to be actively engaged with their states as they make such decisions. In Ohio, for example, the Secretary of State initially appeared to be considering approval of new voting equipment that was unlikely to allow voters with visual impairments to vote independently and confidentially. However, partly as a result of pressure from the disability-rights community, he extended his list of purchases to include technology that could easily be made handicapped accessible. Voting technology decisions can be crucial to the attainment of accessibility.

Although Congress authorized more than $2 billion to be spent on implementation of HAVA, Congress had appropriated only a fraction of that money as of late 2004. Money dedicated to accessibility has been particularly hard hit. Congress allocated only $13 million of the $50 million set aside for making polling places accessible, and only $2 million of the $10 million intended for protection and advocacy systems that were supposed to assist voting by individuals with disabilities. Congress appropriated no money whatsoever for research grants to improve voting technology or for pilot programs.

Enforcement Problems

One problem with creating voting accessibility is that private schools and churches are often used for polling places. Since these entities are not controlled by the public, it is very difficult to ensure their accessibility. As noted earlier in this chapter, as well as in Chapter 5, places of worship were exempted from the Americans with Disabilities Act, so it is particularly difficult to insist that they be accessible. Not surprisingly, the GAO found that 18 percent of all polling places are houses of worship and that 82 percent of these entities have at least one potential impediment to accessibility.[6]

State law supplements federal law with respect to voting accessibility, but it rarely provides meaningful protection, especially for visually impaired voters. Only a few states require the provision of Braille or large-type ballots, and most states do not require even the provision of magnifying instruments.[7] As a practical matter, therefore, visually impaired voters cannot vote independently if audio-visual accommodations are not provided.

Many states try to deal with accessibility problems by encouraging disabled individuals to use absentee ballots. These, however, are not a good solution. Absentee ballots typically require individuals to take the proactive step of deciding whom to vote for in advance of the election. But individuals with disabilities, like everyone else, deserve to be able to make up their minds at the last minute. Moreover, absentee ballots do not help blind voters, who often cannot vote independently with absentee ballots.

Blind voters are trying to get states to adopt easy-to-use audio-voting systems, but few states have such technology. In addition, some people criticize such technology because it may pose security problems. A *New York Times* editorial pointed out that such machines do not create a paper record of votes cast and thus remain vulnerable to vote theft. For example, Maryland purchased some touch-screen voting machines with audio-headphones and determined that it would be an easy matter to reprogram the access cards used by voters and vote multiple times. The use of touch-screen machines without a paper trail remains a controversial issue. In the meantime, states are reluctant to offer private, independent technology to visually impaired voters.

Under state law, blind voters typically have two options at the poll: Bring in a friend or rely on poll workers to assist them, purportedly without suggestion or interference. Unfortunately, poll workers have been known to make suggestions as visually impaired voters try to vote, causing the voters to lose confidence in whether their actual votes are being recorded. Blind voters typically describe voting as demoralizing, embarrassing, or simply an invasion of their privacy. But, ironically, they lack the political clout to get the federal government to allocate sufficient funds to create accessible and confidential balloting for them.

Another enforcement problem is that injunctive relief—as noted earlier, *prospective* relief in which one asks a state official to refrain from certain future conduct or for the court to make a declaration about the unlawfulness of certain conduct—is frequently the only relief available in litigation in the voting rights area. Sometimes, attorney fees are not even available to the prevailing party. Knowing that they have to fear only injunctive relief, governmental entities have little incentive to comply with federal law. Thus, the GAO has found little voting rights compliance. When parties obtain injunctive relief and a governmental entity refuses to comply with the court order, the only recourse is to seek civil or criminal contempt. Contempt is an unusual remedy, but, in that context, a court could order a civil fine until the governmental entity obtains compliance. We are unaware of instances in which that remedy has been used in the disability voting context, but, in theory, it is an option.

Judicial Intervention

In *Tennesee v. Lane*, 541 U.S. 409 (2004), the Supreme Court implied that access to voting booths is a fundamental right under the U.S. Constitution. Possibly, litigants will use that ruling in the future to challenge accessibility barriers that limit their ability to vote.

Prior to the *Lane* decision, however, litigation was not a fruitful option for voters with disabilities. In Michigan, for example, disabled voters challenged a state statute that provided that the state may require a blind person to accept assistance to mark his or her ballot. They argued that this statute violated their right to vote in secrecy, and that they must be provided with technology that would permit them to vote independently and privately. The Sixth Circuit held that the Michigan statute was lawful and constitutional. [*See Nelson v. Miller*, 170 F.3d 641 (6th Cir. 1999). *But see also American Ass'n of People With Disabilities v. Smith*, 227 F.Supp.2d 1276 (M.D. Fla. 2002) (holding that disabled voters stated claims under ADA by alleging that state election officials failed to approve voting systems that would permit visually and manually impaired voters to vote without assistance); *American Ass'n of People with Disabilities v. Hood*, 310 F. Supp. 2d 1226 (M.D. Fla. 2004) (holding that a county elections supervisor violated ADA regulations in utilizing an optical scan voting system; visually impaired voters could not use this system without third-party assistance, and manually impaired voters could have voted unassisted using touch-screen technology).] HAVA contains specific language about the importance of private and independent voting for individuals with visual impairments but, so far, there has been no case law implementing HAVA's requirements (which do not go into effect until 2006).

Nonjudicial Options

In some cases, individuals with disabilities have used the media to publicize their accessibility problems and achieved some positive results. For example, Nina Moore of Fairmont, West Virginia, had voted by absentee ballot all her life because her polling place was not accessible. In 1998, however, her ballot never arrived. She called various local government officials but was told that they could not do anything for her, because the time period for receiving an absentee ballot had passed. She then called the local newspapers, television stations, and radio stations. Some of them met her outside her inaccessible polling place. Suddenly, the city clerk showed up, saying she had obtained "special permission from the capital" to bring Ms. Moore a curbside ballot. Moore's persistence led to a front-page newspaper article and, ultimately, to legislation in West Virginia that was entitled "The Nina Moore Amendment." Under this new state law, voters with disabilities are allowed to vote from their cars if their polling places are inaccessible. Clearly, barriers to voting can capture media attention.

Voting Resources

The following websites offer helpful information for voters with disabilities:

Department of Justice
http://www.usdoj.gov/crt/voting/hava/hava.html

Department of Justice ADA Checklist for Polling Places
www.ada.gov/votingck.htm

American Association of People with Disabilities
www.aapd-dc.org/dvpmain/newdvpindex.html

Center for an Accessible Society
http://www.accessiblesociety.org/topics/voting/

Federal Election Commission
www.fec.gov/hava/hava.htm

HAVAccess Newsletter
http://www.inclusionsolutions.com/main.php?page=hava
  resources

National Organization on Disability "Get Out the Vote" manual
www.nod.org/pdffiles/get_out_the_vote.txt

National Organization on Disability
www.nod.org/election2004.html

Conclusion

The right to vote is fundamental in our society. The Help America
Vote Act is an important development that may enhance the accessibility of voting for individuals with disabilities. As we write this book
in early 2005, however, it is hard to know whether HAVA will be effective. On the one hand, unfortunately, the judicial remedies existing
under voting rights laws for individuals with disabilities are weak. On
the other hand, the media have been important allies in seeking exposure to voting problems. As with other areas of the law, we urge our
readers to document voting accessibility problems and bring them to
the attention of the media and government. We hope that increased
availability of early voting and new technology may improve the situation for voters with disabilities. But history suggests that it will take
much vigilance for progress to continue to occur.

Notes

1. United States, Government Accounting Office, "Voters with
Disabilities: Access to Polling Place and Alternative Voting Methods," vol. 14
(October 2001). Fully accessible version available online at http://www.
gao.gov/special.pubs/d02107.txt.(Hereafter referred to as "GAO Study.")
2. Michael Waterstone, "Civil Rights and the Administration of
Elections—Toward Secret Ballots and Polling Place Access," *Journal of
Gender, Race and Justice*, vol. 8 (2004), pp. 101, 106.
3. See Kay Schriner et al., "Democratic Dilemmas: Notes on the ADA
and Voting Rights of People with Cognitive and Emotional Impairments,"
Berkeley Journal of Employment and Labor Law, vol. 21 (2000), pp. 437,
439, 456 (including Table 2).

4. Waterstone, *Civil Rights and the Administration of Elections*, pp. 101, 107.

5. Hollister Bundy, "Election Reform, Polling Place Accessibility, and the Voting Rights of the Disabled," *Election Law Journal*, vol. 2 (2003), pp. 217, 225.

6. GAO Study at 29.

7. GAO Study at 17.

9
Conclusion

We have enjoyed writing this book because it has given us an opportunity to think of creative solutions to legal problems that don't require hiring an attorney and filing a lawsuit. Indeed, we hope that our readers have benefited from our suggestions by becoming better self-advocates.

In Chapter 2, we discussed the problem of employment discrimination. It was difficult to make constructive suggestions in the employment discrimination area because the courts have been very unsympathetic to most claims of discrimination brought by individuals with disabilities. Nonetheless, we have found that certain steps can enhance the chances of resolving an employment discrimination problem in a voluntary, positive manner. First, we encourage people to get a written report from a licensed medical professional documenting that they are individuals with a disability. It is important that the licensed professional understand the nature of the job that the disabled individual is seeking so that he or she can comment on the individual's ability to perform the job's essential functions. For that matter, it is also a good idea for a disabled employee to request that such a report be made part of his or her employment file so that an employer cannot deny having knowledge that the individual is disabled.

Sometimes, individuals with disabilities require accommodations to perform the essential functions of the job. Many accommodations do not cost anything at all, and the typical accommodation costs only $300. Hence disabled individuals should not be overly concerned about seeking such accommodations.

In fact, it is their responsibility to do so. An employer is required to engage in an interactive process with a disabled individual who requests an accommodation. But it is not fair to blame an employer for not coming up with an accommodation if the employee does not request one. Accordingly, we have included information in Chapter 2 about resources that can help people identify reasonable accommodations. Although we are not so naïve as to think that all employers are willing to provide accommodations, we also know that many employers would feel uncomfortable suggesting an accommodation without a request from the employee. Occasionally, we have even seen employees who are pleasantly surprised with their employer's reaction to a request; they had discounted the employer's interest in keeping loyal, highly qualified employees on the job. Even in situations where an employer believes that he or she could prevail in court and avoid granting a requested accommodation, it may still be in the employer's interest to maintain good workplace morale by providing a reasonable accommodation.

Employees may nonetheless find themselves in difficult situations with no easy solution in sight. Consider, for example, the fact that employers are not permitted to require people applying for employment to take a medical examination *before* being offered a job. Not all employers are aware of that requirement and sometimes unintentionally violate the law. What should a job applicant do if an employer insists that she take a medical exam before being offered a job? If she complains about the requirement, she may look like a less desirable potential employee. But if she takes the exam, she risks having the employer learn about an invisible disability and then engage in discriminatory behavior. In such a situation, the employee must use her best judgment. If she is confident that the employer is likely to offer her the job despite the results of the (illegal) exam, she might take the exam, get offered the position, and then tell the employer afterward that the medical exam was unlawful and should be discontinued in advance of subsequent job offers. If the job is not offered after she takes the exam, she still would have the option of pursuing litigation to challenge an unlawful exam. Although we realize that litigation is a tough route, there is no doubt that requiring a medical exam before offering a job offer is unlawful.

Unfortunately, disabled individuals often find themselves in difficult and unpredictable situations. Should an individual with an invisible disability disclose it to a potential employer? Should a person with a visible disability who has been invited to a job interview disclose the disability in advance of the interview? Should individuals who need accommodations request those accommodations in advance of receiving a job offer, or should they do so shortly thereafter? In general, we have found that employers and others respond better to disclosures about disability status after having a chance to get to know a person. Early disclosure can promote the use of stereotypes. But waiting to disclose (when disclosure is inevitable) can be very stressful and inconsistent with the way someone wants to live his or her life. Thus, we are not trying to give the reader a magic formula. Instead, our aim is simply to suggest that the reader think about the range of options in a given situation and decide what works best for him or her.

In Chapter 3, we discussed K–12 education. The education arena presents a somewhat different set of complications. In the K–12 context, a parent or guardian typically has to make decisions on behalf of a child with a disability. That is a heavy responsibility for a parent. Some parents are reluctant to identify their child as disabled out of the fear that such labeling will engender stereotypical thinking on the part of the teacher. But federal law specifies that parents can ask for special assistance for their child only if the child is first identified as disabled. Privacy is therefore rarely an option if the child needs extra resources.

We have found that, on the whole, parents' active involvement in the educational process creates more positive outcomes for children. But, unfortunately, not all parents are qualified to act as effective advocates for their children. If any of our readers know of a child who is not receiving effective advocacy from a parent, we urge them to try to get involved or (if possible) to assist. Parents are permitted to bring another person with them to meetings held under the auspices of the Individuals with Disabilities Education Act (IDEA)—and, indeed, Professor Colker has been training students in law and allied health to assist parents who recognize that they would benefit from additional assistance. In Chapter 3, we provide a sample letter as well as advocacy tips for people involved in the educational advocacy process. We hope that those suggestions can help provide disabled children with more effective advocates.

In Chapter 4, we discussed postsecondary education. The postsecondary setting presents its own set of challenges. Children with disabilities often grow accustomed to having a parent or guardian advocate on their behalf under IDEA. But when they arrive at postsecondary school, IDEA no longer applies, and the students (and parents) have to learn how to seek accommodations in a new system under a university or other institution's disability coordinator's office. Many universities have good disability coordinator's offices. We encourage students with disabilities who are considering postsecondary education to learn about the quality of those offices *before* enrolling. Once enrolled, students have an obligation to try to take advantage of whatever services are provided. Nonetheless, the university setting can present substantial challenges to students with disabilities because they may have multiple professors who have differing understandings of their obligations toward such students. In addition, the physical campus may be much larger than a high school campus, causing significant transportation and accessibility issues — especially in adverse weather. The university's disability coordinator should be able to help a student navigate the challenges of a large campus. (And if the disability coordinator *cannot* provide that kind of assistance, then the student may have made an error in selecting the university. Unfortunately, the student might have to consider transferring to another university, if doing so is at all possible.)

It is important for a student, nonetheless, to understand the difference between a high school's obligations under IDEA and a university's obligations under ADA. ADA is an antidiscrimination statute, whereas IDEA is an entitlement statute (to some extent). IDEA promises each child a free and appropriate education. ADA promises each student a nondiscriminatory educational environment. Under ADA, a student must be *qualified* to receive services. Under IDEA, all students are entitled to an education. Thus, college students may find that they have to pay for therapy or other services that they received for free under IDEA. On the other hand, universities have an interest in retaining their students so that they can receive their tuition dollars and have successful graduates. We have therefore found that universities are sometimes more cooperative in dealing with students with disabilities than the law would appear to require. They simply perceive that it is good public relations to accommodate students with disabilities.

As part of their classroom work at Ohio State University, Professor Colker's students work directly with the ADA coordinator to make recommendations to improve the accessibility of the campus. The students get enormous satisfaction from seeing the university accept some of their recommendations. They also get a better real-world sense of the law relating to disability discrimination by engaging in such practical work. We do not know of other universities that have created such a connection with an ADA course, but we encourage our readers to try to create a similar connection in their community.

In Chapter 5, we discussed accessibility. Obtaining greater accessibility, particularly at the structures that house public entities (state and local governments), can be very difficult. A decade after Congress enacted the ADA, many public entities had still not created wheelchair-accessible sidewalks as required by the ADA. It took extensive and successful litigation by disability advocates for many branches of local government to make accessible sidewalks a basic feature of the local landscape. Even where curb ramps are provided, they have often been installed incorrectly, and the disability community risks looking like a bunch of whiners for complaining about poorly constructed curb ramps. When construction is obviously faulty, however, we have found that the local media can sometimes be enlisted to demonstrate the inadequacy of the city's work. In this chapter we also provide sample letters and advocacy tips for people involved in the accessibility advocacy process. As before, we hope those suggestions can help people become more effective advocates.

In Chapter 6, we discussed transportation. Transportation problems can also be thorny to deal with. As in many other areas of the law, monetary damages are not likely in transportation cases, and lawyers are rarely willing to take such cases given the low risk of attorney fees. The transportation industry, however, does have an interest in maintaining a good relationship with the public. Indeed, Professor Milani has found that he can sometimes get a voucher for a free ticket when the airlines misplace his power wheelchair. Transportation problems can really ruin vacation plans, and we therefore strongly encourage people to think in advance about what their accessibility needs are so that these can be resolved in advance. We have found that simply because an organized event advertises itself as accessible does not mean that the organizers have genuinely thought through the needs of the community of individuals with disabilities. Disabled individuals must engage in fact gathering *before* a trip in order to avoid disappointment. We sincerely hope that people take such steps so that they can enjoy traveling and not feel confined due to the artificial transportation barriers created by society.

In Chapter 7, we discussed housing. Housing accessibility is possible in privately owned housing, but typically only for those people who can afford to make their own rental units accessible. The Fair Housing Act Amendments require landlords to allow renters with disabilities to make modifications to improve accessibility, but a landlord can request that the structure be returned to its original condition at the expiration of the lease. The individual with a disability may therefore be confronted by *two* expenses—at both the beginning and the end of the lease. Some landlords, however, are not even aware that individuals with disabilities are entitled to modify an apartment to make it more accessible. Self-advocacy may be effective in situations where the landlord understands that he or she does not bear the expense involved. But of course some renters cannot afford to make the accommodations themselves. Federal law provides no recourse for such individuals. Bear in mind, however, that housing financed by the federal government *is* an option in such cases; accordingly, we discuss a HUD website that includes an inventory designed to assist prospective applicants with locating units in HUD-insured and HUD-subsidized multifamily properties that serve the elderly and/or persons with disabilities.

In Chapter 8, we discussed voting. The right to vote may be basic to our system of government but it has not been basic to the lives of many individuals with disabilities. Under the recently enacted Help America Vote Act (HAVA), we should see increased accessibility by 2006. However, it is not clear that state and local governments will follow HAVA given their history of ignoring federal voting law requirements. Visually impaired voters, in particular, should be aware that in 2006 federal law will require that they be provided with a confidential and independent method of voting in local elections. Even now, all voters with disabilities are entitled to curbside voting if they cannot get to the voting booth. Although we are going to press less than a year before the stricter HAVA rules come into effect, we have seen little indication of how various states intend to meet HAVA's requirements. If these requirements are ignored during the next national election, we hope that people engage in self-advocacy through the media to bring this problem to the public's attention. The media have been an effective vehicle in effectuating change with respect to voting. But the judicial system has been too slow and cumbersome to provide much relief here.

We have provided an extensive list of state and federal resources in the Appendix that contain good information about insurance benefits. The reader might want to look at those resources closely to determine whether any of them might help disabled individuals find affordable health insurance. Until our country generally improves its delivery of health care services, it is unlikely that a judicial strategy will be successful for people who have been denied health insurance for disability-related reasons.

At this point, we are concerned that the reader may feel discouraged because each chapter in this book has demonstrated the limited effectiveness of judicial remedies for individuals with disabilities who face discrimination. Although we have been able to suggest some self-help strategies, we have no proof that those strategies are frequently effective. Nonetheless, we do not feel pessimistic about the future for individuals with disabilities. Students in architecture schools are being taught principles of universal design so that they can help to build accessible structures. Schools are generally effective in their efforts to identify disabled children as such and to offer them individualized education plans as part of their education. Employers no longer routinely make job applicants take physical examinations before offering employment. Most cities have curb cuts that allow wheelchair users to get around city streets. Airports routinely make wheelchairs available to the traveling public. And it is even possible that HAVA's reforms will be implemented by 2006 so that more individuals with disabilities can vote confidentially and independently.

The last decade has been a transformative one for individuals with disabilities. With the assistance of some of the information and suggestions found in this book, we hope that the next decade can be equally transformative. Obviously, we are still at a point where such a book is needed. But we hope that there are equally obvious reasons to believe that transformation will continue.

Appendix: National and State Resources

Throughout this book, we have tried to offer practical information concerning the rights of individuals with disabilities. We have explained the legal rules that apply to a particular topic and often suggested strategies other than litigation that might help resolve a problem. The advice that we have been able to offer is limited. An individual with a serious legal problem should consider retaining an attorney. In the pages below, we list resources that exist at both the federal and state level, respectively, to assist individuals with disabilities. We have attempted to provide complete contact information where available, but some of these resources are Internet sites only. We cannot vouch for the quality of each of these organizations, but they should serve as a useful starting point in gathering more information.

Several websites are particularly helpful in listing resources by state. Contact information for local Centers for Independent Living can be found at http://www.ilru.org/Directory. *Disability Resources Monthly*, available at http://www.disabilityresources.org, links to websites for government agencies and private organizations in each state. For a state-by-state list of governor's committees that support employment and rehabilitation of people with disabilities, go to http://www.jan.wvu.edu/cgi-win/TypeQuery. exe?370.

This resource list was prepared by Christina "Cricket" Nardacci, who is a law student at the Moritz College of Law and a Ph.D. student at the School of Education at Ohio State University. We are deeply indebted to Cricket for her extraordinary work on this listing of resources.

National Resources

Civil Rights and General Resources
American Association of People with Disabilities (AAPD)
1629 K Street NW, Suite 503
Washington, DC 20006
Phone: 202-457-0046 (also TDD)
          800-840-8844 (also TDD)
E-mail: aapd@aol.com
Website: www.aapd-dc.org

The AAPD is the largest national nonprofit cross-disability member organization in the United States, dedicated to ensuring economic self-sufficiency and political empowerment for the more than 56 million Americans with disabilities. AAPD works in coalition with other disability organizations for the full implementation and enforcement of disability nondiscrimination laws, particularly the Americans with Disabilities Act (ADA) of 1990 and the Rehabilitation Act of 1973.

Architectural and Transportation Barriers Access Board
Office of Compliance and Enforcement
1331 F St. NW, Suite 1000
Washington, DC 20004-1111
Phone: (202) 272-0080
          (800) 872-2253
          (202) 272-0082 (TDD)
          (800) 993-2822 (TDD)
Fax: (202) 272-0081
Website: http://www.access-board.gov

This office enforces the Americans with Disabilities Act (ADA) and Architectural Barriers Act. The new ADA guidelines can be found at http://www.access-board.gov/ada-aba/Blue%20html/ADAABA%20Guidelines%20Blue.htm, the ADA Architectural Guidelines (ADAAG) can be found at http://www.access-board.gov/adaag/html/adaag.htm, and the ABA's Uniform Federal Accessibility Standards (UFAS) can be found at http://www.access-board.gov/ufas/ufas-html/ufas.htm. Publications from the Access Board, including copies in alternate formats (Braille, large print, audiocassette, or disk) can also be ordered at pubs@access-board.gov. Complaints regarding accessibility problems with buildings covered by ABA may be made to this office online at http://www.access-board.gov/enforcement/form-email.htm, via mail, or by telephone.

Bazelon Center for Mental Health Law
1101 15th Street, NW, Suite 1212
Washington, DC 20005
Phone: (202) 467-5730
Fax: (202) 223-0409
Email: webmaster@bazelon.org
Website: http://www.bazelon.org

Bazelon is a national legal advocacy center for people with mental disabilities. The website provides information sheets that discuss issues such as the "reasonable accommodation" clause of the ADA as it pertains to cases of eviction because of a tenant's "disturbing" behavior, the ADA's application to insurance coverage, and more.

Center for an Accessible Society
2980 Beech Street
San Diego, CA 92102
Phone: (619) 232-2727
Website: www.accessiblesociety.org

This organization provides information to the media about people with disabilities and their lives.

Center for Disability Resources Library
University of South Carolina
School of Medicine Library
Columbia, SC 29208
Phone: (803)733-3361
Fax: (803)733-1509
Email: asklib@med.sc.edu
Website: http://uscm.med.sc.edu/CDR/otherlibraries.htm

This website provides links to state libraries affiliated with University Centers for Excellence in Developmental Disabilities Education, Research, and Service (UCEDD). Some libraries serve residents in more than one state.

Center for Personal Assistance Services
Department of Social & Behavioral Sciences
University of California San Francisco
3333 California Street, Suite 455
San Francisco, CA 94118
Phone: (415) 502-7190
            (866) 727-9577

TDD: (415) 502-5216
Website: http://www.pascenter.org

Provides support and resources for personal assistance service users, along with links to state data.

Center on Human Policy
Syracuse University
805 South Crouse Avenue
Syracuse, NY 13244-2280
Phone: (315) 443-3581
          (800) 894-0826
          (315) 443-4355 (TDD)
          (315) 443-4338 (fax)
Website: http://soeweb.syr.edu/thechp.index.html

This website provides numerous disability-related resources and links.

Disability Rights Education and Defense Fund
2212 Sixth Street
Berkeley, CA 94710
Phone: (510) 644-2555 (also TDD)
E-Mail: dredf@dredf.org
Website: http://www.dredf.org

This organization provides legal resources for people with disabilities and parents of children with disabilities.

Doris Day Animal League
227 Massachusetts Avenue NE, Suite 100
Washington, DC 20002
Phone: (202) 546-1761
Fax: (202) 546-2193
Website: http://www.ddal.org

Describes resources for service animals. Publishes an incredibly thorough pamphlet called Best Friends for Life, which discusses the rights of people with disabilities to have service animal resources in rental housing.

JustCan.com
20 D Tamarac Drive
Greenville, RI 02828
Phone: (401) 949-1119
Fax: (425) 740-9726
Website: http://justcan.com

Describes state-based and local resources for people in the entire disability community.

New Freedom Initiative
Website: http://www.disabilityinfo.gov

This is the federal government guide to disability resources. The website contains links to information about civil rights, education, employment, health, housing, income support, independent living, technology, and transportation.

U.S. Department of Justice (DOJ)
Civil Rights Division
Disability Rights Section
950 Pennsylvania Avenue, NW
Washington, DC 20530
Phone: (800) 514-0301
          (800) 514-0383 (TDD)
Website: http://www.usdoj.gov/crt/drs/drshome.htm

This website provides numerous links to documents about ADA regulations, building codes, and technical assistance materials, including forms that can assist in filing a complaint with the Department of Justice. It also contains a guide to disability rights laws including information on Section 508 of the Rehabilitation Act, Executive Order 12250, and frequently asked questions about the Americans with Disabilities Act. For information regarding requirements about accessibility of electronic and information technology, go to http://www.usdoj.gov/crt/508/report/exec.htm. A list of agencies designated to investigate disability-related discrimination complaints can be found at http://www.usdoj.gov/crt/ada/investig.htm. Some information is available in Spanish, and printed materials can be ordered 24 hours a day by calling the automated ADA information line.

Community and Family Services
ADAPT
201 S. Cherokee
Denver, CO 80223
Phone: (303) 733-9324
or
1339 Lamar Square Drive, Suite 101
Austin, TX 78704

Phone: (512) 442-0252
Website: http://www.adapt.org

ADAPT focuses on promoting community services for people with disabilities and their families. The website contains links to other national and state contacts. Text version also available.

Family Village Community Center
Website: http://www.familyvillage.wisc.edu/index.htmlx

A guide to regional disability-related resources including accessible schools, universities, bookstores, recreation centers, community centers, libraries, hospitals, and houses of worship.

Focus Adolescent Services
Phone: (410) 341-4342
           (877) 362-8727
Website: http://www.focusas.com/index.html

Internet clearinghouse of information, resources, and support for families with troubled and at-risk teens.

The MENTOR Network
Website: http://www.thementornetwork.com

This network brings together people and services to create community-based programs for adults and children with developmental disabilities, children with emotional and behavioral challenges, and individuals with acquired brain injury. The website offers links to states in which the MENTOR network has offices (does not include all 50 states).

National Center on Education, Disability, and Juvenile Justice
University of Maryland
1224 Benjamin Building
College Park, MD 20742
Phone: (301) 405-6462
Fax: (301) 314-5757
E-mail: edjj@umail.umd.edu
Website: http://www.edjj.org/conf/featuredspeakers.htm

This website offers resources for parents of children with disabilities in the juvenile justice system. Some information is translated into Spanish.

National Organization on Disability
910 16th Street, NW, Suite 600
Washington, DC 20006

Phone: (202) 293-5960
            (202) 293-5968 (TDD)
Fax: (202) 293-7999
E-mail: ability@nod.org
Website: http://www.nod.org

This website offers a large range of links in three categories: community involvement, economic participation, and access to independence.

Special Olympics
1325 G Street, NW, Suite 500
Washington, DC 20005
Phone: (202) 628-3630
Website: http://www.specialolympics.org/Special+Olympics+Public+
            Website/ default.htm

The Special Olympics website includes links for schools and youth and for family leadership and support, with a primary focus on supporting families with youth who participate in Special Olympics programs.

Education
Advocacy Consortium for College Students with Disabilities
Community Learning Development Center
2550 Baird Road
Penfield, New York 14526
Phone: (585) 264-1090
Website: http://www.ggw.org/users/advocacyconsortium

Educational Testing Service (ETS)
Rosedale Road
Princeton, NJ 08541
Phone: (609) 921-9000
Fax: (609) 734-5410
Website: http://www.ets.org/disability

This website offers information about accommodations for tests administered by ETS, such as the AP, GMAT, GRE, and SAT. Other related sites include: ACT at http://www.act.org/aap/disab/policy.html; College Boards at http://www.collegeboard.com/disable/students/html/indx000.html; LSAT at http://www.lsat.org/LSAC.asp?url=lsac/accommodated-testing.asp; and MCAT at http://www.aamc.org/students/mcat/about/ada2003.pdf. Financial aid information can be found at http://www.heath.gwu.edu/PDFs/financialaid.pdf.

GreatSchools.net
Website: http://www.greatschools.net

This website provides school information for public, private, and charter schools nationwide. There are links available for all fifty states; detailed school profiles available for Arizona, California, Florida, Texas, and Washington.

Individualized Education Program (IEP) meeting
   preparation tips
Websites: http://www.parentsunitedtogether.com/page22.html
             http://www.geocities.com/Athens/Oracle/1580/preparing_
                for_iep.html
             http://add.about.com/cs/education/a/iepmeetings.htm

Individualized Family Service Plan (IFSP) meeting
   preparation tips
Websites: http://nncf.unl.edu/nncf.go.ifsp.html
             http://www.answers4families.org/IFSPWeb
             http://ericec.org/digests/e605.html

Internet Special Education Resources (ISER)
Phone: (301) 230-9010
            or (301) 649-6207
Fax: (240) 465-0050
Website: http://www.iser.com

Nationwide directory of professionals who serve the learning disabilities and special education communities.

LDonLine
c/o WETA
2775 South Quincy St.
Arlington, VA 22206
Phone: (703) 998-2600
Fax: (703) 998-3401
Website: http://www.ldonline.org

This website provides information on learning disabilities for parents, teachers, and other professionals. It includes separate links specifically for parents, kids, teachers, and volunteers. The site provides a state-by-state index for finding help, which also includes some territories and the District of Columbia.

Learning Disabilities Association of America (LDA)
4156 Library Road

Pittsburgh, PA 15234-1349
Phone: (412) 341-1515
Fax: (412) 344-0224
Website: http://www.ldanatl.org

This organization provides information for parents and teachers of children with learning disabilities.

National Center on Secondary Education and Transition
Institute on Community Integration
University of Minnesota
6 Pattee Hall
150 Pillsbury Drive SE
Minneapolis, MN 55455
Phone: (612) 624-2097
Fax: (612) 624-9344
E-mail: ncset@umn.edu
Website: http://www.ncset.org

This website discusses supports and accommodations for people with disabilities preparing for postsecondary education.

National Dissemination Center for Children with Disabilities
P.O. Box 1492
Washington, DC 20013
Phone: (800) 695-0285 (also TDD)
Fax: (202) 884-8441
E-mail: nichcy@aed.org
Website: http://www.nichcy.org

This website contains information about Individuals with Disabilities Education Act (IDEA), No Child Left Behind (as it relates to children with disabilities), and effective educational practices for students with disabilities. Services are offered in both English and Spanish via mail, telephone, and e-mail.

Rehabilitation Research and Training Center
University of Hawaii at Manoa
2500 Campus Road
Honolulu, HI 96822
Phone: (808) 956-9199
Website: http://www.rrtc.hawaii.edu

This national center works on building new systems of educational support for people with disabilities. It liaises with teachers and agency providers to help them improve individualized supports and technologies.

Transition Coalition
University of Kansas
Department of Special Education
Joseph R. Pearson Hall
1122 West Campus Road, Room 521
Lawrence, KS 66045-3101
Phone: (785) 864-0686
Fax: (785) 864-4149
Website: http://www.transitioncoalition.org

This department provides resources about the transition from special education to adult life.

Transition Research Institute
University of Illinois at Urbana-Champaign
College of Education
113 Children's Research Center
51 Gerty Drive
Champaign, IL 61820
Phone: (217) 333-2325
Fax: (217) 244-0851
Website: http://www.ed.uiuc.edu/SPED/tri/institute.html

This department identifies effective practices, conducts intervention and evaluation research, and provides technical assistance activities that promote the successful transition of youth with disabilities from school to adult life.

U.S. Department of Education (DOE)
Office of Civil Rights
Education Resource Organizations Directory
550 12th Street, SW
Washington, DC 20202-1100
Phone: (800) 421-3481
           (202) 245-6840 (fax)
           (877) 521-2172 (TDD)
E-mail: OCR@ed.gov
Website: http://www.ed.gov/about/offices/list/ocr/topics.html?src=rt

This agency enforces the ADA as it applies to federal and state-funded schools. The DOE's regulations are explained at http://www.ed.gov/policy/rights/reg/ocr/edlite-34cfr104.html. Information about how to file a complaint with the Office of Civil Rights can be found at http://www.ed.gov/about/offices/list/ocr/complaintprocess.html. Reports on compliance levels for each state is available at http://www.ed.gov/about/offices/list/osers/osep/index.html?src=mr. For publications regarding the rights of disabled students in higher education, go to http://www.ed.gov/about/offices/list/ocr/publications.html.

Employment
Association of Medical Professionals with Hearing Losses (AMPHL)
1602 Rosina Drive
Miamisburg, OH 45342
Website: http://www.amphl.org

National Center on Workforce and Disability/Adult
Institute for Community Inclusion
University of Massachusetts Boston
100 Morrissey Blvd.
Boston, MA 02125
Phone: (617) 287-4300
           (617) 287-4350 (TDD)
Fax: (617) 287-4352
E-mail: ici@umb.edu
Website: http://www.onestops.info

U.S. Department of Labor (DOL)
Office of Disability Employment Policy
Website: http://www.dol.gov/odep/state/directry.htm

This website provides a directory of state liaisons regarding employment of people with disabilities and related concerns. For information about the DOL's Job Accommodation Network (JAN), call 800-526-7234 (also TDD) or go to http://www.jan.wvu.edu. For information about the Mental Health Parity Act, which provides for parity in mental health benefits, go to http://www.dol.gov/ebsa/faqs/faq_consumer_mentalhealthparity.html.

U.S. Equal Employment Opportunity Commission (EEOC)
1801 L Street, NW
Washington, DC 20507
Phone: (202) 663-4900
                (202) 663-4494 (TDD)
Field offices: (800) 669-4000
                (800) 669-6820 (TDD)
Website: http://www.eeoc.gov/types/ada.html

The EEOC website contains information about Titles I and V of the ADA, the Family and Medical Leave Act, and Title VII of the Civil Rights Act of 1964. It explains EEOC enforcement guides and policy documents, the employment rights of employees with disabilities, and answers frequently asked questions about the ADA and the workplace regarding diabetes, epilepsy, and people with intellectual disabilities, and more. The website tells people with disabilities how to file a charge of employment discrimination or mediate the situation. A related site for information about the ADA as it applies to workplaces can be found at http://www.usdoj.gov/crt/ada/workta.htm, and information on Section 508 of the Rehabilitation Act is available at http://www.section508.gov.

Health Care

Actors' Fund of America
729 Seventh Avenue, 10th Floor
New York, NY 10019
Phone: (800) 798-8447
Website: http://www.actorsfund.org/ahirc/index.html

This database operates as health insurance resource for artists and people in the entertainment industry as well as self-employed, low-income, underinsured, uninsured, and other workers. Internet links are provided for all fifty states.

American Association on Health and Disability (AAHD)
110 N. Washington Street, Suite 340
Rockville, MD 20850
Phone: (301) 545-6140
Fax: (301) 545-6144
Website: http://www.aahd.us/index.htm

This organization supports health promotion and wellness initiatives for people with disabilities at the federal, state, and local level. The website includes links to AAHD initiatives in some states as well as to organizations, resources, and clearinghouses about disability rights.

National Association of Insurance Commissioners (NAIC)
2301 McGee Street, Suite 800
Kansas City, MO 64108-2662
Phone: (816) 842-3600
Fax: (816) 783-8175
Website: http://www.naic.org

This website contains information about insurance companies and how to file a consumer complaint with your state insurance department at http://www.naic.org/consumer. Other helpful insurance-related websites include http://www.dol.gov/odep/archives/ek96/insurance.htm and http://www.odc.state.or.us/tadoc/ada67.htm.

National Center on Birth Defects and Developmental Disabilities (NCBDDD)
Centers for Disease Control and Prevention
1600 Clifton Rd.
Atlanta, GA 30333
Phone: (404) 639-3311
            or (800) 311-3435
Website: http://www.cdc.gov/ncbddd

This website contains links regarding birth defects, developmental disabilities, human development, disability and health, and hereditary blood disorders. It offers a link to the CDC's autism-related information and includes links to state activities.

PlanetAmber.com
Website: http://www.planetamber.com

Global health and disability resource center offers information for people with health impairments, their families, and those who provide services and support. Rates Internet resources, indicating country and quality of information provided.

U.S. Department of Health and Human Services (HHS)
370 L'Enfant Promenade, SW
Washington, DC 20447
Website: http://www.hhs.gov

For a state-by-state mental health services locator, go to the department's related website at http://mentalhealth.org. For women's health information, go to http://www.4woman.gov/wwd. For information about the Mental Health Parity Act, which provides for parity in mental health benefits, go to http://www.cms.hhs.gov/hipaa/hipaa1/content/mhpa.asp. For information for individuals with developmental disabilities and their families, go to http://www.acf.dhhs.gov/programs/add/index.htm. For information on individual states' Medicaid programs, go to http://www.cms.hhs.gov/medicaid/statemap.asp. Another related website, http://www.statelocalgov.net/50states-health.htm, includes links for state departments of health.

U.S. Social Security Administration (SSA)
Office of Public Inquiries
Windsor Park Building
6401 Security Blvd.
Baltimore, MD 21235
Phone: (800) 772-1213

(800) 325-0778 (TDD)
Website: http://www.ssa.gov

This website includes links for help with disability applicants. For information about youth with disabilities, go to http://www.ssa.gov/work/Youth/youth.html. Information for advocates is available at http://www.ssa.gov/work/Advocates/advocates.html.

Housing
Center for Universal Design
North Carolina State University
College of Design
Campus Box 8613
Raleigh, NC 27695-8613
Phone: (919) 515-3082
          (800) 647-6777
Fax: (919) 515-8951
E-mail: cud@ncsu.edu
Website: http://www.design.ncsu.edu/cud

National research, information, and technical assistance center. Evaluates, develops, and promotes universal design in housing, public and commercial facilities, and related products. Publications include *Tenant's Guide to Apartment Modifications: An Idea Source Pamphlet to Simple, Low-cost Modifications to Increase Accessibility in Apartments.* Related websites regarding accessible design are http://www.extension.iastate.edu/Pages/housing/uni-design.html; http://www.aarp.org/life/homedesign; http://www.makoa.org/accessable-design.htm; and http://www.abledata.com/Site_2/accessib.htm.

U.S. Department of Housing and Urban
   Development (HUD)
Office of Fair Housing and Equal Opportunity
451 7th Street, SW, Room 5204
Washington, DC 20410-2000
Phone (English and Spanish):   (800) 767-7468
                                   (800) 877-8339 (TDD)
Housing Discrimination Hotline: (800) 800-3088
                                   (800) 927-9275 (TDD)
Website: http://www.hud.gov/groups/disabilities.cfm

From this site, you can file a complaint regarding housing discrimination at http://www.hud.gov/complaints/housediscrim.cfm or print a complaint form, fill it out, and drop it off or mail it to your nearest fair housing office or the national office. Regional addresses are available through links on the

HUD website. A chart of the HUD complaint process is available at http://
www.fhosc.org/discrimination/hud_chart.html. Related websites that provide legal resources for tenants with disabilities include http://www.dlp-
pa.org/pubs/manuals/TR_2003.pdf;   http://www.oradvocacy.org/pubs/
housingfacts1.htm; http://www.povertylaw.org/legalresearch/articles/free/
trafford.htm; and http://www.vlpnet.org/legalresources/LandlordTenant-
Law/HandBook/chapter3.htm.

To locate HUD-insured and HUD-subsidized properties, go to http://
www.hud.gov/offices/hsg/mfh/hto/inventorysurvey.cfm. Information on
group homes for people with disabilities is available on a number of websites, including http://www.advocacyinc.org/HS2_text.htm; http://www.ci.
mesa.az.us/citymgt/mayorcc/FAQ'sD1.asp; and http://www.oxfordhouse.
org/fairhouse.html. Websites offering information about service animals in
rental housing include http://www.deltasociety.org/dsz102.htm and http://
www.metrokc.gov/dias/ocre/animals.htm.

Transportation
Federal Aviation Administration (FAA)
800 Independence Avenue, SW
Washington, DC 20591
Phone: (866) 835-5322
Website: http://www.faa.gov

The FAA is the division of the federal Department of Transportation responsible for enforcing air travel regulations. Overviews of the Air Carrier Access
Act of 1986 (ACAA) and its regulations can be found at http://www.
faa.gov/passengers/Disabilities.cfm and http://airconsumer.ost.dot.gov/rules/
382SHORT.htm. For helpful publications regarding air travelers with disabilities, visit http://airconsumer.ost.dot.gov/publications/disabled.htm. For information about the implications of air travel under the Transportation Security Administration (TSA) Screening of Persons with Disabilities Program
developed after the September 11, 2001, attacks, go to http://www.tsa.
gov/public/display?theme=156. Passengers who experience discrimination
can file a complaint with the Department of Transportation (see entry below).

Society for Accessible Travel and Hospitality (SATH)
347 Fifth Ave, Suite 610
New York, NY 10016
Phone: (212) 447-7284
Fax: (212) 725-8253
E-mail: sathtravel@aol.com
Website: http://www.sath.org

SATH is a nonprofit educational organization that has actively represented
travelers with disabilities since 1976. Its Internet site provides links to the

access information for several airlines. Specific travel tips may be found at http://www.access-able.com/tips/air.htm or a related website, http://www.mossresourcenet.org/travel.htm.

U.S. Department of Transportation (DOT)
Aviation Consumer Protection Division
400 7th Street, SW
Washington, DC 20590
Phone: (888) 446-4511 (ADA Assistance Line)
          (800) 877-8339 (TDD)
          (800) 778-4838 (general DOT hotline)
          (800) 455-9880 (TDD)
E-Mail: ada.assistance@fta.dot.gov
Website: http://www.dot.gov

The U.S. Department of Transportation, through its hotlines and website, provides consumers with general information about the rights of air travelers with disabilities, responds to requests for printed consumer information, and assists air travelers with time-sensitive disability-related issues. Complaints regarding discrimination by airlines may be made via letter or a form found at http://airconsumer.ost.dot.gov/forms/382form.pdf. The complaint can also be filed by e-mail at airconsumer@ost.dot.gov.

The Federal Transit Authority (FTA), a division of the DOT, provides Internet links to the full ADA Title II and Rehabilitation Act regulations governing all transportation provided by public and private entities at http://www.fta.dot.gov/transit_data_info/ada. Another helpful website that provides an overview of the rules regarding bus, lightrail, and paratransit services is http://www.ada-infonet.org/documents/transportation. Riders' complaints may be filed with the FTA using a form found at http://www.fta.dot.gov/14531_14889_ENG_HTML.htm.

Voting
Federal Election Commission (FEC)
999 E Street, NW
Washington, DC 20463
Phone: (202) 694-1100
          (800) 424-9530
          (202) 219-3336 (TDD)
E-mail: webmaster@fec.gov
Website: http://www.fec.gov

The FEC is the federal agency responsible for enforcing election regulations. For the full text of the Help America Vote Act (HAVA) passed in 2002, go to www.fec.gov/hava/hava.htm. For a newsletter concerning the most recent developments in implementing HAVA, go to http://www.inclusionsolutions. com/havanews.htm.

National Association of State Election Directors
c/o Council of State Governments
Hall of the States
444 N. Capitol Street, NW, Suite 401
Washington, DC 20001-1512
Phone: (202) 624-5460
Fax: (202) 624-5452
Website: http://www.nased.org

This website lists current state election commissioners, who can direct voters with disabilities to services and election regulations in their states.

U.S. Department of Justice (DOJ)
Office of Civil Rights
Voting Section
P.O. Box 66128
Washington, DC 20035-6128
Phone: (800) 253-3931 (also TDD)
Website: www.usdoj.gov/crt/voting

For the ADA rules regarding accessibility of polling places, go to http:// www.usdoj.gov/crt/ada/votingck.htm Voters with disabilities can file complaints about discrimination at the polls with the U.S. attorney general at the address above.

State Resources

Alabama
Disabilities Advocacy Program
Box 870395
Tuscaloosa, AL 35487-0395
Phone: (205) 348-4928
          (800) 826-1675 (TDD)
Fax: (205) 348-3909
Website: http://www.adap.net

Governor's Office on Disability
100 North Union Street, Suite 586
Montgomery, AL 36130-2761
Website: http://www.good.state.al.us

Legal Services
Website: http://www.alabamalegalservices.org

Alaska
ADA Coordinator's Office
Department of Labor and Workforce Development
Division of Vocational Rehabilitation
801 W. 10th Street, Suite A
Juneau, AK 99801
Phone: (907) 465-2814
Fax: (907) 465-2856
Website: http://www.labor.state.ak.us/ada/home.htm

Disability Law Center of Alaska
3330 Arctic Boulevard, Suite 103
Anchorage, AK 99503
Phone: (800) 478-1234 (also TDD)
Website: http://www.dlcak.org

Governor's Council on Disabilities and Special Education
Website: http://health.hss.state.ak.us/gcdse/aboutus/default.htm

Legal Services
Website: http://www.alsc-law.org

Arizona
Center for Disability Law
100 North Stone Ave., Suite 305
Tucson, AZ 85701
Phone: (520) 327-9547 (also TDD)
          or (800) 922-1447 (also TDD)
or
3839 N. Third St., Suite 209
Phoenix, AZ 85012
Phone: (602) 274-6287 (also TDD)
          or (800) 927-2260 (also TDD)
Website: http://www.acdl.com

Department of Education, Exceptional Student Services
Website: http://www.ade.state.az.us/ess/ESSHome.asp

Governor's Council on Developmental Disabilities
1717 West Jefferson, Suite SC074Z
Phoenix, AZ 85007
Phone: (602) 542-4049
          or (800) 889-5893
          (602) 542-8920 (TDD)
Fax: (602) 542-5320
Website: http://www.azgcdd.org

Office for Americans with Disabilities
Website: http://www.know-the-ada.com/links.htm

Rehabilitation Services Administration
Website: http://www.de.state.az.us/rsa

Arkansas
Department of Human Services
Website: http://www.state.ar.us/dhs/ddds

Disability Coalition
Website: http://www.adcpti.org/

Disability Rights Center
1100 N. University, Suite 210
Little Rock, AR 72207
Phone: (501) 296-1775 (also TDD)
          or (800) 482-1174 (also TDD))
Website: http://www.arkdisabilityrights.org/links.html

Governor's Developmental Disabilities Council
Website: http://www.ddcouncil.org

Partners for Inclusive Communities
Website: http://www.uams.edu/UAP/resources.htm

California
Child Health and Disability Program
Website: http://www.dhs.ca.gov/pcfh/cms/chdp

Department of Developmental Services
Website: http://www.dds.ca.gov

Support and services to children of developmental disabilities

Department of Rehabilitation
Website: http://www.rehab.ca.gov

Developmental Disabilities Netlink
Website: http://www.npi.ucla.edu/uap/cddn

Protection and Advocacy
100 Howe Avenue, Suite 185-N
Sacramento, CA 95825
Phone: (916) 488-9955
           or (800) 776-5746
           (800) 719-5798 (TDD)
or
3580 Wilshire Blvd., Suite 902
Los Angeles, CA 90010
Phone: (213) 427-8747
           or (800) 776-5746
           (800) 781-4546 (TDD)
or
433 Hegenberger Road, Suite 220
Oakland, CA 94621
Phone: (510) 430-8033
           or (800) 776-5746
           (800) 649-0154 (TDD)
or
1111 Sixth Avenue, Suite 200
San Diego, CA 92101
Phone: (619) 239-7861
or (800) 776-5746
           (800) 576-9269 (TDD)
Website: http://www.pai-ca.org

Colorado
Division of Developmental Disabilities
Website: http://www.cdhs.state.co.us/ohr/dds/DDS_center.html

**Legal Center for People with Disabilities and
   Older People**
455 Sherman Street, Suite 130
Denver, CO 80203-4403

Phone: (303) 722-0300
            (303) 722-3619 (TDD)
            (800) 288-1376 (also TDD)
Fax: (303) 722-0720
or
322 N. 8th Street
Grand Junction, CO 81501-3406
Phone: (970) 241-6371
            (800) 531-2105 (also TDD)
Fax: (970) 241-5324
Website: http://www.thelegalcenter.org/contact.html

Legal Services
Website: http://www.coloradolegalservices.org

Parent Information and Resource Center
Website: http://www.cpirc.org/tips/disability.htm

Connecticut
Commission on Human Rights and Opportunities (CHRO)
Website: http://www.state.ct.us/chro

Department of Social Services
Website: http://www.dss.state.ct.us/svcs/adults.htm

Disability Resource Directory
Website: http://www.state.ct.us/opapd/disresources.htm

Legal Services
Website: http://www.connlegalservices.org

Office of Protection and Advocacy for Persons with Disabilities
60B Weston Street
Hartford, CT 06120-1551
Phone: (860) 297-4380 (TDD)
            (800) 297-4300
            (800) 842-7303 (TDD)
Fax: (860) 566-8714
Website: http://www.ct.gov/opapd/site/default.asp

Statewide Legal Services of Connecticut
Website: http://www.slsct.org

Delaware
Disabilities Law Program
Community Service Building
100 West 10th Street, Suite 801
Wilmington, DE 19801
Phone: (302) 575-0690
           (302) 575-0696 (TDD)

or

840 Walker Road
Dover, DE 19904
Phone: (302) 674-8503
           (302) 674-8500 (TDD)

or

144 E. Market Street
Georgetown, DE 19947
Phone: (302) 856-3742
           (302) 856-0038 (TDD)
Website: http://www.declasi.org/dis.html

Health and Social Services
Website: http://www.state.de.us/dhss/main/disabil.htm

Legal Services
Website: http://www.lscd.com/Home/PublicWeb

State Council for Persons with Disabilities
Website: http://www2.state.de.us/scpd

Florida
Advocacy Center for Persons with Disabilities
2671 Executive Center Circle W., Suite 100
Tallahassee, FL 32301-5092
Phone: (850) 488-9071
           (800) 342-0823
           (800) 346-4127 (TDD)
Website: http://www.advocacycenter.org

Central Florida Legal Services
Website: http://www.cfls.org

Clearinghouse on Disability Information and the Real Choice Partnership Project
Phone: (850) 922-4103

(877) 232-4968 (TDD)
Website: http://www.abilityforum.com/rcp.shtml

Developmental Disabilities Council
Website: http://www.fddc.org/Home/index1.asp

Governor's Americans with Disabilities Act Working Group (ADAWG)
4030 Esplanade Way, Suite 315A
Tallahassee, FL 32399-0950
Phone: (850) 487-3423
Website: http://www.abilityforum.com

Health and Human Services Agency for Persons with Disabilities
Website: http://apd.myflorida.com

Legal Services
Websites: http://www.floridalegal.org; http://www.lsnf.org

Georgia
ADA Coordinator's Office
Georgia State Financing and Investment Commission
2 Martin Luther King Jr. Drive, Suite 1002
Atlanta, GA 30334
Phone: (404) 657-7313
          (404) 657-9993 (TDD)
Fax: (404) 657-1741
E-mail: gaada@gsfic.ga.gov
Website: http://www.state.ga.us/gsfic/ada

Advocacy Office
100 Crescent Centre Parkway, Suite 520
Tucker, GA 30084
Phone: (404) 885-1234
          (800) 537-2329
Website: http://www.thegao.org

Governor's Council on Developmental Disabilities
Website: http://www.gcdd.org

Legal Services
Website: http://www.glsp.org

Hawaii

Department of Health
Website: http://www.hawaii.gov/health/disability-services

Department of Human Services
Website: http://www.state.hi.us/dhs

Disability and Communication Access Board
919 Ala Moana Blvd., Room 101
Honolulu, HI 96814
Phone: (808) 586-8121 (also TDD)
Fax: (808) 586-8129
E-mail: accesshi@aloha.net
Website: http://www.state.hi.us/health/dcab

Disability Rights Center
900 Fort Street Mall, Suite 1040
Honolulu, HI 96813
Phone: (808) 949-2922 (also TDD)
        (800) 882-1057 (also TDD)
Fax: (808) 949-2928
Website: http://www.hawaiidisabilityrights.org

Legal Aid Society
Website: http://www.legalaidhawaii.org

Volunteer Legal Services
Website: http://www.vlsh.org/01/index.htm

Idaho

Comprehensive Advocacy
4477 Emerald, Suite B-100
Boise, ID 83706
Phone: (208) 336-5353 (also TDD)
Fax: (208) 336-5396
Website: http://users.moscow.com/co-ad

Department of Health and Welfare
Website: http://www.healthandwelfare.idaho.gov

Legal Services
Website: http://www.idaholegalaid.org/Home/PublicWeb

Parents Unlimited
Website: http://www.ipulidaho.org/perc.html

Partners in Policymaking
Website: http://idahopartners.state.id.us

Illinois
Department of Human Rights
James R. Thompson Center
100 West Randolph Street, Suite 10-100
Chicago, IL 60601
Phone: (312) 814-6200
          (312) 263-1579 (TDD)
Website: http://www.state.il.us/dhr

Equip for Equality
20 N. Michigan Avenue, Suite 300
Chicago, IL 60602
Phone: (312) 341-0022
          (800) 537-2632
          (800) 610-2779 (TDD)
Fax: (312) 341-0295
or
1612 Second Avenue
Rock Island, IL 61204
Phone: (309) 786-6868 (also TDD)
          (800) 758-6869 (also TDD)
Fax: (309) 786-2393
or
235 S. Fifth Street
Springfield, IL 62705
Phone: (217) 544-0464 (also TDD)
          (800) 758-0464 (also TDD)
Fax: (217) 523-0720
Website: http://www.equipforequality.org

Guardianship and Advocacy Commission/Legal
  Advocacy Service
Website: http://gac.state.il.us/las

Legal Aid
Website: http://www.illinoislegalaid.org/index.cfm

Living in Illinois
Website: http://www.illinois.gov/living/disability.cfm

Indiana
Family and Social Services Administration, Division of Disability, Aging and Rehabilitative Services
Phone: (800) 545-7763
Website: http://www.state.in.us/fssa/servicedisabl/index.html

Governor's Council for People with Disabilities
Website: http://www.in.gov/gpcpd

Legal Services
Website: http://www.indianajustice.org/Home/PublicWeb

Protection and Advocacy Services
4701 N. Keystone Ave., Suite 222
Indianapolis, IN 46205
Phone: (800) 838-1131 (also TDD)
            (800) 622-4845, ext. 234
Website: http://www.in.gov/ipas

Iowa
Division of Persons with Disabilities
Website: http://www.state.ia.us/government/dhr/pd

Governor's Developmental Disabilities Council
Website: http://www.state.ia.us/government/ddcouncil

Legal Services
1111 9th Street, Suite 230
Des Moines, IA 50314
Phone: (515) 243-2151
Website: http://www.iowalegalaid.org

Protection and Advocacy Services
950 Office Park Rd., Suite 221
West Des Moines, IA 50265
Phone: (515) 278-2502
            (800) 779-2502
            (515) 278-0571 (TDD)
            (866) 483-3342 (also TDD)
Website: http://www.ipna.org

Workforce Development Partnership
Website: http://www.iowaworkforce.org/region13/disability

Kansas
ADA Coordinator
Website: http://da.state.ks.us/ada

Commission on Disability Concerns
1430 SW Topeka Boulevard
Topeka, KS 66612-1877
Phone: (785) 296-1722
            (800) 295-5232
            (785) 296-5044 (TDD)
            (877) 340-5874 (TDD)
Fax: (785) 296-0466
Website: http://www.hr.state.ks.us/dc

Disability Rights Center
3745 S.W. Wanamaker
Topeka, KS 66610
Phone: (785) 273-9661 (also TDD)
            (877) 776-1541 (also TDD)
Fax: (785) 273-9414
Website: http://drckansas.org

Legal Services
Website: http://www.kansaslegalservices.org/main.html

Kentucky
Children's Law Center
Website: http://www.childrenslawky.org

Children's Services and Programs
Website: http://kentucky.gov/Portal/Category/hea_pediatric

Specific information for children's services.

Council on Developmental Disabilities
Website: http://www.chs.ky.gov/kcdd/Links/default.htm

Disability Resources
Website: http://kentucky.gov/Portal/Category/hea_disability

Disability Resources Manual
Website: http://www.ihdi.uky.edu/kydrm

KATS Network
Website: http://www.katsnet.org/kylinks.html

Legal Services
Website: http://www.accesstojustice.org

Protection and Advocacy
100 Fair Oaks Lane, Third Floor
Frankfort, KY 40601
Phone: (502) 564-2967 (also TDD)
            (800) 372-2988 (also TDD)
Website: http://www.kypa.net

Louisiana
Advocacy Center
225 Baronne Street, Suite 2112
New Orleans, LA 70112-1724
Phone: (504) 522-2337
            (800) 960-7705
Fax: (504) 522-5507
Website: http://www.advocacyla.org

Department of Social Services
Website: http://www.dss.state.la.us/departments/lrs/Vocational_
            Rehabilitation.html

Developmental Disabilities Council
Website: http://www.laddc.org

Disability Information Resources
Website: http://www.ladir.org

Governor's Disability Affairs Area
P.O. Box 94004
Baton Rouge, LA 70804
Phone: (225) 219-7550
Websites: http://gov.louisiana.gov/office_detail.asp?id=8; http://www.
            gov.state.la.us/disabilityaffairs/default.asp

Legal Services
Website: http://www.lawhelp.org/LA; http://www.lawhelp.org/
      program/921

Office for Citizens with Developmental Disabilities
Website: http://www.dhh.state.la.us/offices/?ID=77

Office of Public Health
Website: http://www.oph.dhh.state.la.us/childrensspecial

Maine
Ability Maine
Website: http://www.abilitymaine.org

Accessibility and Disability Resources
Website: http://www.maine.gov/portal/accessibility.html

Bureau of Health
Website: http://www.state.me.us/dhs/boh/index.htm

Developmental Disabilities Council
Website: http://www.maineddc.org

Disability Rights Center
P.O. Box 2007
Augusta, ME 04338-2007
Phone: (207) 626-2774 (also TDD)
      (800) 452-1948 (also TDD)
Fax: (207) 621-1419
Website: http://www.drcme.org

Disability Services
Website: http://www.youthwork.com/LA/disability.html

Legal Services
Websites: http://www.helpmelaw.org; http://www.mbf.org/provider.htm;
      http://www.ptla.org/index.html

Free legal services for low-income Maine residents.

Maryland
Committee for Children
Website: http://mdchildcare.org/mdcfc/for_parents/specialneeds.html

Developmental Disabilities Council
Website: http://www.md-council.org

Disability Law Center
1800 N. Charles St., 4th Floor
Baltimore, MD 21201
Phone: (410) 727-6352
            (410) 727-6387 (TDD)
            (800) 233-7201
Fax: (410) 727-6389
Website: http://www.mdlcbalto.org

Governor's Office for Children, Youth, and Families
Website: http://www.ocyf.state.md.us

Legal Services
Websites: http://www.mdlab.org/rights.html; http://www.dhr.state.
            md.us/legal; http://www.mlsc.org/

**Office for Genetics and Children with Special Health
    Care Needs**
Website: http://www.fha.state.md.us/genetics

Technology Assistance Program
Website: http://www.mdtap.org/oid.html

Massachusetts
Association of Special Education Parent Advisory Councils
P.O. Box 167
Sharon, MA 02067
Phone: (617) 962-4558
E-mail: info@maspac.org
Website: http://www.masspac.org

Citizens' Guide to State Services
Website: http://www.sec.state.ma.us/cis/ciscig/f/f11f14.htm

Department of Health and Human Services
Website: http://www.mass.gov/portal/index.jsp?pageID=eohhs2
            utilities&L=1&sid=Eeohhs2&U=catalog#Disabilities%20
            Services

Disability Law Center
11 Beacon Street, Suite 925
Boston, MA 02108
Phone: (617) 723-8455
            (617) 227-9464 (TDD)
            (800) 872-9992
            (800) 381-0577 (TDD)
or
30 Industrial Drive East
Northampton, MA 01060
Phone: (413) 584-6337
            (800) 222-5619
            (413) 582-6919 (TDD)
Website: http://www.dlc-ma.org

Legal Services
Website: http://www.masslegalhelp.org

Office on Disability
One Ashburton Place, Room 1305
Boston, MA 02108
Phone: (617) 727-7440
            (800) 322-2020 (also TDD)
Website: http://www.mass.gov/mod

Rehabilitation Commission
27 Wormwood St., Suite 600
Boston, MA 02210-1616
Phone: (617) 204-3600
            (800) 245-6543 (TDD)
Website: http://www.mass.gov/mrc

Michigan
Bridges4Kids
Website: http://www.earlyonmichigan.org/counties/MDRD.htm

Commission on Disability Concerns
Michigan Division of Deaf and Hard of Hearing
Phone: (517) 334-8000 (also TDD)
            (877) 499-6232 (also TDD)

Disability Resources Directory
Website: http://mdrd.state.mi.us/

Disability Rights Coalition
80 West Lake Lansing Road, Suite 200
Lansing, MI 48823
Phone: (517) 333-2477
           (800) 760-4600
Website: http://www.copower.org/mdrc/MDRC.htm

Michigan Works! Association
2500 Kerry Street, Suite 210
Lansing, MI 48912
Phone: (517) 371-1100
Website: http://www.michiganworks.org/page.cfm/302

Rehabilitation Services
Website: http://www.michigan.gov/mdcd/0,1607,7-122-25392—-,00.html

University of Michigan Health Systems
Website: http://www.med.umich.edu/1libr/yourchild/ld.htm#else

Minnesota
Department of Health
85 East 7th Place
St. Paul, MN 55164-0882
Phone: (651) 215-8956
           (800) 728-5420
E-mail: mcshnweb@health.state.mn.us
Website: http://www.health.state.mn.us/fas/tipsheets/disability-
           resources.html

Department of Human Services
Website: http://www.dhs.state.mn.us/main/groups/disabilities/
           documents/pub/dhs_Disabilities.hcsp

Disability Law Center
430 First Avenue North, Suite 300
Minneapolis, MN 55401-1780
Phone: (612) 334-5970
           (800) 292-4150
           (612) 332-4668 (TDD)
Website: http://www.mndlc.org

Governor's Council on Developmental Disabilities
370 Centennial Office Building

658 Cedar Street
St. Paul, MN 55155
Phone: (651) 296-4018
             (877) 348-0505
             (651) 296-9962 (TDD)
E-mail: admin.dd@state.mn.us
Website: http://www.mncdd.org

Legal Services
Websites: http://www.lawhelpmn.org; http://www.hbci.com/~smrlswi/
             mnlegaid.htm

State Disability Information Network
121 E. 7th Place, Suite 107
St. Paul, MN 55101
Phone: (651) 296-6785 (also TDD)
             (800) 945-8913 (also TDD)
E-mail: council.disability@state.mn.us
Website: http://www.disability.state.mn.us

Mississippi
Department of Rehabilitation Services
Website: http://www.mdrs.state.ms.us/client/

Institute for Disability Studies
Website: http://www.ids.usm.edu/interest.asp

Legal Services
Website: http://www.mslegalservices.org/

Protection and Advocacy System
5305 Executive Place
Jackson, MS 39206
Phone: (601) 981-8207(also TDD)
             (800) 772-4057
Website: http://www.mspas.com

North Mississippi Rural Legal Services
Website: http://www.nmrls.com

State Disability Resources
Website: http://www.mississippi.gov/ms_sub_sub_template.jsp?
             Category_ID=47

Missouri
Bar Association
Website: http://www.mobar.org/pamphlet/asstprnt.htm

Department of Mental Health
Website: http://www.dmh.mo.gov/mrdd/help/faqs.htm

Developmental Disability Resource Center
Website: http://www.moddrc.com

Developmental Disabilities
Website: http://missourifamilies.org/features/disabilitiesfeatures/
disabilities2.htm

Disability Resources
Website: http://bellasartes.8m.net/society/Disability.html

Governors Council on Disabilities
Website: http://www.gcd.oa.mo.gov

Legal Services
Website: http://www.mobar.org/legalser/offices.htm

Protection and Advocacy Program
925 South Country Club Drive
Jefferson City, MO 65109
Phone: (573) 893-3333
            (800) 392-8667
            (800) 735-2966 (TDD)
Website: http://www.moadvocacy.org/textver.htm

Montana
Advocacy Program
400 North Park, 2nd Floor
Helena, MT 59624
Phone: (406) 449-2344 (also TDD)
            (800) 245-4743 (also TDD)
Website: http://www.mtadv.org/index.htm

A.W.A.R.E.
Website: http://www.aware-inc.org

Disability and Health Program
Website: http://mtdh.ruralinstitute.umt.edu/OurPlan.htm

Independent Living Council
Website: http://www.dphhs.state.mt.us/MontLive/Montana_
              Independent_Living.htm

Legal Services
Websites: http://www.montanalawhelp.org; http://www.mtlsa.org/

Mental Disabilities Board of Visitors
Website: http://www.discoveringmontana.com/gov2/css/boards/
              mdbv/links.asp

State Disability Services Division
Website: http://www.dphhs.state.mt.us/dsd

**Research and Training Center on Disability in Rural
 Communities**
Website: http://rtc.ruralinstitute.umt.edu

Support and Techniques for Empowering People (STEP)
Website: http://www.step-inc.org/

Nebraska
Advocacy Services
Center for Disability Rights, Law, and Advocacy
134 South 13th Street, Suite 600
Lincoln, NE 68508
Phone: (402) 474-3183 (also TDD)
              (800) 422-6691
Website: www.nebraskaadvocacyservices.org

Answers 4 Families
Website: http://nncf.unl.edu/common/us

Assistive Technology Partnership/Nebraska ChildFind
Website: http://www.nde.state.ne.us/ATP/childfind.asp

Early Intervention Program Services Coordination
Website: http://www.connectfremont.org/COMSER/earlyip.htm

Department of Education
Website: http://www.nde.state.ne.us/SPED/iepproj/appd/que.html

Health and Human Services System's Disability Programs
Website: http://www.hhs.state.ne.us/dip/dipindex.htm

Hotline for Disability Services
Phone: (402) 471-0801
Website: http://www.uwmidlands.org/Directory/uwml0489aw.html

Legal Services
Website: http://www.nebls.com

Speech-Language-Hearing Association
Website: http://www.nslha.org/links.phtml

PTI Nebraska
Phone: (402) 346-0525
            (800) 284-8520
Fax: (402) 934-1479
E-mail: info@pti-nebraska.org
Website: http://www.pti-nebraska.org/index.htm

Nevada
Department of Cultural Affairs, Disability Related Services
Website: http://dmla.clan.lib.nv.us/docs/nsla/tbooks/ada/nv-dis.htm

Department of Employment, Training, and Rehabilitation
Website: http://detr.state.nv.us/rehab/reh_vorh.htm

Department of Human Resources, Office of Disability Services
Website: http://hr.state.nv.us/directors/disabilitysvcs/dhr_odsprog.htm

Disability Advocacy and Law Center
6039 Eldora Avenue, Suite C
Las Vegas, NV 89146
Phone: (702) 257-8150
            (888) 349-3843
            (702) 257-8160 (TDD)
or
1311 North McCarran, Suite 106
Sparks, NV 89431
Phone: (775) 333-7878

(800) 922-5715
(775) 788-7824 (TDD)
Website: http://www.ndalc.org

Legal Services
Websites: http://lawhelp.org/nv; http://www.nvlawdirectory.org/
linksdisability.html

Parent Training and Information Center
2355 Redrock Street, Suite 106
Las Vegas, NV 89146
Phone: (800) 216-5188
E-mail: pepinfo@nvpep.org
Website: http://www.nvpep.org/template.php?page=front

New Hampshire
Autism Society
Website: http://www.autism-society-nh.org

Developmental Disabilities Services System, Family and
   Children's Services
105 Pleasant Street
Concord, NH 03301
Phone: (603) 271-5122
Website: http://www.nhdds.org/programs/famchild/earlysupports

Disabilities Rights Center
18 Low Avenue
Concord, NH 03301-4971
Phone: (603) 228-0432
            (800) 834-1721 (TDD)
Fax: (603) 225-2077
Website: http://www. drcnh.org/contactus.htm

Governor's Commission on Disability
Website: http://www.state.nh.us/disability

Legal Services
Websites: http://www.nhla.org; http://www.larcnh.org/Home/Public
            Web/LegalSvcs

New Hampshire Challenge
Website: http://www.nhchallenge.org/resources/links.htm

New Hampshire Family Voices
Website: http://www.nhfv.org

New Jersey
Department of Human Services
Division of Disability Services
P.O. Box 700
Trenton, N.J. 08625-0700
Phone: (609) 292-7800
            (888) 285-3036
            (609) 292-1210 (TDD)
Fax: (609) 292-1233
Website: http://www.state.nj.us/humanservices/disable/index.html

Epilepsy Foundation
Website: http://www.efnj.com/index.shtml

Inclusive Child Care Project
Website: http://www.spannj.org/njiccp

Legal Services
P.O. Box 1357
Edison, NJ 08818
Phone: 888-LSNJ-LAW
Website: http://www.lsnj.org

Protection and Advocacy
210 South Broad Street, Third Floor
Trenton, NJ 08608
Phone: (609) 292-9742
            (609) 633-7106 (TDD)
Fax: (609) 777-0187
Website: http://www. njpanda.org

New Mexico
A.W.A.R.E.
Website: http://www.aware-inc.org

Governor's Committee on Concerns of the Handicapped
Phone: (505) 827-6465
            (505) 827-7329 (TDD)
Website: http://www.state.nm.us/gcch

Healthier Schools
Website: http://www.healthierschools.org/index.html

Legal Services
Website: http://www.fscll.org/Freelegal.htm

Protection and Advocacy
1720 Louisiana Blvd NE, Suite 204
Albuquerque, NM 87110
Phone: (505) 256-3100
(800) 432-4682
Website: http://www.nmpanda.org

Public Education Department, Special Education Office
Website: http://www.ped.state.nm.us/seo/index.htm

University of New Mexico Health Sciences Center, Center for Development and Disability
Website: http://cdd.unm.edu/deafblind

New York
ARC
393 Delaware Avenue
Delmar, NY 12054
Phone: (518) 439-8311
E-mail: info@nysarc.org
Website: http://www.nysarc.org

Commission on Quality of Care
401 State Street
Schenectady, NY 12305-2397
Phone: (800) 624-4143
Website: http://www. cqc.state.ny.us

Department of Education, Vocational and Educational Services for Individuals with Disabilities
Website: http://www.vesid.nysed.gov/all/contact.htm

Developmental Disabilities Planning Council
Website: http://www.ddpc.state.ny.us/

Disability and Health
Website: http://www.health.state.ny.us/nysdoh/prevent/main.htm

Institute for Special Education (NYISE)
Website: http://www.nyise.org

Legal Services
Websites: http://www.legal-aid.org; http://www.lsny.org; http://www.
            nylegalservices.org; http://www.nls.org

Office of Advocate for Persons with Disabilities
1 Empire State Plaza, Suite 1001
Albany, NY 12223
Phone: (518) 474-5567
            (518) 473-4231 (TDD)
            (800) 522-4369 (also TDD)
E-mail: oapwdinfo@oawpd.org
Website: http://www.advoc4disabled.state.ny.us

Office of Mental Retardation and Developmental Disabilities
Website: http://www.omr.state.ny.us

Office of Temporary and Disability Assistance
Website: http://www.otda.state.ny.us

School for the Blind's Blindness Resource Center
Website: http://www.nyise.org/blind.htm

Western New York Disabilities Forum
Website: http://www.wnydf.bfn.org

North Carolina
ARC
4200 Six Forks Road, Suite 100
Raleigh, NC 27609
Phone: (919) 782-4632
            (800) 662-8706
E-mail: arcofnc@arcnc.org
Website: http://www.arcnc.org

Governor's Advocacy Council for Persons with Disabilities
1314 Mail Service Center
Raleigh, NC 27699-1314
Phone: (919) 733-9250
            (800) 821-6922
            (888) 268-5535 (TDD)

Fax: (919) 733-9173
Website: http://www.gacpd.com

Legal Services
Website: http://www.legalaidnc.org

NAMI
Website: http://www.naminc.org

Office on Disability and Health
Website: http://www.fpg.unc.edu/~ncodh/AdolescentsYoungAdult/
            adolescentsresources.htm

Pisgah Legal Services
P.O. Box 2276
Asheville, NC 28802
Phone: (800) 489-6144
            (828) 253-0406 (Asheville)
            (828) 247-0297 (Forest City)
            (828) 692-7622 (Hendersonville)
E-mail: legalaid@pisgahlegal.org
Website: http://www.main.nc.us/pls

North Dakota
Association for the Disabled
Website: http://www.ndad.org

Department of Human Services
Developmental Disabilities, Suite 1A or
Vocational Rehabilitation, Suite 1 B
600 S Second Street
Bismark, ND 58504-5729
Phone: (800) 755-8529 (developmental disabilities)
            (800) 755-2745 (vocational rehabilitation)
E-mail: dhsds@state.nd.us
Website: http://www.state.nd.us/humanservices/services/disabilities

Gateway to Civil Legal Services for Low-Income and
   Elderly Persons
Website: http://www.legalassist.org

Legal Services
P.O. Box 217

345 Main Street
New Town, ND 58763
Phone: (701) 627-4719
E-mail: ndls@newtown.ndak.net
Website: http://web.ndak.net/~ndls

Protection and Advocacy Project
5124 4th Avenue E., Room 220
Williston, ND 58802-2472
Phone: (701) 774-4345
Fax: (701) 774-4302
Website: http://www. ndpanda.org

State Library
Website: http://ndsl.lib.state.nd.us/Subject/disability.html

Ohio
Ability Center
Website: http://www.abilitycenter.org

Assistive Technology
Website: http://www.atohio.org/disability_resources.htm

Center for Independent Living Options
Website: http://www.cilo.net/ciloservices.htm

Cleveland Clinic
Website: http://www.clevelandclinic.org/socialwork/RESOURCES
           FORSPEICALNEEDSMRDD.htm#WEBSITES

Council for Exceptional Children
Website: http://www.cec-ohio.org/Links.htm

Governor's Council on People with Disabilities
Website: http://gcpd.ohio.gov/links.asp

Legal Rights Service
8 East Long Street, Suite 500
Columbus, OH 43215-2999
Phone: (614) 466-7264
           (614) 728-2553 (TDD)
           (800) 282-9181

(800) 858-3542 (TDD)
Website: http://olrs.ohio.gov/ASP/HomePage.asp

Legal Services
Website: http://www.oslsa.org/OSLSA/PublicWeb/LegalSvcs

Oklahoma
ABLE Tech
Website: http://okabletech.okstate.edu/

AgrAbility Project
Website: http://www.agrability.okstate.edu/

Department of Rehabilitation Services
3535 N.W. 58th Street, Suite 500
Oklahoma City, OK 73112-4815
Phone: (800) 845-8476
Website: http://www.okrehab.org

Disability Law Center
2915 Classen Blvd.
300 Cameron Building
Oklahoma City, OK 73106
Phone: (800) 880-7755
            (800) 880-7755 (also TDD)
or
2828 East 51st Street, Suite 302
Tulsa, OK 74105
Phone: (918) 743-6220 (also TDD)
            (800) 226-5883 (also TDD)
Website: http://www.oklahomadisabilitylaw.org

Indian Legal Services
4200 Perimeter Center Drive, Suite 222
Oklahoma City, OK 73112
Phone: (405) 943-OILS
            (800) 658-1497
E-mail: oils@oilsonline.org
Website: http://thorpe.ou.edu/OILS

Legal Services
Website: http://www.lawhelp.org/program/1610/index.cfm?pagename=
            homepage

Office of Handicapped Concerns
Website: http://www.ohc.state.ok.us

Oregon
Advocacy Center
620 S.W. Fifth Avenue, 5th Floor
Portland, OR 97204-1428
Phone: (503) 243-2081
            (503) 323-9161 (TDD)
            (800) 452-1694
            (800) 556-5351 (TDD)
Website: http://www.oradvocacy.org

Disabilities Commission
Website: http://www.odc.state.or.us/odctac.htm

Family Law Courts
Website: http://www.ojd.state.or.us/osca/cpsd/courtimprovement/
            familylaw/legalaid.htm

Family Support Network
Website: http://www.ofsn.org/internetsites.html

Lane County Senior and Disabled Services
Website: http://www.sdslane.org

Legal Services
Website: http://www.lanecountylegalservices.org/Offices.htm

Office on Disability and Health
PO Box 574
Portland, OR 97207-0574
Phone: (503) 494-3331
            (800) 735-2900 (TDD)
E-mail: roberamb@ohsu.edu
Website: http://cdrc.ohsu.edu/oodh

Parents United
Website: http://www.oregonparentsunited.org

**Washington County Developmental Disabilities/
Community Resources**

Website: http://www.co.washington.or.us/deptmts/hhs/dev_dsab/
resource.htm

Pennsylvania
Accessible PA
Website: http://www.accessiblepa.state.pa.us/accessiblepa/site/default.asp

Department of Labor and Industry
Website: http://www.dli.state.pa.us/landi/cwp

Department of Public Welfare
Website: http://www.dpw.state.pa.us/Disable

Governor's Disability Policy Team
Website: http://www.parac.org/resources.html

Legal Services
Websites: http://www.dlp-pa.org; http://palawhelp.org; http://www.
palegalservices.org

Protection and Advocacy
1414 North Cameron Street, Suite C
Harrisburg, PA 17103
Phone: (717) 236-8110
            (717) 346-0293 (TDD)
            (800) 692-7443
            (877) 375-7139 (TDD)
Website: http://www.ppainc.org

Rhode Island
Department of Elementary and Secondary Education
Website: http://www.ridoe.net/Special_needs/Default.htm

Developmental Disabilities Council
Website: http://www.riddc.org

Disability Law Book
Website: http://www.gcd.state.ri.us/RI_Laws/Table_of_Contents.htm

Disability Law Center
349 Eddy Street
Providence, RI 02903

Phone: (401) 831-3150
          (401) 831-5335 (TDD)
          (800) 733-5332

Legal Services
56 Pine Street, 4th Floor
Providence, RI 02903
Phone: (800) 662-5034
or
50 Washington Square
Newport, RI 02840
Phone: (800) 637-4529
Website: http://www.rils.org

Office of Rehabilitation Services
Website: http://www.ors.state.ri.us

South Carolina
Autism Society
Website: http://www.scautism.org/links.html

Centers for Equal Justice
Website: http://www.centersforequaljustice.org/

Commission for the Blind
Website: http://www.sccb.state.sc.us/

Department of Disabilities and Special Needs
Website: http://www.centersforequaljustice.org/

Developmental Disabilities Council
Website: http://www.scddc.state.sc.us/who.htm

Family Connection
Website: http://www.familyconnectionsc.org

Protection and Advocacy for People with Disabilities
3710 Landmark Drive, Suite 208
Columbia, SC 29204
Phone: (803) 782-0639 (also TDD)
          (866) 275-7273
Website: http://www.protectionandadvocacy-sc.org

Sciway Mental Health Resources
Website: http://www.sciway.net/med/disabilities.html

Services Information System
Phone: (803) 935-5300
          (800) 922-1107 (also TDD)
Website: http://www.state.sc.us/ddsn/pubs/scsis/scsis.htm

State Website
Website: http://www.myscgov.com/SCSGPortal/static/health_tem1.html

Support Groups
Website: http://www.state.sc.us/ddsn/service/sectionfour/section4.html

Vocational Rehabilitation Department
Website: http://www.scvrd.net

University of South Carolina School of Law
Website: http://www.law.sc.edu/refdessc.htm

South Dakota
Advocacy Services
221 South Central Avenue
Pierre, SD 57501
Phone: (605) 224-8294 (also TDD)
          (800) 658-4782 (also TDD)
Website: http://www.sdadvocacy.com

Department of Education
Website: http://www.state.sd.us/deca

Department of Health, Children's Special Health Services
Website: http://www.state.sd.us/doh/Famhlth/child.htm

Department of Human Services
Website: http://www.state.sd.us/dhs

Parent Connection
Website: http://www.sdparent.org/Who%20We%20Are.htm

State Resources
Website: http://www.autism-pdd.net/LINKS/sdakota.html

University of South Dakota, School of Medicine and Health Sciences, Center for Disabilities
Website: http://www.usd.edu/cd/links/southdakota.htm

Tennessee

Autism Society
Website: http://www.autismmidtenn.org/html

Brain Resource and Information Network (B.R.A.I.N.)
Website: http://www.tndisability.org/brain/index.html

Council on Developmental Disabilities
Website: http://www.state.tn.us/cdd/ylf.html

Department of Mental Health and Developmental Disabilities
Website: http://www.state.tn.us/mental/reslinks.html

Disability Coalition
Website: http://www.tndisability.org/

Disability Information and Referral Office
Website: http://mingus.kc.vanderbilt.edu/devents/kcresults.asp

Disability Pathfinder
Website: http://kc.vanderbilt.edu/kennedy/pathfinder

Family Voices
Website: http://www.tndisability.org/familyvoices/default.html

Health Care Campaign
Website: http://www.thcc2.org/tenncare/tclegal.html

Legal Services
Website: http://www.tals.org/PublicWeb

Memphis Center for Independent Living (MCIL)
Website: http://www.mcil.org/mcil/news/news.htm

Protection and Advocacy
2416 21st Avenue S.
Nashville, TN 37212
Phone: (615) 298-1080 (also TDD)

(800) 342-1660
(888) 852-2852 (TDD)
Website: www.tpainc.org

Texas
Advocacy
7800 Shoal Creek Blvd. Suite 171-E
Austin, TX 78757
Phone: (512) 454-4816 (also TDD)
(800) 252-9108 (also TDD)
Website: http://www.advocacyinc.org

Commission for the Blind
Website: http://www.tcb.state.tx.us/

Council for Developmental Disabilities
Website: http://www.txddc.state.tx.us/menus/fset_cncl_1.asp

Department of Assistive and Rehabilitation Services
Website: http://www.dars.state.tx.us

Department of Licensing and Regulation: Architectural Barriers
Website: http://www.license.state.tx.us/ab/ab.htm

Department of State Health Services
Website: http://www.tdh.state.tx.us/disability/families.html

Division for Deaf and Hard of Hearing Services
Website: http://www.tcdhh.state.tx.us

Governor's Committee on People with Disabilities
Website: http://www.governor.state.tx.us/disabilities

Legal Services
Websites: http://www.texaslawhelp.org; http://www.tlsc.org; http://
www.trla.org

Rehabilitation Commission
Website: http://www.rehab.state.tx.us/

State Law Library
Website: http://www.sll.state.tx.us/legalaid.asp

Technology Access Project
Website: http://techaccess.edb.utexas.edu/

Workforce Commission, Civil Rights Division
Website: http://tchr.state.tx.us

Turning Point
Website: http://www.turningpointtechnology.com/Texas%20Programs
            %20for%20the%20Disabled.htm

Utah
Deafblind Project
Website: http://www.usdb.org/departments/deafblind/project.asp

Department of Human Services
Website: http://www.dhs.utah.gov/default.htm

Disability Law Center
205 North 400 West
Salt Lake City, UT 84103
Phone: (801) 363-1347
            (801) 924-3185 (TDD)
            (800) 662-9080
            (800) 550-4182 (TDD)
Website: http://www.disabilitylawcenter.org

Legal Services
Phone: (801) 328-8891
            (800) 662-4245
Websites: http://www.uls.state.ut.us/uls; http://www.lasslc.org; http://
            www.weberpl.lib.ut.us/legalServicesAccessGuide.htm

Office of Rehabilitation
Website: http://www.usor.utah.gov/index.htm

Parent Center
Website: http://www.utahparentcenter.org

TURN Community Services
850 South Main
Salt Lake City, UT 84101
Phone: (866) 359-8876
Website: http://www.turn.nu

United Cerebral Palsy
P.O. Box 65219
3550 South 700 West
Salt Lake City, UT 84119
Phone: (801) 266-1805
Website: http://www.ucputah.org/services.php

Utah State University Center for Persons with Disabilities
Website: http://www.cpd.usu.edu/projects

Vermont
**Agency of Human Services, Department of Aging and
    Independent Living**
Website: http://www.dad.state.vt.us/ConsumerPages/Legal.htm

Assistive Technology
Website: http://www.dad.state.vt.us/atp/

Department of Developmental and Mental Health Services
103 South Main Street
Waterbury, VT 05671-1601
Phone: (802) 241-2610
            (800) 253-0191 (TDD)
Website: http://www.ddmhs.state.vt.us/programs/ds/ds-services.html

Department of Education
120 State Street
Montpelier, VT 05620-2501
Phone: (802) 828-3130
E-mail: edinfo@education.state.vt.us
Website: http://www.state.vt.us/educ/new/html/pgm_sped.html#
            guidelines

Department of Health, Agency of Human Services
108 Cherry Street
Burlington, VT 05402-0070
Phone: (802) 863-7200
            (800) 464-4343
Website: http://www.healthyvermonters.info/

Developmental Disabilities Council
103 South Main Street
Waterbury, VT 05671-0206

Phone: (802) 241-2612
           (888) 317-2006 (also TDD)
E-mail: vtddc@ahs.state.vt.us
Website: http://www.ahs.state.vt.us/vtddc

Legal Services
264 North Winooski Avenue, Burlington, VT 05402
7 Court Street, Montpelier, VT 05601
57 North Main Street, Rutland, VT 05701
56 Main Street, Suite 301, Springfield, VT 05156
1111 Main Street, Suite B, St. Johnsbury, VT 05819
Vermont State Hospital (no client intake)
Phone: (800) 889-2047
Websites: http://www.vtlawhelp.org/Home/PublicWeb; http://www.
           vtlegalaid.org

Parent Information Center
1 Mill Street
Suite A7
Burlington, VT 05401
Phone: (802) 658-5315 (also TDD)
           (800) 639-7170
E-mail: vpic@vtpic.com
Websites: http://www.vtpic.com; http://www.wested.org/nerrc/vermont.
           htm

Parent to Parent
600 Blair Park Road, Suite 240
Wiliston, VT 05495-7549
Phone: (802) 764-5290
           (800) 800-4005
E-mail: p2pvt@partoparvt.org
Website: http://www.partoparvt.org

Protection and Advocacy
141 Main Street, Suite 7
Montpelier, VT 05602
Phone: (802) 229-1355
           (802) 229-2603 (TDD)
           (800) 834-7890
Website: http://www.vtpa.org

University of Vermont, Center on Disability and
   Community Inclusion
Mann Hall, Third Floor
208 Colchester Avenue
Burlington, VT 05405-1757
Phone: (802) 656-4031 (also TDD)
Website: http://www.uvm.edu/~cdci

VocRehab
Website: http://www.vocrehabvermont.org

Virginia
Accessible Travel
Websites: http://www.virginia.org/site/features.asp?FeatureID=146;
            http://www.travelguides.org/vaguide.html

Assistive Technology System
Website: http://www.vats.org/default.htm

Board for People with Disabilities
202 N. 9th Street, 9th Floor
Richmond, VA 23219
Phone: (800) 846-4464
            (804) 786-0016 (also TDD)
Website: http://www.vaboard.org/default.htm

Commission on Youth
Website: http://coy.state.va.us/Initiatives.htm

Department for the Blind and Vision Impaired
397 Azalea Avenue
Richmond, VA 23227-3623
Phone: (804) 371-3140 (also TDD)
            (800) 622-2155 (also TDD)
Website: http://www.vdbvi.org

Department of Health
Website: http://www.virginia.gov/cmsportal/employment_850/
            professional_941/health_1376/

Department of Rehabilitative Services
Website: http://www.vadsa.org

HandiNet
Website: http://www.handinet.org

Legal Services
P.O. Box 6058
513 Church Street
Lynchburg, VA 24505
Phone: (434) 528-4722
or
227 West Cherry Street
Marion, VA 24354
Phone: (276) 783-8300
          (800) 277-6754
E-mail: svlas@svlas.org
Websites: http://www.vlas.org; http://www.cvlas.org; http://www.svlas.
          org

Protection and Advocacy
1910 Byrd Avenue, Suite 5
Richmond, VA 23230
Phone: (804) 225-2042 (also TDD)
          (800) 552-3962 (also TDD)
Website: http://www.vopa.state.va.us

University of Virginia, Curry School of Education
Website: http://curry.edschool.virginia.edu/sped/projects/ose/categories/
          ld.html

Voices in Action
Website: http://www.vavoicesinaction.com

Washington
Aging and Disability Services Administration
Website: http://www.aasa.dshs.wa.gov/default.htm

Coalition of Citizens with disAbilities
4649 Sunnyside Ave. N., Suite 100
Seattle, WA 98103
Phone: (206) 545-7055
          (866) 545-7055
          (206) 632-3456 (TTY)
E-mail: info@wccd.org
Website: http://www.wccd.org

disAbility Resource Network
16315 NE 87th St., Suite B-3
Redmond, WA 98052
Phone: (425) 558-0993
           (800) 216-3335
           (425) 861-4773 (TDD)
E-mail: dnetredmond@yahoo.com

disAbility Resource Center
607 SE Everett Mall Way, Suite 6C
Everett, WA 98208
Phone: (425) 347-5768 (also TDD)
           (800) 315-3583
E-mail: sean@wa-ilsc.org

**Division of Developmental Disabilities, Department of Social &
   Health Services**
Website: http://www1.dshs.wa.gov/ddd/index.shtml

Equal Justice
P.O. Box 21026
Seattle, WA 98111
Phone: (206) 447-8168
Website: http://www.ejc.org

Legal Services
Website: http://www.washingtonlawhelp.org/

Protection and Advocacy System
315 Fifth Avenue South, Suite 850
Seattle, WA 98104
Phone: (206) 324-1521
           (800) 562-2702
           (206) 957-0728 (TDD)
           (800) 905-0209 (TDD)
Website: http://www.wpas-rights.org

**University of Washington, Disabilities, Opportunities,
   Internetworking, and Technology**
Website: http://www.washington.edu/doit

West Virginia
Advocates
Litton Bldg, 4th Floor
1207 Quarrier Street
Charleston, WV 25301
Phone: (304) 346-0847 (also TDD)
            (800) 950-5250 (also TDD)
Website: http://www.wvadvocates.org

Autism Training Center,
Website: http://www.marshall.edu/coe/atc

Developmental Disabilities Council
110 Stockton Street
Charleston, WV 25312
Phone: (304) 558-0416
            (304) 558-2376 (TDD)
Website: http://www.wvddc.org

Division of Rehabilitation Services
Website: http://www.wvdrs.org

Legal Services
Website: http://www.wvlegalservices.org

Wisconsin
Brain Injury Association
2900 N. 117th Street, Suite 100
Wauwatosa, WI 53222
Phone: (414) 778-4144
            (800) 882-9282
E-Mail: biaw@execpc.com
Website: http://www.biaw.org/links.html

Disability Advocates
201 West Washington Avenue, Suite 110
Madison, WI 53703
Phone: (608) 266-7826
            (608) 266-6660 (TDD)
E-mail: help@wcdd.org
Website: http://www.dawninfo.org

Coalition for Advocacy
16 North Carroll Street, Suite 400
Madison, WI 53703
Phone: (608) 267-0214 (also TDD)
               (800) 928-8778
Website: http://www.w-c-a.org

Department of Health and Family Services
Website: http://dhfs.wisconsin.gov/Disabilities/INDEX.HTM

Department of Workforce Development Accessibility Resources
Website: http://www.dwd.state.wi.us/accessres/

Judicare, Inc.
Website: http://www.judicare.org/wils.html

Legal Services
Phone: (920) 432-4645 (Green Bay)
               (608) 785-2809 (La Crosse)
               (608) 256-3304 (Madison)
               (414) 278-7722 (Milwaukee)
               (920) 233-6521 (Oshkosh)
               (262) 635-8836 (Racine)
Website: http://www.legalaction.org

Wyoming
Contacts
Website: http://www.k12.wy.us/svi/wycontacts.html

Department of Health Programs and Services
Website: http://wdhfs.state.wy.us/WDH/Programs.htm

Developmental Disabilities Division
186E Qwest Building
6101 Yellowstone Blvd.
Cheyenne, WY 82002
Phone: (307) 777-7715
               (307) 777-5578 (TDD)
Website: http://ddd.state.wy.us

Governor's Planning Council on Developmental Disabilities
122 West 25th Street, Room 1608
Cheyenne, WY 82002

Phone: (307) 777-7230
           (800) 438-5791
E-mail: cweisb@state.wy.us
Website: http://ddcouncil.state.wy.us

New Options in Technology
1000 E. University Avenue, Dept. 4298
Laramie, WY 82071
Phone: (307) 766-2084 (also TDD)
           (800) 861-4312 (also TDD)
E-mail: wynot.uw@uwyo.edu
Website: http://wind.uwyo.edu/wynot/inforesource/wyoming.asp

Parent Information Center
5 North Lobban
Buffalo, WY 82834
Phone: (307) 684-2277
           (800) 660-9742
Website: http://wpic.org

Protection and Advocacy System
320 West 25th Street, 2nd Floor
Cheyenne, WY 82001
Phone: (307) 632-3496
Fax: (307) 638-0815
Website: http://wypanda.vcn.com

Index

About the Authors

Ruth Colker holds the Heck-Faust Memorial Chair in Constitutional Law at Ohio State University. **Adam Milani** was Associate Professor of Law at Mercer University. They coauthored (with Bonnie Poitras Tucker) *The Law of Disability Discrimination* (4th ed., Anderson Publishing, 2003). In addition, Colker authored *Disability Pendulum: The First Decade of the Americans with Disabilities Act* (New York University Press, 2005), and Milani coauthored (with Bonnie Poitras Tucker) *Federal Disability Law in a Nutshell* (3rd ed., West, 2004).

GLENVIEW PUBLIC LIBRARY

3 1170 00721 6868